EARLY NUMERACY

EARLY Numeracy

Assessment for Teaching and Intervention
Second Edition

Robert J. Wright, Jim Martland and Ann K. Stafford

P·C·P

Paul Chapman Publishing

Paul Chapman Publishing
A SAGE Publications Company
1 Oliver's Yard
55 City Road
London EC1Y 1SP

SAGE Publications Inc
2455 Teller Road
Thousand Oaks, California 91320

SAGE Publications India Pvt Ltd
B-42, Panchsheel Enclave
Post Box 4109
New Delhi 110 017

Photographs provided by Carole Cannon, Joan McCarthy, Jim
Martland and Ann K. Stafford

Library of Congress Control Number: 2005905281

A catalogue record for this book is available from the British
Library

ISBN 10 1-4129-1019-6
ISBN 10 1-4129-1020-X (pbk)
ISBN 13 978-1-4129-1019-4
ISBN 13 978-1-4129-1020-0 (pbk)

Typeset by Pantek Arts Ltd, Maidstone, Kent
Printed and bound by Athenaeum Press, Gateshead, Tyne & Wear
Printed on paper from sustainable resources

To Monica and the memory of Jack.
To Wendy, Alison and Helen.
To Shannon.

Contents

List of Figures

List of Photographs

List of Tables

Contributors

AUTHORS

Dr Robert J. Wright holds the position of Professor in Mathematics Education at Southern Cross University in Australia and is an internationally recognized leader in understanding and assessing young children's numerical knowledge and strategies, publishing many articles and papers in this field. His work in the past 15 years has included the development of the Mathematics Recovery Programme which focuses on providing specialist training for teachers to advance the numeracy levels of young children assessed as low attainers. In Australia, the UK, the USA and elsewhere, this programme has been implemented widely and applied extensively to classroom teaching and to average and able learners as well as low attainers. He has conducted several research projects funded by the Australian Research Council including a current project on assessment and intervention for 8–10-year-olds.

Jim Martland is a member of the International Board of Mathematics Recovery and Director of Mathematics Recovery Programme (UK) Limited. He is Senior Fellow in the Department of Education at the University of Liverpool. In his long career in education he has held headships of primary and middle schools and was Director of Primary Initial Teacher Training. In all his posts he continued to teach and pursue research in primary mathematics. His current work is with education authorities in the UK and Canada, delivering professional development courses on assessing children's difficulties in numeracy and evaluating teacher intervention.

Ann Stafford's academic background includes graduate study at Southern Cross University, Australia, graduate study at the University of Chicago and Clemson University in the USA, a Master's degree from Duke University and undergraduate degree in Elementary Education and Mathematics from the University of North Carolina at Greensboro. Her professional expertise includes administrative roles for gifted and remedial students, mathematics supervision in the School District of Oconee County in South Carolina, teaching positions in Early Childhood and Middle School Mathematics, and teaching and research positions at Clemson University.

Ann has received professional awards and grants for outstanding contributions to the region and state for mathematics and leadership. She received Teacher of the Year while at Walhalla Middle School. She has been the recipient of state grants for the implementation of an Early Childhood Gifted Programme, the Elementary Mathematics Specialist Programme, and annual grants for the implementation of the Mathematics Recovery (MR) Programme in Oconee County and the state of South Carolina. She currently directs the implementation of MR in the USA.

CONTRIBUTORS TO CHAPTER 8

Dr Joanne Mulligan holds the position of Senior Lecturer in Mathematics Education at Macquarie University, Sydney, Australia. She is internationally recognized for her work on children's number learning. In particular her research on multiplication and division concepts has been implemented through publications and professional development. Over the past 15 years her work has included contributions to the development of the Count Me In Too Professional

Development Programme in New South Wales schools and a large-scale Australian Research Council project on children's imagery and number learning.

Peter Gould is the Chief Education Officer in mathematics with the New South Wales Department of Education and Training. He has been instrumental in designing the Count Me In and Count Me In Too projects. His major interest is the effective use of research in the design and delivery of mathematics education.

Acknowledgments

This book is a culmination of several interrelated projects conducted over the past 15 years, many of which come under the collective label of Mathematics Recovery. All these projects have involved one or more of the authors undertaking research, development and implementation in collaboration with teachers, schools and school systems. These projects have also received significant support from the participating schools and school systems. The authors wish to express their sincere gratitude to all the teachers, students and project colleagues who have participated in and contributed to these projects. We also wish to thank the following organizations for funding and supporting one or more projects that have provided a basis for writing this book: the government and Catholic school systems of the north coast region of New South Wales, Australia, and the Australian Research Council; the New South Wales Department of Education and Training; the School District of Oconee County and the South Carolina State Department of Education in the USA; many other school districts across the USA; the University of Liverpool and Wigan, Sefton, Salford, Stockport, Knowsley and Cumbria Educational Authorities in England; Flintshire County Council in Wales; the University of Strathclyde and Glasgow, West Dunbartonshire, Edinburgh and Stirling Education Authorities in Scotland; Frontier School Division in the Province of Manitoba, Canada; and the Ministry of Education in the Bahamas.

We also wish to thank the staff and pupils of Westwood Primary School, Flintshire, for permission to appear in the photographs.

Series preface

If you ask educationalists and teachers whether numeracy intervention deserves equal attention with literacy intervention the overwhelming answer is 'Yes, it should'. If you then ask whether this happens in their experience the answer is a resounding 'No!' What then are the reasons for this discrepancy? Research shows that teachers tend to regard addressing difficulties in literacy as more important than difficulties in early numeracy. Teachers also state that there is a lack of suitable tools for assessing young children's numeracy skills and knowledge and appropriate programmes available to address the deficits.

The three books in this series make a significant impact to redress the imbalance by providing practical help to enable schools and teachers to give equal status to early numeracy intervention. The books are:

▶ *Early Numeracy Assessment for Teaching and Intervention, 2nd Edition*, Robert J. Wright, Jim Martland and Ann K. Stafford, available December 2005
▶ *Teaching Number: Advancing Children's Skills and Strategies, 2nd Edition*, Robert J. Wright, Jim Martland, Ann K. Stafford and Garry Stanger, available August 2006
▶ *Teaching Number in the Classroom with 4–8 year-olds*, Robert J. Wright, Garry Stanger, Ann K. Stafford and Jim Martland, available December 2005.

The authors are internationally recognized as leaders in the field of early numeracy intervention. They draw on considerable practical experience of delivering training courses and materials on how to assess young children's mathematical knowledge, skills and strategies in addition, subtraction, multiplication and division. This is the focus of *Early Numeracy*. The revised version contains six comprehensive diagnostic assessment tools to identify children's strengths and weaknesses and has a new chapter on how the assessment provides the direction and focus for teaching intervention. *Teaching Number* sets out in detail nine principles which guide the teaching together with 180 practical, exemplar teaching activities to advance children to more sophisticated strategies for solving numeracy problems. The third book, *Teaching Number in the Classroom with 4–8 year-olds*, extends the work of assessment and teaching intervention with individual and small groups to working with whole classes. In this new text the lead authors have been assisted by expert, primary practitioners from Australia, America and the United Kingdom who have provided the best available instructional activities for each of eight major topics in early number learning.

The three books in this series provide a comprehensive package on

1. The identification, analysis and reporting on children's numerical knowledge, skills and strategies
2. How to design, implement and evaluate a course of teaching intervention
3. How to incorporate both assessment and teaching in the daily numeracy programme in differing class organizations and contexts.

The series is distinctive from others in the field because it draws on a substantial body of recent, theoretical research supported by international, practical application. Because all the assessment and teaching activities portrayed have been empirically tested the books have the additional, important distinction that they indicate to the practitioner ranges of responses and patterns of behavior which children tend to make.

The book series provides a package for professional growth and development and an invaluable comprehensive resource for both the experienced teacher concerned with early numeracy intervention and for the primary teacher who has responsibility for teaching numeracy in kindergarten to upper junior level. Primary numeracy consultants, mathematics advisers, special education teachers, teaching assistants and initial teacher trainees around the world will find much to enable them to put numeracy intervention on an equal standing with literacy. At a wider level the series will reveal many areas of interest to educational psychologists, researchers and academics.

Find out more about Math Recovery by visiting our website at http://www.mathrecovery.com/index.shtml

Preface

This book has as its major focus the comprehensive assessment of children's early numerical knowledge and strategies and their advancement. Practical and theoretical aspects of assessment are explained in detail. A major feature of the book is a learning framework in early number that is applied in analyzing the results of assessment and planning for teaching. The book is particularly relevant to the assessment and teaching of children in the early years of school, that is, 4–9-year-olds, as well as older children.

The book provides a comprehensive approach to assessing a range of aspects of early number knowledge. This includes children's counting strategies, their strategies for adding and subtracting, their knowledge of number word sequences and numerals, their ability to reason in terms of tens as well as ones and their developing strategies for multiplication and division. The book describes several other significant aspects of children's early numerical knowledge such as the use of finger patterns, combining and partitioning small numbers, the role of spatial and temporal patterns, and the use of five-based strategies as well as base-ten strategies.

The theory and methods underlying this approach have resulted from research projects conducted since the early 1980s, which had the goal of comprehensively assessing children's number knowledge and documenting its development over time. Over the past 15 years these methods have been learned and applied by thousands of teachers who have participated in a range of research and development projects conducted by the authors and colleagues, in Australia, the USA, the UK and Canada as well as several other countries. The approach is distinctive and embodies an extensive focus on teacher development.

The book is of interest to all who are concerned with finding ways to better understand and develop children's early numerical thinking. Teachers, advisers, numeracy consultants, mathematics supervisors and learning support personnel, as well as teacher educators and researchers whose work relates to this field will find much of interest and practical help to develop confidence and skill in the assessment and teaching of early numeracy.

Introduction

Summary

In this introduction we set out the background to the Mathematics Recovery Programme and the need for early intervention. We describe the key aspects of the programme – assessment, teaching intervention and professional development – and the purpose and structure of this book.

Over recent years in the English-speaking world there has been a concern to raise standards of numeracy. Britain, America, Australia, New Zealand and Canada have placed increased emphasis on numeracy in educational policy and practice. Initially, gains were made in the general levels of numeracy. However, the gains have not either been maintained or reached the set targets. What is apparent is that some children continue to experience difficulty in numeracy, and that these difficulties can take several forms and are equally common in boys and girls. The causes for such difficulties are varied and include individual characteristics, inadequate or inappropriate teaching, absence from school resulting in gaps in mathematical learning, and lack of pre-school or home experience with mathematical activities and language (DfES, 2004; Dowker, 2003; 2004).

A further obstacle to progress was reported in a study of primary children with learning difficulties. The report indicated there is a tendency by teachers to regard addressing difficulties in literacy learning as more urgent and important than difficulties in mathematics learning. The report also showed how schools do not have a systematic focus on learning difficulties in numeracy and that children with learning difficulties were not identified in the early years of schooling. Part of the problem was that there was a lack of suitable assessment tools. Even when schools recognized that they had significant numbers of children with learning difficulties in numeracy they failed to provide programmes to address the difficulties (DETYA, 2000).

If we make the assertion that numeracy intervention deserves equal status with literacy intervention, then it follows that help and guidance must be available to schools. The first task for the head teacher/principal or mathematics specialist is to find out how many children are experiencing difficulties in numeracy and the nature of those difficulties. Therefore diagnostic tools are required to identify the specific problems children are experiencing and to profile strengths and weaknesses. The tools should also indicate children's particular misconceptions and incorrect strategies. Only then can interventions be planned and resources targeted towards the individual's needs. We would add that while interventions can take place at any time it is desirable that interventions should take place at an early age. This is because difficulties in numeracy can affect performance in other aspects of the curriculum. Also, correcting difficulties can help prevent the development of negative attitudes and mathematical anxiety.

Over the past 15 years several interrelated and collaborative projects under the collective label of the Mathematics Recovery Programme and the Count Me in Too Programme in New South Wales, Australia, the UK and the USA have developed diagnostic tools for early numeracy assessment. All these projects have involved research, development and implementation with teachers, school districts and school systems. However, before setting out the detail of these we begin by relating the origins and development of the Mathematics Recovery Programme. We describe the key features, including the need for early intervention, and show how Mathematics Recovery has expanded internationally. We conclude by indicating what is special about this book and how the chapters are structured.

BACKGROUND TO THE MATHEMATICS RECOVERY PROGRAMME

The initial development of Mathematics Recovery (MR) occurred over a three-year period (1992–95) in the Australian State of New South Wales. The development was funded by the Australian Research Council and the school system. Since 1995 the Mathematics Recovery Programme has been widely implemented in 21 states in the USA, in 21 education authorities in Britain and Ireland, in the Bahamas and in the province of Manitoba, Canada.

THE KEY FEATURES

The key features of MR can be summed up under four headings – Early Intervention, Assessment, Teaching and Professional Development. The assessment and teaching strands use a strong underpinning theory of young children's mathematical learning which leads to a comprehensive and integrated framework for both assessment and teaching. The programme has a detailed approach to, and specific diagnostic tools for, the assessment of children's early number strategies and knowledge. Following the assessment, teachers can employ an especially developed instructional approach and distinctive instructional activities which can be applied to individuals in small-group or class situations. The programme also has an intensive, short-term teaching intervention for low-attaining 5–8-year-old children by specialist teachers. The entire programme provides an extensive, professional development course to prepare the specialist teachers, and ongoing collegial and leader support for these teachers.

THE NEED FOR EARLY INTERVENTION

In the 1990s several research studies focused on assessing the number knowledge of children in the early years of school (Aubrey, 1993; Wright, 1991b; 1994; Young-Loveridge, 1989; 1991). Some of these studies have assessed the knowledge of school entrants and some have documented children's progress by assessing the children several times within one school year or annually for several years. Apparent from these studies is that there are significant differences in the numerical knowledge of children when they begin school. A study by Wright (1994) described the three-year difference in children's early number knowledge, that is, some 4-year-olds have attained a level of number knowledge that others will not attain until they are 7 years old.

What these studies also show is that, by and large, these differences in number knowledge increase as the children progress through the early learning years and beyond. Thus children who are low-attaining in the early years tend to remain so throughout their schooling, and the knowledge gap between low-attaining children and average or able children tends to increase over the course of their years at school. A three-year difference in the early years of school becomes a seven-year difference for low-attaining children after about ten years of school. The notion of a seven-year difference was identified in the influential Cockcroft Report (Cockcroft, 1982) on school mathematics in the UK. What also seems to be the case is that, even in the early years of schooling, low-attaining children begin to develop strong negative attitudes to mathematics. It is reasonable to suggest that these negative attitudes result from a lack of understanding of school mathematics and rare experience of success in school mathematics.

In the 1990s, governments and school systems in several countries focused increasing attention on the extent to which their schools teach mathematics well and how well their children achieve in mathematics. One aspect of this has been the close attention paid to the results of international comparisons of aspects of mathematics education such as student achievement, curriculum content and teaching methods. Most recently in the UK and Australia, for example, there has been a particular focus by governmental agencies in education on mathematics in the early years. Of particular interest has been the need for, and feasibility of, intervention programmes for low attainers in the early years.

Recently in the UK guidance has been set out to help teachers provide for children who are experiencing difficulties. This has arisen from research which shows that targeted interventions in numeracy can have significant impact on children's performance and self-confidence. The provision is seen as three 'waves' of intervention:

Wave 1 refers to the effective inclusion of all children in high-quality learning and teaching in the daily mathematics lesson.

Wave 2 relates to the provision of additional time-limited support in the form of small-group intervention to accelerate progress and enable children to work at age-related expectations.

Wave 3 again provides time-limited teaching to enhance the progress for those children who are not benefiting from the provision in Waves 1 and 2. These children will require focused teaching activities which tackle fundamental errors and misconceptions that are preventing progress (DfES, 2005).

The document cites the Mathematics Recovery Programme as one of only two examples of successful intervention for low-attaining 6–7-year-olds. The research report upon which the guidance was framed reinforces the following points. These are the same identifiable aspects of the Mathematics Recovery Programme.

▶ Early intervention is important because it provides an opportunity for educationally disadvantaged children before the gap between their knowledge and that of average and high-attaining children is too wide, and before they experience too much failure.
▶ Children's arithmetical difficulties are highly susceptible to intervention.
▶ Individualized work with children who are falling behind in arithmetic has a significant impact on their performance.
▶ The amount of time given to such individualized work does not, in many cases, need to be very large to be effective (Dowker, 2004).

DEVELOPMENT AND OVERVIEW OF MATHEMATICS RECOVERY

The Mathematics Recovery Programme was developed as a systemic response to the problem of chronic failure in school mathematics. The programme involves: (1) identification of the lowest attainers at the first-grade level, that is, the second year of school, and (2) provision of a programme of intensive, individualized and group teaching to these children in order to advance them to a level at which they are likely to learn successfully in a regular class.

The initial development of the Mathematics Recovery Programme was undertaken in the north-eastern region of New South Wales, Australia, from 1992 to 1995. This development was a nationally funded research project and was undertaken collaboratively with regional government and Catholic school systems.

ASSESSMENT IN MR

Mathematics Recovery incorporates a distinctive approach to assessing young children's numerical knowledge and strategies in addition, subtraction, multiplication and division. This method does not involve pencil and paper tests. It is interview based and involves presenting numerical tasks and engaging with the child in order to determine the extent of the child's knowledge and the relative sophistication of the child's numerical strategies. The assessment results in a profile of the child's knowledge across several aspects of early number and additional information about the current numerical strategies used by the child. Thus MR assessment accords with a profiles-based approach to assessment, with the advantage that it provides much more detailed assessment information than that typically provided by profiles. The profiling aspect of the assessment is particularly useful for documenting children's progress over time, for example, for the duration of the teaching cycle or over the course of a school year. The assessment also results in specific and detailed guidance for teaching via the Learning Framework in Number (LFIN) and the Instructional Framework for Early Number (IFEN). These are described in Chapters 2 and 10 respectively.

MR TEACHING

Mathematics Recovery teaching takes full account of the results of assessment and focuses simultaneously on a range of aspects in early number. In MR teaching sessions the child is presented with tasks that are genuine problems for them. The tasks are carefully chosen to elicit numerical thinking that is just beyond the limitations of the child's current knowledge. The teaching sessions typically involve the child in thinking hard and thinking reflectively about aspects of early number. The experience in MR is that teaching sessions of this kind are those most likely to result in significant advancement in the child's early numerical knowledge and strategies. Mathematics Recovery teachers are continually assessing children's progress during the teaching sessions through careful observation and review of teaching sessions. Mathematics Recovery assessment and teaching are fully integrated. Thus assessment informs teaching and teaching provides additional assessment information. Planning for teaching involves the application of the Instructional Framework for Early Number which provides crucial directionality for teaching and ensures that teaching is at the cutting edge of the child's current knowledge and strategies. Development of the Mathematics Recovery Programme also included the development of a set of guiding principles for teaching in the programme, and a working method for teaching, which takes account of the guiding principles.

Guiding Principles for MR Teaching

1. The teaching approach is enquiry based, that is, problem based. Children are routinely engaged in thinking hard to solve numerical problems that for them are quite challenging.

2. Teaching is informed by an initial, comprehensive assessment and ongoing assessment through teaching. Assessment through teaching refers to the teacher's informed understanding of the child's current knowledge and problem-solving strategies, and continual revision of this understanding.

3. Teaching is focused just beyond the 'cutting edge' of the child's current knowledge.

4.   Teachers exercise their professional judgment in selecting from a bank of instructional settings and tasks, and varying this selection on the basis of ongoing observations.

5.   The teacher understands children's numerical strategies and deliberately engenders the
development of more sophisticated strategies.

6.   Teaching involves intensive, ongoing observation by the teacher and continual micro-
adjusting or fine-tuning of teaching on the basis of her or his observation.

7.   Teaching supports and builds on the child's intuitive, verbally based strategies and these are
used as a basis for the development of written forms of arithmetic that accord with the
child's verbally based strategies.

8.   The teacher provides the child with sufficient time to solve a given problem. Consequently
the child is frequently engaged in episodes that involve sustained thinking, reflection on
her or his thinking and reflecting on the results of her or his thinking.

9.   Children gain intrinsic satisfaction from their problem-solving, their realization that they
are making progress and from the verification methods they develop.

EXTENSION OF MR TO THE USA, BRITAIN AND IRELAND, AND CANADA

One of the characteristics of the Mathematics Recovery Programme is its applicability to a multitude of situations and contexts. The focus on strategies and concept development is consistent
with the *Principles and Standards for School Mathematics* published by the National Council for
Teachers of Mathematics in 2000. Mathematics Recovery meets guidelines for the national No
Child Left Behind Act 2001 (PL 107–110) legislation by having a strong research foundation.

The extension of Mathematics Recovery (MR) to the USA began in 1995 with its adoption by
Oconee County in South Carolina. By 1999 the programme had spread to the states of North
Carolina, Virginia, Maryland, Wyoming and the Bahamas. Over the past five years implementa-
tions have included school districts in 24 states across America and the Bahamas. In total this
has involved 350 teachers, 60 leaders of Training and over 3,000 participating children. In 2003
the US Mathematics Recovery Council (USMRC) was established. It is a non-profit organization
which ensures the quality of Mathematics Recovery, provides oversight and management of
training, materials and related intellectual property, validates courses and certifies leaders and
teachers. The Council coordinates a comprehensive staff development programme and makes
research and knowledge of young children's mathematical thinking available to a wider audience through publications and conference presentations.

The expansion of the Mathematics Recovery Programme to the UK came about when Wigan
Metropolitan Borough Council commissioned the University of Liverpool's Department of
Education to research international early years intervention projects. The research report recommended the adoption of the Mathematics Recovery Programme. The first cohort of teachers was
selected from schools which had identified in their development plan the need to tackle under-
achievement in mathematics at Year 1. Following the successful training of the first cohort of
Mathematics Recovery teachers, the group continued to train as MR leaders. The leadership training involved visits with US trainers and leaders, presentations at the annual MR conference and
visits to schools both in the USA and in England. In 1997 MR coverage extended to the
Metropolitan Borough of Sefton. This was particularly significant because Sefton Metropolitan
Borough Council clearly saw Mathematics Recovery complementing the work of the National

Numeracy Project which was beginning to come on stream. Thirty-six teachers from 14 schools undertook the courses. The key idea was to establish learning teams within a school, typically these included the Mathematics Coordinator, the Year 1 teacher and either the Special Needs Coordinator or Classroom Assistant. The advent of a learning team was a very positive agent for change both for the school and for the personnel involved. By 2005, 21 education authorities had implemented the Mathematics Recovery Programme to be used alongside the centrally funded National Numeracy Strategy (NNS). The NNS gives a broad-brush approach to raising attainment but Mathematics Recovery provides a necessary, in-depth assessment tool and intervention for the early years and Wave 2 and Wave 3 children.

In Scotland almost 200 teachers at all levels of the education system have been trained in assessment and intervention. This usually involves the teacher's school writing Mathematics Recovery into its development plan. Six of the 32 education authorities have included Mathematics Recovery in their plans for developing mathematics teaching and a number of teachers have continued to use the instructional framework with individual children. Large numbers of teachers have adapted the framework for use with groups of children or with whole classes. A university accredited course that covers basic and advanced assessment, individual teaching and implementation in schools has been developed and validated. It now operates as a distance learning course through the university's virtual learning environment as an extension to the continuing professional development for teachers. The assessment schedules have been translated into Welsh, and the Flintshire Education Department, like their Scottish counterparts, have developed digital training materials using the latest technology. In 2005 the Mathematics Recovery Council for the United Kingdom and Ireland was established.

Further international development commenced in 2003 when the Province of Manitoba, Canada, became involved through the work of the Frontier School Division. Frontier Division covers the area north of Winnipeg with many of its schools located in remote northern communities. The work of the superintendent, and regional and district numeracy consultants has been particularly significant in raising attainment in early numeracy.

COUNT ME IN TOO – A SYSTEMIC, CLASSROOM-BASED PROJECT ADAPTING THE KEY ASPECTS OF MATHEMATICS RECOVERY

In 1996 the Mathematics Recovery Programme (MRP) which was running in New South Wales was adapted by the NSW Department of Education and Training as the basis of a systemic initiative in mathematics in the early years of schooling and was called Count Me In Too (CMIT). The main focus of CMIT is the development of teachers' understanding of children's strategies in early number and how teachers can help children to develop more advanced numerical strategies. The evolution of CMIT involved adaptation of key aspects of the theory and methods of MR including:

- ▶ the guiding framework (Learning Framework in Number);
- ▶ the approach to assessment and the assessment tasks;
- ▶ the underlying theory of early numerical learning;
- ▶ the guiding principles for teaching; and
- ▶ approaches to teacher professional development.

Count Me In Too was piloted in 13 schools and then implemented progressively across the state. By 2004 the programme had been implemented in almost all of the 1,700 schools in the system. The programme is also widely used in non-government schools in NSW, and by school systems in other states and territories in Australia. In 2000, it formed the basis of a nationally funded pilot project in New Zealand involving 81 schools and now has been adapted for use in all schools in New Zealand.

According to an independent evaluation of CMIT in its pilot year, the project was highly successful in terms of teacher professional development and student learning (Bobis, 1996). The success of CMIT and the high regard in which it is held by educational administrators, principals and teachers provided strong evidence that the MRP is readily adaptable to classroom teaching and to average and high attainers as well as low attainers.

A study by Mitchelmore and White (2003) examined the impact of implementation of CMIT on schools' results in the statewide Basic Skills Test (BST) in New South Wales. The study involved surveying the BST results of 71 schools that had been implementing CMIT for two or more years. As described by Bobis et al. (2005), 'the BST are standardized tests in literacy and numeracy implemented in Year 3 and Year 5 across the state of NSW ... [The authors] concluded that the implementation of CMIT in NSW public schools had caused a definite improvement in Year 3 BST numeracy performance' (p. 32).

In each of the years since its inception, the Mathematics Recovery Programme has significantly influenced general classroom teaching of mathematics and many of the participating schools have successfully applied MR theory and techniques to classroom mathematics. This influence has been particularly significant in schools where the MR teacher has a leadership role and where the programme is well supported in the school. Such applications of MR to classroom teaching typically have occurred at the level of the individual school. Count Me In Too, by way of contrast, is a large-scale and systemic initiative.

Considered together the international applications of MR theory and techniques to classroom teaching provide compelling evidence of the suitability of this approach to the teaching of number in the early years of school. A list of selected publications relating to both the Mathematics Recovery Programme and Count Me In Too is included in the Bibliography.

PROFESSIONAL DEVELOPMENT

The initial training in the Mathematics Recovery Programme has an emphasis on individual assessment interviews and teaching. However, even before the assessment modules are complete teachers report that they begin to make changes in their practice. They begin to revise their teaching objectives to place greater emphasis on previously neglected, or less emphasized, aspects of the curriculum such as the backward number word sequence and number word before activities. They report that they change their teaching style to allow more time to respond to questions and have more class discussion. They begin to group the children based on the results of the assessments. Most importantly, they talk about having gained a greater understanding of how children learn and they recognize the difficulties they encounter. The teachers state openly how they have increased confidence to advise colleagues on children's strategies and misconceptions and on the intervention necessary.

A particularly effective professional development initiative came about when groups of two, three or four teachers worked collaboratively when conducting the videotaped assessment training sessions. The trainees became more confident in using the digital technology, shared the assessment workload, reached group agreement on the analysis of the child's performance and gave supportive feedback to members. The collaborative group work had the benefit of equipping the trainees to involve colleagues, including teaching assistants, when they began to disseminate the work in their school.

Mathematics Recovery teachers and leaders have applied the MR methods to different age groups and directed numerous workshops aimed at kindergarten through to 12-year-olds. They have formed networks that provide ongoing support and additional professional development within school districts, education authorities and regional areas. Mathematics Recovery conferences are held annually for administrators, teachers and leaders, and are increasingly gaining an international audience.

The principles of MR are being incorporated into undergraduate- and graduate-level courses but it is at school district level where the biggest benefit is felt. As the districts embrace the National Council for the Teaching of Mathematics (NCTM) Standards the Mathematics Recovery Programme gives a direction to the assessment and subsequent teaching by increasing teachers' knowledge of how young children think and reason. The programme is consistent with the efforts that individual states and districts are making to provide children with the opportunities to develop mathematical power, a central theme of the NCTM Standards.

PURPOSE OF THIS BOOK

This book has three main aims. The first is to equip primary teachers, numeracy consultants and educational support staff with a practical and theoretical understanding of how to assess children's early number knowledge and strategies. The second is to raise teachers' understanding of early numeracy by providing a Learning Framework In early Number. The LFIN provides a comprehensive approach to assessing a range of aspects of early number knowledge and shows how they are related. The aspects include children's counting strategies, their strategies for adding and subtracting, their knowledge of number word sequences and numerals, their ability to reason in terms of tens as well as ones, and their developing strategies for multiplication and division. We also describe several other significant aspects of children's early numerical knowledge such as the use of finger patterns, combining and partitioning small numbers, the role of spatial and temporal patterns, and the use of base-five as well as base-ten strategies. The third element is to demonstrate how an intervention programme can be planned and implemented so that each child can be given a positive learning experience and success in early numeracy.

THE STRUCTURE OF THE BOOK

The introduction has shown that change can be made, and that low attainment can be challenged and standards raised. Our task is to enable you to have access to the full programme. In Chapter 1 we present the real stories of three children in different educational contexts in order to give you evidence of how the Mathematics Recovery Programme has been used for assessment and intervention around the world. Chapter 2 provides a detailed description of the Learning Framework in Number (LFIN) which is common to all of these programmes. The LFIN provides a blueprint for the assessment and indicates the likely paths for children's learning. The LFIN consists of 11 interrelated aspects of early number, which are organized into four parts: A, B, C and D. The most important aspect of the LFIN is the Part A which includes Stages of Early Arithmetical Learning (SEAL) and relates to the relative sophistication of the child's strategies for counting, adding and subtracting.

Assessment Schedules and LFIN

Chapter 3 illustrates how the assessment schedules relate to the LFIN and discusses the distinctive approach to assessment in the Mathematics Recovery Programme. We explain that the key outcomes of the assessment are to elicit the child's most advanced numerical knowledge and strategies and to determine the child's stage of development in terms of Stages of Early Arithmetical Learning. We describe the techniques necessary for the preparation of the assessment interviews and how the assessment interviews differ from pencil and paper tests. We explain how to administer the Assessment Interview Schedule 1.1 and how to use Part B, the models for the number words and numerals to analyze the information gathered. A particular feature of this revised edition is that because the assessment schedules have been used by hundreds of teachers around the English-speaking world we have been able to gather information on the types of responses children make. We present examples of these to alert the trainee and experienced interviewer to non-standard responses. We do this so that the assessor is prepared to recognize and to note the incidence or persistence of them.

SEAL

In Chapter 4, we present, explain and exemplify each of the six Stages of Early Arithmetical Learning (SEAL). This includes an introduction to the particular sense in which the term 'counting' is used in SEAL, explanations of the terms 'stages' and 'levels', and a discussion of the means by which children's numerical strategies may be observed. Progression across the stages involves the child using increasingly sophisticated ways to solve number problems. For each stage we give a definition and provide the profile of a typical child. We conclude the explanation of each stage with two examples of children's problem-solving activity relevant to the stage. These examples take the form of video excerpts, that is, objective descriptions of the child's problem-solving activity. Each video excerpt is followed by a discussion of the problem-solving activity portrayed in the excerpt.

Teacher Learning

Analysis of the MR assessment involves a good deal of learning on the part of teachers. This learning is best undertaken through practice, reflection and discussion, and Chapter 5 introduces the reader to this process. Twelve scenarios of children's problem-solving activity in early number are presented. These scenarios are based on actual assessments by MR teachers, and focus specifically on additive and subtractive tasks. The exercise for the reader is to study each scenario carefully in order to determine the child's stage of development in terms of the SEAL model. This exercise serves several purposes. As well as providing important practice for the reader in analyzing children's problem-solving activity, it provides insights into the ways in which teachers present tasks and interact with children during MR assessment, and exemplifies the diverse ways children respond to the assessment tasks.

Readers should bear in mind that MR assessment aims to determine the most advanced strategy available to the child. This is equally important in the administration of the assessment interview and its analysis. The child's use of this strategy should be spontaneous, that is, unassisted either directly or indirectly by the teacher. As a general rule the child should use the strategy in solving several tasks, rather than only the introductory task. Each of the 12 scenarios in this chapter has been selected because, in the view of the authors, it provides a reasonably clear-cut example of children's problem-solving at a given stage. Readers should aim to identify carefully each strategy used by the child and then determine the most advanced strategy available to the child. When a decision has been reached the reader's solution can be checked at the end of the chapter where each scenario is explained in detail and the particular stage identified.

Assessment Interview Schedules

Chapter 6 includes the specific instructions required to prepare for and administer the second aspect of Part A, that is, Assessment Interview Schedule 1.2. This will introduce the reader to the model for tens and ones and how to identify base-ten strategies. Included in schedule 1.2 is a task group termed non-count-by-ones which will enable more information to be gathered on a child's counting strategies and will indicate whether the child has attained Stage 5. In Chapter 7 we turn to Part C of the LFIN, which is concerned with structuring number. Part C has two assessment schedules labeled 2.1 and 2.2. Part C contains five aspects which are considered important in children's early number learning. The five aspects are combining and partitioning; spatial patterns and subitizing; temporal sequences; finger patterns and base-five (quinary-based) strategies. Not only are these aspects closely integrated with Part A and Part B but also the aspects themselves share close interrelationships. In Chapter 8 we turn to Part D of the Learning Framework in Number. This addresses early and advanced multiplication and division. It has two assessment schedules, 3.1 and 3.2. An overview of the development of children's early multiplication and division knowledge and strategies is provided, together with an associated model consisting of five levels. For each level, an explanation and an illustration in the form of a protocol of a child's solutions of multiplicative or divisional tasks is provided. We also include five scenarios taken from classroom situations and challenge the reader to identify the child's level, solutions and explanations. Assessment schedule 3.1 for early multiplication and division knowledge and strategies is set out together with guidance for administration. This is followed by assessment schedule 3.2 for advanced multiplication and division knowledge and strategies. We conclude the chapter with summary guidelines for determining levels of early multiplication and division knowledge.

Chapter 9 has further advice for coding and analyzing the assessment schedules together with information on how to operate the digital video camera to secure quality recording. In the final chapter, Chapter 10, we return to the three children who were struggling with early numeracy and show how a teaching intervention programme is planned by linking the results of the assessment to an Instructional Framework for Early Numeracy.

The Appendices contain the full Diagnostic Assessment Interview Schedules, 1.1 and 1.2, 2.1 and 2.2 and 3.1 and 3.2 together with lists of equipment, reference guides for the allocation of Stages and Levels, and Record Keeping sheets. Finally, we provide a Glossary of terms used in Mathematics Recovery Assessment. These terms are printed in bold type at their first occurrence in the text.

Development of Mathematics Recovery and related programmes such as *Count Me In Too* has shown that it is applicable to a multitude of situations and contexts. So now we move from the overview to school-based specifics. We start by looking at the three children in widely different contexts who are beginning to fall behind their classmates in numeracy, and how early intervention via the Mathematics Recovery Programme has helped them.

1

Children, Numeracy and Mathematics Recovery

Summary

We present the stories of three children in different countries who were struggling with early number. The governmental initiatives to raise standards are discussed but questioned as to whether they would meet the needs of children experiencing difficulty in the bottom 20 per cent of attainment. We show all three children have grown mathematically as a result of a detailed assessment leading to a teaching intervention which possessed clearly defined objectives and distinctive teaching approaches. Not only did each child attain, or surpass, the age-related norm but also as a result of the exercise teachers reported changes in their coverage of the curriculum and in their teaching style. The teachers also professed confidence to advise colleagues and to disseminate their learning and results.

We would like you to meet three young children. Judy is Australian and attends school in New South Wales, Denise lives in the North West of England and Michael is from South Carolina in the USA. Their classrooms are thousands of miles apart, in opposite hemispheres and in different time zones. Though they receive schooling under different educational administrations, Judy, Denise and Michael have several features in common. First, they are approximately the same age, between 6 and 7 years. Secondly, at the time of the interviews all three have been in school for almost a year and a half. They are regular attendees and well adjusted to school. However, they also share a problem. They are all experiencing difficulty with basic numeracy and are already falling behind the expected performance level of their year group.

Judy, Denise and Michael had been assessed in mathematical attainment and placed in the bottom 10 to 25 per cent bracket within their year group.

We know there is ample evidence (Aubrey, 1993; Wright, 1991b; 1994; Young-Loveridge, 1989; 1991) to show that there are significant differences in the numerical knowledge of children when they begin school and that these differences increase as they progress through school. In other words, children who are low attainers at the beginning of schooling tend to remain so, and the gap between them and the average to high attainers tends to increase. Thus the question arises: what will happen to these children if they do not receive additional support in numeracy other than that given by the class teacher as part of their normal duties? Further, since the vast majority of primary and elementary teachers are not specialist teachers of mathematics one might also ask whether the teachers are in a position to remediate the children's problems even if they know what these are. Since neither Judy, Denise nor Michael is disruptive, rather classified as 'cooperative', there is a strong possibility that their difficulties may be overlooked. Let us look at the actual attainment of each child and, though they are in different school systems, see if they experience common difficulties in numeracy lessons.

JUDY

Judy has completed one and a half year's schooling. Her teacher assessed her knowledge of the **number word** sequence, the ability to name **numerals**, and **strategies** for solving addition and subtraction involving two small collections of counters both of which were covered from view.

Judy showed she had a sound knowledge of the number word sequence in the range of one to ten. She could 'count' from one to ten and backwards from ten to one. She could also say the number before or after any number word in the range one to ten. However, she was not able to do this for the **numbers** in the teens or twenties. When numeral cards were shown to Judy she was able to identify the numerals in the range 1 to 20 but was not able to name many beyond 20.

Judy was given two verbal addition **tasks**, 5 + 4 and 8 + 3. First, she was presented with five red counters as a group, which were covered, and then four green counters which were placed under a separate screen. She was asked how many counters were there altogether. She successfully solved these tasks but it is revealing to consider the strategy she used in doing so. She invariably counted from one using her fingers or making pointing actions over the screened collections. Her strategy could be described as counting one of the screened collections from one and then continuing her count to include the other screened collection. 'One, two, three, four, five . . . six, seven, eight, nine . . . Nine!'

Judy demonstrates that she possesses one-to-one correspondence and has good counting skills but these are limited to the range one to ten. She identifies numerals up to twenty. She understands the operation of addition but not subtraction. It is important to note that her current number knowledge does not include number facts to ten. She uses a strategy of counting from one to solve additive tasks. Mathematically this is a low-level strategy. Given that she has difficulty with counting in the teens, her strategy is likely to fail her when larger quantities are introduced such as 9 + 6 for example.

DENISE

Denise was 7 years and 1 month at the time of assessment and had been in school for four terms. She could say the number words up to 27 but she had difficulty when saying the number that came after a number when it was above twelve. She also had a lack of fluency when crossing the decade number twenty. Her counting backwards skills were limited to saying the words from ten. When she was asked to start at fifteen and count backwards she said '15, 51, 52, 53'. She could say the number word that comes before a number but only if the number was less than ten. When asked to produce the number before a certain number between ten and twenty she always gave the number one more than, even when the task was repeated. For example, she would respond 'eighteen' when asked for the number before 17 and 'twenty-one' for 20.

Her numeral identification skills were limited to numbers less than 10. She said 'fourteen' for 47, 'fifty-five' for 15 and 'thirty-three' for 13. When Denise was given the same addition problem with the screened counters as Judy, that is, 5 + 4, her strategy was to guess 'seven'. The task was re-presented and this time she stated 'six'. Other than guessing Denise did not have a strategy for solving the addition tasks. The teacher reduced the complexity of the problem by showing her five counters which were then placed under a screen. Two more counters of a different colour were displayed alongside but this time they were not covered. She was asked, 'How many are there altogether?' The teacher indicated the total collection by a circular motion of the hand. Denise failed to answer three tasks, 5 + 2, 4 + 4 and 7 + 5, correctly. The level of the tasks was reduced even further by checking if Denise had one-to-one correspondence. First, a linear collection of 13 counters was presented and, secondly, one of 18 counters. Denise successfully demonstrated that she had good one-to-one correspondence in this range.

MICHAEL

Michael could count forwards up to 29 but halted at twenty. He could not say the number that came after a number within the range one to 29. He was not able to count backwards and as a consequence could not give the number which comes before a number. He was shown numeral cards to identify and was proficient in identifying the numbers up to 10. However, he had difficulties with the larger numbers especially the teens. For example, he said 'twenty' for 12 and 'fifty' for 15. He also failed to identify decade numbers.

When assessed on the additive tasks 5 + 4 and 8 + 3, he portrayed the same behaviours as Denise. He guessed. He was not able to solve tasks involving partially covered collections and he did not appear to be interested in trying to find a solution. He was successful, however, in demonstrating one-to-one correspondence with collections of 13 and then 18 items.

WHAT DO THE THREE HAVE IN COMMON?

We have presented the individual characteristics of the children but what attainments do they have in common? The number word and **numerals** knowledge and the strategies used for addition give us the clues. Collectively the three children have some proficiency in saying the forward number word sequence into the high twenties but all experience problems with teen and decade numbers. Judy and Denise can count backwards from ten but Michael is lost here. The lack of facility with number word sequences is also shown in the poor skills at saying the number which comes after or before a number word. Judy can identify numerals up to 20 but Denise and Michael's numeral identification skills are good only in the 1–10 range. Of the three children, Judy shows the most advanced strategy for the addition of two screened collections by the fact that she counts from one to arrive at the total. However, this is still a low-level strategy. Denise and Michael could not solve these problems, not even when they were posed using partially screened collections. But, they did have one-to-one correspondence. Overall, it is clear that they are performing at a low level of numeracy given the standard that is expected for their year group.

Our experience in assessing children in the three countries has led us to believe that Judy, Denise and Michael are not unusual in their level of mathematical knowledge. We are sure that teachers everywhere will readily be able to substitute the name of one, or more, of their children for the above.

The problem is not being neglected. The desire to raise standards of numeracy is a stated national education priority for many nations. Certainly Australia, the USA and England are currently undertaking systemic initiatives in early mathematics and numeracy.

In Australia, for example, the Commonwealth Government worked jointly with the states and territories to establish agreed National Numeracy Benchmarks for 8-year-olds. Commonwealth, state and territory ministers responsible for education have agreed the following literacy and numeracy goals: 'That every child leaving primary school should be numerate, and be able to read, write and spell at an appropriate level. That every child commencing school from 1998 will achieve a minimum acceptable literacy and numeracy standard within four years'. (*Numeracy = Everyone's Business*, p. 3, 1997).

In the past eight years many of the state and territory education systems in Australia, as well as the national education system in New Zealand, have developed and implemented major new programmes in early numeracy. A detailed description of some of the most significant examples of these can be found in Bobis et al. (2005).

In the USA the Standards 2000 Project released the National Council of Teachers of Mathematics updated Standards entitled *Principles and Standards for School Mathematics*. The publication includes ten standards for children's learning which span pre-school through to grade 12. The Standards emphasize how learning should grow across the four grade bands – K–2, 3–5, 6–8 and 9–12 – and are seen as statements of criteria for excellence in school mathematics. Standard 1: Number and Operation, for example, states that mathematics instructional programmes should foster the development of number and operation sense so that all students:

▶ understand numbers, ways of representing numbers, relationships among numbers, and number systems.
▶ understand the meaning of operations and how they relate to one another.
▶ use computational tools and strategies fluently and estimate appropriately.

In the UK the government launched the National Numeracy Strategy which set out a Framework for Teaching Mathematics (DfEE, 1999a). The Framework provides a year-on-year list of key objectives that are expected to be attained by the 'great majority' of children.

Examination of the published documents for each country reveals a commonality in describing numerate children. The publications indicate the need for children to be confident and competent in working with numbers, money and measurement. Statements, listing the skills, knowledge and understanding to be attained, show that children should be able to calculate accurately and efficiently, both mentally and on paper, and have a sense of the size of a number and where it fits in the number system. They should have a knowledge of number facts and have strategies for solving problems. They should also be able to check the reasonableness of an answer and be able to explain their methods. They should recognize when it is appropriate to use calculators and have the skills to use them effectively.

We cannot disagree with these aims though clearly Judy, Denise and Michael are considerably behind in meeting the targets. Although the aims are laudable it is less clear how the improvement in attainment is to be achieved. How will the aims be translated into action to help Judy, Denise and Michael? The UK government's National Numeracy Strategy embarked on a rigorous training programme and published guidance on teaching mental calculation strategies (QCA, 1999a), exemplification of key learning objectives (QCA, 1999b), sample lessons (NNP, 1999) and lists of associated mathematical vocabulary (DfEE, 1999b). Let us now examine this initiative in greater detail.

The National Numeracy Strategy's Framework for Teaching Mathematics (DfEE, 1999a) provided a year-on-year list of key objectives which the 'great majority' of children were expected to attain. Each local education authority (LEA) has been given a target for improvement. The LEAs in turn have set targets for individual schools.

The National Numeracy Strategy has also provided schools with a mechanism for attaining the objectives based upon best practice from European and Pacific-rim countries. The mechanism is a structured three-part daily mathematics lesson. The sections are referred to as 'Introduction', 'Main Teaching Activity' and 'Plenary'.

A typical lesson commences with five to ten minutes' oral work and mental calculation with the whole class, which is conducted at a brisk pace. The aim here is to rehearse, sharpen and develop mental and oral skills that may be called upon in the lesson. This is followed by the main teaching activity lasting 30–40 minutes where the teacher works directly on new input with the whole class. They then have the opportunity to split into group work or individual and paired work, thus providing consolidation and differentiation. The lesson concludes with a plenary session where the children explain their work and discuss the efficiency of different solution strategies. It is also the opportunity for the teacher to help the children to assess their developing skills against the targets they have been set and to record their progress, to make links with other work and to set homework.

Even if the target is reached by 75 per cent of the children, by implication 25 per cent are seen to be failing. Initially, prominence in the strategy was placed on whole-class introductions and summaries, with additional emphases on pace, mental agility and articulation of solutions and method. However, by 2004, despite some improvement being evident with underachieving pupils, greater recognition was being given to the fact that a significant number of children needed small-group intervention to accelerate progress and to allow the children to reach age-related expectations. Further some children would need individual provision to tackle fundamental errors and misconceptions that are preventing progress. Judy, Denise and Michael clearly fall into these categories and, if they do not receive help, will continue to experience failure and begin to feel that they are not part of the mathematics community in the classroom.

The National Numeracy standards indicate that children at Year 1 should have the following understanding of numbers and the number system, calculations and problem-solving skills:

1. Count reliably at least 20 objects.
2. Count-on and back in ones from any small number and in tens from and back to zero.
3. Read, write and order numbers from 0 to at least 20; understand and use the vocabulary for comparing and ordering these numbers.
4. Understand the operation of addition, and subtraction (as 'take away' and 'difference') and use the related vocabulary.
5. Know by heart all pairs of numbers with a total of ten.
6. Within the range 0 to 30, say the number that is one or ten more or less than any given number (QCA, 1999a, p. 6).

Clearly though Judy, Denise and Michael could meet 1 above, and partially meet 2, 3 and 6, they could not meet 5, and only Judy has a strategy for addition and this is a low-level one. Our concern is that teachers do not have sufficient skills to diagnose children's difficulties in numeracy and that in the desire to reduce the 'burden of assessment' greater emphasis is being placed on teacher assessment. We feel strongly that teachers need help in diagnosing errors and misconceptions and practical help and support firmly grounded in theory, to provide for the less able children in the early years. Such help was provided for Judy, Denise and Michael via the Mathematics Recovery Programme.

HELP FOR JUDY, DENISE AND MICHAEL VIA THE MATHEMATICS RECOVERY PROGRAMME

Judy, Denise and Michael, and their respective teachers, did receive help, support and training because each, in their own country, was selected to participate in the Mathematics Recovery Programme. A key feature of this programme is that it provides teachers with an extensive professional development course to improve their understanding, knowledge and skill in the teaching and assessment of early numeracy. This is achieved through participation in intensive, individualized teaching programmes for low-attaining children. The skills learned on the one-to-one basis can then be applied effectively to groups and whole classes of children.

Before explaining the short-term intervention programme in full detail let us show how it helped our three children by explaining the-progress each made. We will also relate how knowledge of the assessment tasks, administrative style and the implementation of the intervention impacted on the teachers involved.

JUDY REVISITED

Following the Mathematics Recovery assessment Judy received individual teaching sessions of 25 minutes' duration, four times per week, for a total of seven weeks. This was a total of 11 hours and 40 minutes. The teaching activities were to enhance Judy's knowledge of the number word sequence and numerals, and to further develop her strategies for adding and subtracting. In selecting teaching activities the teacher's intention was to present problems that, on the one hand, were quite challenging but, on the other, were reasonably likely to be solved by the child. For the first three weeks of the teaching cycle Judy continued to adhere to her count-from-one strategy to solve addition and subtraction tasks.

During the fourth week of the teaching cycle Judy made a significant development in her strategies for adding and subtracting – she developed a strategy of **counting-on** rather than counting from one. Judy seemed to become aware of counting-on during her solution of the task of 20 + 3, which was presented verbally using two screened collections. She solved this task by counting from one to twenty and then continuing her counts from twenty-one to twenty-three, while keeping track of three counts. In an ensuing discussion with her teacher after having solving the task, Judy said 'twenty and three (pause), twenty-three!' Her statement seemed indicative of mental reflection on her solution to the task. From that point onward Judy routinely used counting-on to solve addition tasks and subtraction tasks. By the time of the fourth week of her teaching session Judy had also developed proficiency with the number word sequence in the range one to one hundred. Judy could now use counting-on to solve addition tasks presented verbally (that is, without use of written symbols), for example 87 + 5, and **missing addend** tasks presented verbally such as 42 + [ ] = 46.

By the end of the fourth week of the teaching cycle, it was apparent Judy had made significant progress in her **early number** knowledge, and there was little doubt that her progress was attributable to her participation in the MR teaching sessions. Also apparent was a very significant and positive change in Judy's general attitude to the MR teaching sessions. It was clear that Judy was keenly aware of her progress and success in Mathematics Recovery, and this awareness was accompanied by a very positive attitude towards participating in the teaching sessions. In her initial interview and in the early teaching sessions Judy tended to be somewhat quiet and withdrawn. Over the course of the teaching cycle there was a gradual and substantial change in her general disposition. By the time of the fourth week, for example, she seemed to relish undertaking tasks and solving problems. She would as much as challenge her teacher to present a difficult problem. Judy's MR teacher was fully aware of this change in Judy's attitude to the teaching sessions. Her classroom teacher observed that Judy was performing better in mathematics, exhibited an increased confidence in her approach to mathematics activities in the classroom and was more positive in her approach to all classroom activities.

DENISE REVISITED

Meanwhile Denise, in England, received four 25-minute lessons each week for a period of ten weeks. During that time she learned to count forwards and backwards from 112. She could say the number that came before, or after, a number in the range 1 to 100. She still had some hesitancy with certain decade numbers. She could identify all two-digit numerals and, like Judy, had developed a count-on strategy proudly exclaiming that she did not need to use her fingers. Denise's teacher had developed a game where a numeral card was turned over and a die was thrown to generate a subtraction problem. Denise turned over 14 and then threw a six.

Denise: That is a hard one, taking six away. I don't think I want to see that!
  (Denise counts up to six.)
Denise: Took 14 away, 13 away, 12 away, 11 away, 10 away, 9 away, 8.
  (As Denise was counting back she made a regular six pattern on the table.)

Denise had developed a **count-down-from** strategy which she used to explain how she answered the next problem, 18 – 5 = [ ].
  Three lessons later Denise's teacher hid 14 bears in a cave. She told Denise there were 14 bears and asked her to close her eyes as she was going to remove some bears. She did this and informed Denise that there were only 11 bears left in the cave. How many had gone out? This can be summarized as a missing **subtrahend** 14 – [ ] = 11 and is a very challenging task.

Denise: Three!
Teacher: How did you do that?
Denise: I jumped in my head. Because 14 is not a jump we go 13, then 12, then 11.

Denise later solved 16 to 13, 20 to 16, 27 to 25 and 30 to 26. For 16 to 13 she showed double counting skills as she counted down to.

Denise: 15 that's one, 14 that's two, 13 that's three.

Denise had advanced her numerical skill and strategies for addition. She was now adept at counting-on and could **count-up-to** for missing addends. She had a count-down-from strategy for subtraction and was beginning to develop a **count-down-to** strategy though as yet she did not always choose the most appropriate strategy to solve a particular problem. Like Judy, she grew in confidence and enthusiasm. Most pleasing to see was the way in which she relished the challenge of mathematics and her ability to articulate her strategies.

MICHAEL REVISITED

Michael received a similar teaching programme to those of Judy and Denise. He showed tremendous gains in arithmetical strategies, in **forward** and **backward number word sequences**, and in **numeral identification**, all of which improved his self-confidence. When he was being assessed at the end of the programme he said, 'I'm going to do good thinking this time'. He was presented with a very difficult symbolic subtraction problem. The task on the card was 16 – 12. He read the problem out loud without hesitation.

Teacher: Do you have a way of figuring that out?
  (Michael looked at the problem for about 15 seconds thinking hard. He looks up and says) Four.

Teacher: How did you figure that out?
            (Michael shrugs his head and smiles broadly.)
Teacher: Your mouth was moving.
Michael: I took away 12 and there was four.
            (As he was saying this he made a clenched fist with his left hand. His thumb and knuckles are facing him. He points to the little finger and says) Eleven was right there.

What is significant about this is that Michael was demonstrating a count-down-to strategy. He knew where 12 was and that if it had been 'subtract eleven' the answer would have been five. Michael also developed some 'known facts' which he used in addition and subtraction. Overall he showed considerable gains in strategies. His parents were delighted with the progress he had made and wished to share in it. Michael regularly took home a homework and communication book for numeracy. The lessons for the three children were routinely videotaped. Michael's parents watched some of the taught sessions to gain an understanding of the tasks and how they could reinforce the learning. Needless to say, Michael does not receive special education remediation and he has exceeded the standard expected of his age group.

CONCLUSION

It can be said that any child receiving individualized teaching should make progress. However, the progress of all three children, in different contexts and educational systems, is highly significant. They have achieved considerable gains and now possess advanced strategies for the solution of challenging addition and subtraction tasks. Also the Mathematics Recovery Programme can be seen to have had a very significant influence on the children's attitude to learning and their self-esteem. They no longer see themselves as failing.

Moreover, the programme has changed teachers' perceptions of what can be achieved and they have delighted in the ability to move children on from low-level to advanced strategies. During the course of their training in assessment and teaching they taught children individually. This was essentially to cut down control and management factors in order to concentrate on the teaching moves involved and the child's responses, a form of teaching experiment which can be described as microteaching. Teachers began to grow in confidence even before the teaching course input. The change came about when they began to work on the assessment schedules and associated frameworks. They reported that the aspects of the assessment schedules gave them a greater content knowledge of early numeracy together with greater insights into how children learn mathematically. They felt the training gave them clear direction in their teaching in that they knew exactly what the child could, and could not, do. They knew what objectives to set and how to achieve them. They began to put greater emphasis on less-used aspects of the curriculum such as backward number word sequences and number word before tasks. The assessment course not only changed their view of the curriculum but they reported how it began to impact on their teaching style. Because the emphasis in the assessment is on observation and interaction with the child, they began to pick up on the verbal and non-verbal clues the children give when solving tasks. They began to appreciate why children need time to answer and to check and reflect on their thinking. They told how they began to ask more probing questions to explore the children's responses. A significant effect was they professed a confidence and a willingness to help colleagues and to disseminate the new learning in their schools and districts.

We return to the children and their teachers in Chapter 10 to show how progress was made. In Chapter 2 we explain how you too may attain this knowledge and ability by presenting a learning framework for early numeracy.

2

The Learning Framework in Number

Summary

This chapter describes the Learning Framework in Number (LFIN).

The LFIN consists of 11, interrelated aspects of early number, which are organized into four parts. The Stages of Early Arithmetical Learning in Part A are the most important aspect of the LFIN and relate to the relative sophistication of the child's strategies for counting, adding or subtracting. The six aspects of Parts A, B and D are set out in tabular form and show a progression of stages or levels. Determining the child's stages and levels results in a comprehensive profile of the child's early number knowledge.

The four parts of the LFIN generate six assessment schedules. Schedules 1.1 and 1.2 cover the Parts A and B. Schedules 2.1 and 2.2 relate to Part C, and 3.1 and 3.2 to Part D.

Development of Mathematical Recovery included the development of a learning framework which provides essential guidance for assessment and teaching in early number.

The **Learning Framework in Number** (LFIN) is organized into four parts – A, B, C and D. The parts are further subdivided and span 11 aspects of children's early numerical knowledge. All the eleven aspects of the LFIN are considered to be important in children's early numerical learning. They should not be regarded as early number topics which are widely separate from each other. Rather we would like to highlight their closely integrated nature. Assessing one aspect typically provides information about other aspects. For example, the integrated nature of LFIN can be demonstrated as follows. A child solves an addition task, for example 7 + 4, by counting-on, a strategy that is classified in the Stages of Early Arithmetical Learning (Part A). In solving the task the child uses the forward number word sequence, that is 'seven, . . . eight, nine, ten, eleven', which is an aspect of Number Words and Numerals (Part B) and uses their fingers to keep track of their counting. Use of finger patterns is an aspect which appears in Structuring Number (Part C). This comprehensive and integrated framework is referred to as the Learning Framework in Number and is presented in Table 2.1.

Teaching in the Mathematics Recovery Programme (MRP) typically focuses on several aspects simultaneously rather than just a single aspect. In the following section we provide a description of the aspects in each part and then present them in a numbered, tabulated form – referred to as a model. Each model sets out stages and levels of children's numerical knowledge and facilitates profiling of the children's knowledge as well as indicating likely progressions in the children's learning. Teachers have used the framework to predict the types of advancement their children are likely to make. The LFIN provides important directionality in setting the learning objectives.

Table 2.1 The Learning Framework in Number

Part A	Part B	Part C	Part D
Early Arithmetical Strategies Base-Ten Arithmetical Strategies	Forward Number Word Sequences and Number Word After Backward Number Word Sequences and Number Word Before Numerals	Structuring Number 1 to 20	Early Multiplication and Division
Stages: **Early Arithmetical Strategies**	**Levels:** **Forward Number Word Sequences (FNWSs) and Number Word After**	Combining and Partitioning Spatial Patterns and Subitizing	**Levels:** 1 Initial Grouping 2 Perceptual Counting in Multiples 3 Figurative Composite Grouping 4 Repeated Abstract Composite Grouping 5 Multiplication and Division as Operations
0 – Emergent Counting 1 – Perceptual Counting 2 – Figurative Counting 3 – Initial Number Sequence 4 – Intermediate Number Sequence 5 - Facile Number Sequence	0 – Emergent FNWS. 1 – Initial FNWS up to 'ten'. 2 – Intermediate FNWS up to 'ten'. 3 – Facile with FNWSs up to 'ten'. 4 – Facile with FNWSs up to 'thirty'. 5 – Facile with FNWSs up to 'one hundred'.	Temporal Sequences Finger Patterns Five-based (Quinary-based) Strategies	
Levels: **Base-Ten Arithmetical Strategies**	**Levels:** **Backward Number Word Sequences (BNWSs) and Number Word Before**		
1 – Initial Concept of Ten 2 – Intermediate Concept of Ten 3 – Facile Concept of Ten	0 – Emergent BNWS. 1 – Initial BNWS up to 'ten'. 2 – Intermediate BNWS up to 'ten'. 3 – Facile with BNWSs up to 'ten'. 4 – Facile with BNWSs up to 'thirty'. 5 – Facile with BNWSs up to 'one hundred'.		
	Levels: **Numeral Identification** 0 – Emergent Numeral Identification. 1 – Numerals to '10' 2 – Numerals to '20' 3 – Numerals to '100' 4 – Numerals to '1000'		

Source: adapted from Wright et al. 2002, p. 10.

TECHNICAL TERMS

In order for the reader to become familiar with LFIN it is necessary to learn a range of technical terms. These terms relate mainly to children's early numerical knowledge and strategies, and associated instructional techniques. The terms are explained in the following section and, for the convenience of the reader, many of the terms also appear in the Glossary at the end of this book.

PART A OF THE LFIN – STAGES OF EARLY ARITHMETICAL LEARNING (SEAL) AND BASE-TEN ARITHMETICAL STRATEGIES

Part A contains two **aspects** and their attendant models. Of these, SEAL is the primary and most significant aspect of LFIN.

Aspect 1: Stages of Early Arithmetical Learning (SEAL)

Stage 0 – Emergent Counting
Stage 1 – Perceptual Counting
Stage 2 – Figurative Counting
Stage 3 – Initial Number Sequence
Stage 4 – Intermediate Number Sequence
Stage 5 – Facile Number Sequence

The Stages of Early Arithmetical Learning sets out a progression of the strategies children use in early numeracy situations that are problematic for them, for example, being required to figure out how many in a collection, and various kinds of additive and subtractive situations. The SEAL model appears in Table 2.2 and consists of a progression of five **stages** in children's development of early arithmetical strategies. The label 'Stage 0' is used for children who have not attained the first stage. The SEAL model has been adapted from research by Steffe and colleagues (Steffe, 1992a; Steffe and Cobb, 1988; Steffe et al., 1983) and related research by Wright (1989; 1991a). Finally, descriptions in the SEAL model include reference to particular tasks (e.g. missing addend) and strategies (for example, **count-on**). Descriptions of these tasks and strategies are provided in the Glossary at the end of this book.

Aspect 2: Base-Ten Arithmetical Strategies

Level 1 – Initial Concept of Ten
Level 2 – Intermediate Concept of Ten
Level 3 – Facile Concept of Ten

Around the time they attain Stage 4 or 5 on the SEAL, children typically begin to develop knowledge of the tens and ones structure of the numeration system. Of course, children can and should solve addition and subtraction tasks involving two-**digit** numbers long before they develop knowledge of the tens and ones structure. For children who have attained Stage 5, development of knowledge of the tens and ones structure becomes increasingly important. Table 2.3 outlines a progression of three levels in children's development of base-ten arithmetical strategies. The model for the development of base-ten arithmetical strategies is adapted from research by Cobb and Wheatley (1988).

Table 2.2 The SEAL Model for Stages of Early Arithmetical Learning

Stage 0: Emergent Counting. Cannot count visible items. The child either does not know the number words or cannot coordinate the number words with items.

Stage 1: Perceptual Counting. Can count perceived items but not those in screened (that is, concealed) collections. This may involve seeing, hearing or feeling items.

Stage 2: Figurative Counting. Can count the items in a screened collection but counting typically includes what adults might regard as redundant activity. For example, when presented with two screened collections, told how many in each collection and asked how many counters in all, the child will count from 'one' instead of counting on.

Stage 3: Initial Number Sequence. Child uses counting-on rather than counting from 'one', to solve addition or missing addend tasks (for example, 6 + [ ] = 9). The child may use a count-down-from strategy to solve removed items tasks (for example, 17 − 3 as 16, 15, 14 − answer 14) but not count-down-to strategies to solve missing subtrahend tasks (for example, 17 − 14 as 16, 15, 14 − answer 3).

Stage 4: Intermediate Number Sequence. The child counts-down-to to solve missing subtrahend tasks (for example, 17 − 14 as 16, 15, 14 − answer 3). The child can choose the more efficient of count-down-from and count-down-to strategies.

Stage 5: Facile Number Sequence. The child uses a range of what are referred to as **non-count-by-ones** strategies. These strategies involve **procedures** other than **counting-by-ones** but may also involve some counting-by-ones. Thus in additive and subtractive situations, the child uses strategies such as compensation, using a known result, adding to ten, commutativity, subtraction as the inverse of addition, awareness of the 'ten' in a teen number.

Table 2.3 Model for the development of base-ten arithmetical strategies

Level 1: Initial Concept of Ten. The child does not see ten as a unit of any kind. The child focuses on the individual items that make up the ten. One ten and ten ones do not exist for the child at the same time. In addition or subtraction tasks involving tens, children at this level count forward or backward by ones.

Level 2: Intermediate Concept of Ten. Ten is seen as a unit composed of ten ones. The child is dependent on re-presentations (like a mental replay or recollection) of units of ten such as hidden ten-strips or open hands of ten fingers. The child can perform addition and subtraction tasks involving tens where these are presented with materials such as covered strips of tens and ones. The child cannot solve addition and subtraction tasks involving tens and ones when presented as written number sentences.

Level 3: Facile Concept of Ten. The child can solve addition and subtraction tasks involving tens and ones without using materials or **re-presentations** of materials. The child can solve written number sentences involving tens and ones by adding or subtracting units of ten and ones.

Note: A necessary condition for attaining Level 1 is attainment of at least Stage 3 in the Stages of Early Arithmetical Learning.

PART B OF THE LFIN − FORWARD NUMBER WORD SEQUENCES (FNWSs), BACKWARD NUMBER WORD SEQUENCES (BNWSs) AND NUMERAL IDENTIFICATION (NUM. ID.)

There are three aspects in Part B of the LFIN. They are concerned with important specific aspects of children's early number knowledge. These models resulted from research by Wright (1991b; 1994).

Understanding children's specific strategies on tasks relating to these aspects is still important but perhaps less so than in SEAL. There is also less emphasis on the idiosyncratic nature and diversity of the strategies relating to these aspects.

Aspects 1 and 2: FNWSs and BNWSs

The term 'number words' refers to the spoken and heard names of numbers. In LFIN an important distinction is made between counting and reciting a sequence of number words. This distinction was made by Steffe and Cobb (1988). The term 'counting' is used only in cases that involve coordination of each spoken number word with an actual or imagined (that is, conceptualized) item. Thus counting typically occurs in situations that are problematic for students, for example, solving an **additive** or **subtractive task** or establishing the **numerosity** of a collection of items. The activity of merely saying a sequence of number words is not referred to as counting.

The term 'forward number word sequence' refers to a regular sequence of number words forward, typically but not necessarily by ones, for example, the FNWS from one to twenty, the FNWS from eighty-one to ninety-three or the FNWS by tens from twenty-four. The term 'backward number word sequence' is used in similar vein, for example, the BNWS from twenty to ten. From the point of view of fully understanding children's early numerical knowledge, it is useful to construe as distinct the two aspects, concerned with number word sequences, that is, forward and backward. Nevertheless, because of the many similarities between these two aspects, their presentations here are integrated to some extent. Models associated with these aspects are shown in Tables 2.4 and 2.5. The label 'Level 0' is used for children who have not attained the first **level**.

Table 2.4 Model for the construction of Forward Number Word Sequences

---

Level 0: Emergent FNWS. The child cannot produce the FNWS from 'one' to 'ten'.

Level 1: Initial FNWS up to 'ten'. The child can produce the FNWS from 'one' to 'ten'. The child cannot produce the number word just after a given number word in the range 'one' to 'ten'. Dropping back to 'one' does not appear at this level. Children at Levels 1, 2 and 3 may be able to produce FNWSs beyond 'ten'.

Level 2: Intermediate FNWS up to 'ten'. The child can produce the FNWS from 'one' to 'ten'. The child can produce the number word just after a given number word but drops back to 'one' when doing so.

Level 3: Facile with FNWSs up to 'ten'. The child can produce the FNWS from 'one' to 'ten'. The child can produce the number word just after a given number word in the range 'one' to 'ten' without dropping back. The child has difficulty producing the number word just after a given number word, for numbers beyond ten.

Level 4: Facile with FNWSs up to 'thirty'. The child can produce the FNWS from 'one' to 'thirty'. The child can produce the number word just after a given number word in the range 'one' to 'thirty' without dropping back. Children at this level may be able to produce FNWS beyond 'thirty'.

Level 5: Facile with FNWSs up to 'one hundred'. The child can produce FNWS in the range 'one' to 'one hundred'. The child can produce the number word just after a given number word in the range 'one' to 'one hundred' without dropping back. Children at this level may be able to produce FNWS beyond 'one hundred'.

Table 2.5 Model for the construction of Backward Number Word Sequences

---

Level 0: Emergent BNWS. The child cannot produce the BNWS from 'ten' to one'.

Level 1: Initial BNWS up to 'ten'. The child can produce the BNWS from 'ten' to 'one'. The child cannot produce the number word just before a given number word. Dropping back to 'one' does not appear at this level. Children at Levels 1, 2 and 3 may be able to produce BNWSs beyond 'ten'.

Level 2: Intermediate BNWS up to 'ten'. The child can produce the BNWS from 'ten' to 'one'. The child can produce the number word just before a given number word but drops back to 'one' when doing so.

Level 3: Facile with BNWSs up to 'ten'. The child can produce the BNWS from 'ten' to 'one'. The child can produce the number word just before a given number word in the range 'ten' to 'one' without dropping back. The child has difficulty producing the number word just before a given number word, for numbers beyond ten.

Level 4: Facile with BNWSs up to 'thirty'. The child can produce the BNWS from 'thirty' to 'one'. The child can produce the number word just before a given number word in the range 'one' to 'thirty' without dropping back. Children at this level may be able to produce BNWS beyond 'thirty'.

Level 5: Facile with BNWSs up to 'one hundred'. The child can produce BNWS in the range 'one hundred' to 'one'. The child can produce the number word just before a given number word in the range 'one' to 'one hundred' without dropping back. Children at this level may be able to produce BNWSs beyond 'one hundred'.

Aspect 3: Numeral Identification

Numerals are the written and read symbols for numbers, for example '3', '27', and '360'. Learning to identify, recognize and write numerals can rightly be regarded an important part of early literacy development. At the same time it is important to realize that this learning is equally, if not more so, an important part of early numerical development. The term 'identify' is used here with precise meaning, that is, to state the name of a displayed numeral. The complementary task of selecting a named numeral from a randomly arranged group of displayed numerals is referred to as 'recognizing'. Thus we make the distinction between '**numeral identification**' and '**numeral recognition**'. Using these terms in this way accords with typical use in psychology and in early literacy. Table 2.6 outlines a progression of four levels in children's development of numeral identification. As with the models above, the label 'Level 0' is used for children who have not attained the first level.

Table 2.6 Model for the development of Numeral Identification

---

Level 0: Emergent Numeral Identification. Cannot identify some or all numerals in the range '1' to '10'.

Level 1: Numerals to '10'. Can identify numerals in the range '1' to '10'.

Level 2: Numerals to '20'. Can identify numerals in the range '1' to '20'.

Level 3: Numerals to '100'. Can identify one- and two-digit numerals.

Level 4: Numerals to '1000'. Can identify one- two- and three-digit numerals.

PART C OF THE LFIN – COMBINING AND PARTITIONING, SPATIAL PATTERNS AND SUBITIZING, TEMPORAL SEQUENCES, FINGER PATTERNS AND FIVE-BASED (QUINARY-BASED) STRATEGIES

There are five aspects in Part C. They often arise incidentally in children's solutions to tasks on the assessment. As a consequence, they are not presented in tabular form. Nevertheless, these aspects should be regarded as important and interrelated with Parts A, B and D of the LFIN. There are also close interrelationships among the aspects within Part C. For example, **combining** and **partitioning** are interrelated with spatial patterns and finger patterns, temporal patterns are interrelated with spatial patterns and finger patterns are interrelated with the five-based aspect.

Each of the five aspects in Structuring Number Strand is potentially important in children's early numerical development. The description of each of the five aspects in Structuring Number Strand typically includes examples of children's strategies.

Aspect 1: Combining and Partitioning

Counting strategies are an important aspect of children's early numerical knowledge. Nevertheless, at the same time as they develop counting strategies, children may also develop knowledge of simple combinations and partitions of numbers, which does not rely on counting. Examples of these combinations are the addition of two numbers in the range one to five. Doubles of the numbers in the range one to five and beyond (for example, four and four is eight) are prominent examples of these combinations. The process of partitioning (for example, eight is four and four, six is four and two) is the complement of combining. Children learn to provide answers almost immediately to questions such as three plus three, using procedures that do not involve counting-by-ones. Numerical knowledge of this kind has been labeled 'automatized' or 'habituated'. Recent research provides strong indications that teaching children to habituate simple addition facts through combining and partitioning of small numbers can significantly facilitate development of advanced numerical strategies, that is, non-count-by-one strategies. Combining and partitioning can also be important for the development of five-based strategies. Consider for example that a child is asked to say two numbers that make seven when added and the child immediately answers 'five' and 'two'. We might conclude that the child can partition seven into five and two without counting by ones. Combining and partitioning is included in the LFIN because development of this aspect of early number can form an important basis for further learning. The development of this aspect has drawn on research by Cobb and colleagues (Cobb et al., 1991; 1992; Yackel et al., 1991).

Aspect 2: Spatial Patterns and Subitizing

This aspect relates to strategies that arise in situations involving spatial configurations of various kinds, for example domino patterns, pairs patterns, ten frames, playing card patterns, regular plane figures and random arrays. Activities involving spatial patterns and **subitizing** have an important role in young children's numerical development. Subitizing is a technical term in psychology. The *Penguin Dictionary of Psychology* defines 'subitize' thus: 'to apprehend directly the number of dots in an unstructured stimulus display without counting them. The limit on this process is about seven or eight dots.' Von Glasersfeld (1982, p. 214) described subitizing as 'the immediate, correct assignation of number words to small collections of perceptual items'. In his discussion of subitizing, von Glasersfeld points out that when a young child says, for example, 'three' in response to a briefly displayed spatial array, the child may be doing no more than recognizing and naming a spatial arrangement. One cannot assume that this child has a concept of 'three'. Nevertheless, being able to name spatial arrays in this way is an important basis. No doubt at some point the child will see a correspondence between the name of the array, that is, 'three', and the last number word when they count the dots in the array, for example 'one, two, three'.

'Subitizing' is a technical term with a specific meaning whereas, in the context of early arithmetic, the term 'spatial patterns' is more general or more inclusive. In early number there is a range of instructional settings for which spatial pattern or spatial arrangement seems to be a dominant feature. These include dot cards with random or irregular arrays, the various dots cards with regular patterns (see below); rows of counters arranged by twos or fives and with colour differentiating each group of ten, the ten frame, plane figures (triangles, squares, and so on).

Aspect 3: Temporal Sequences

Temporal sequences involve events that occur sequentially in time, for example sequences of sounds and movements. Sequences of sounds may be rhythmical, arrhythmic or monotonic. Instructional settings in which the child's task is to count or copy a sequence of sounds or count a sequence of movements are considered likely to enhance early numerical knowledge. There has been little systematic study of children's strategies associated with temporal sequences. Experience has shown that, as a general rule, children are not as facile at counting temporal sequences as they are at counting items occurring in spatial sequence. When counting a sequence of sounds, the child has no control of the speed of perception of the individual items which is in contrast to counting a row of dots. Children will count slow monotonic sequences of sounds and sequences of movements similarly to the way they count a row of items, that is, to coordinate a number word in sequence with their perception of each item. When counting rapid, rhythmical sequences of up to six sounds any one of three strategies might be used:

▶ counting the individual sounds from one as they occur;
▶ recognizing the pattern in terms of its number of beats and thus answer without counting; and
▶ mentally replaying or re-presenting the pattern, after its completion, and counting the number of beats in re-presentation.

Development of this aspect has drawn on research by Wright (for example, 1989).

Aspect 4: Finger Patterns

Children's use of fingers is very prominent in early number. Fingers are used in a range of ways and with varying levels of facility and sophistication. Let us consider a low-level strategy to solve 4 + 3. A child may work out 4 + 3 by sequentially raising four fingers on one hand in coordination with counting from one to four, then raising three fingers on the other hand in coordination with counting from one to three and, finally, counting their raised fingers from one to seven. We would call this 'counting from one three times' or 'counting-all'. The child does not have a facile finger pattern for three or four and necessarily establishes finger patterns for these numbers prior to working out 4 + 3. An example of a reasonably advanced strategy is using fingers to keep track of counting-on. Thus in working out 7 + 4, a child might raise four fingers sequentially in coordination with saying 'eight, nine, ten, eleven'. The fingers serve the purpose of keeping track of the count and the child stops at eleven because they realize that they have made four counts and this is indicated by having four fingers raised. As children progress across the Stages of Early Arithmetical Learning, they typically develop increasingly sophisticated finger strategies. One expects that, ultimately, children will no longer rely on using finger patterns. We believe that instruction in early number must accord with and take account of children's spontaneous finger-based strategies. Finger patterns play an important role in early numerical strategies, and their use and development is to be encouraged.

Aspect 5: Five-based (Quinary-Based) Strategies

These strategies involve using the number five as a base and arise in instructional settings involving the arrangement of items in fives, for example, the **arithmetic rack** and the ten frame, and also settings where use of fingers is prominent (because there are five fingers on each hand). Using five as a base (reference point, anchor) means that combining and partitioning numbers involving five is given special emphasis in children's learning, and is therefore likely to be incorporated by children into additive and subtractive strategies. Typically in these settings, the number ten is also a base, for example two rows of five can be seen as ten. Thus five does not replace ten as a base. Rather, five, as well as ten, is an essential reference point. In early number there is a major potential advantage associated with five being used as an additional base along with ten, that is, using five as a base has the potential to greatly reduce reliance on counting-by-ones. Development of this aspect has drawn on research by Gravemeijer (1994; Gravemeijer et al., 2000) and Cobb and colleagues (1995).

Examples of five-based strategies are: working out 3 + 4 by saying 'three and two is five, and two more is seven' and working out 8 – 4 by saying 'eight take three is five and one more back is four'. Development of five-based strategies is closely linked to the development of combining and partitioning strategies (see Aspect 1). In the first example above (3 + 4), four is partitioned into 2 and 2, and in the second example (8 – 4), four is partitioned into 3 and 1. Promoting the use of five-based strategies in early number is considered likely to facilitate development of advanced numerical strategies and to support children's advancement across the stages of SEAL.

PART D OF THE LFIN – MULTIPLICATION AND DIVISION

In 2000 the Learning Framework in Number was extended to include a focus on young children's development of multiplication and division knowledge, and drew on a range of research (see Mulligan, 1998).

The multiplication and division aspect is presented in tabular form consisting of five levels. As in the above aspects these are regarded as levels of progression and are used to profile children's knowledge (Mulligan, 1998). The model is presented in Table 2.7.

Table 2.7 Model for the levels of Multiplication and Division

---

Level 1: Initial Grouping
Level 2: Perceptual Counting in Multiples
Level 3: Figurative Composite Grouping
Level 4: Repeated Abstract Composite Grouping
Level 5: Multiplication and Division as Operations

Level 1: Initial Grouping. The child at Level 1 can establish the numerosity of a collection of equal groups when the items are visible and counts by ones when doing so, that is, the child uses perceptual counting (see Stage 1 of SEAL). The child can make groups of a specified size from a collection of items, for example, given 12 counters the child can arrange the counters into groups of three thereby obtaining four groups. This is referred to as quotitive sharing, and is also known as the grouping aspect of division. The child can also share a collection of items into a specified number of groups, for example, given 20 counters the child can share the counters into five equal groups. This is referred to as partitive sharing or as the sharing aspect of division. The child does not count in multiples.

Level 2: Perceptual Counting in Multiples. The child at Level 2 has developed counting strategies that are more advanced than those used in Level 1. These multiplicative counting strategies involve implicitly or explicitly counting in multiples. After sharing a collection into equal groups, the child uses one of these strategies to count all the items contained in the groups, which must be visible. The child is not able to count the items in situations were the groups are screened. These counting strategies include rhythmic, double and skip counting, and each is given the label 'perceptual' (for example, perceptual rhythmic counting) because of the child's reliance on visible items.

Level 3: Figurative Composite Grouping. The child at Level 3 has developed counting strategies which do not rely on items being visible and which do not involve counting by ones. For example, if the child is presented with four groups of three counters, where each group is separately screened, the child may use skip counting by threes to determine the number of counters in all, that is, 'three, six, nine, twelve'. From the child's perspective each of the four screens symbolizes a collection of three items but the individual items are not visible. There is a correspondence between not having to count by ones on tasks involving equal groups and counting-on in the case of an additive task, for example 6 + 3 presented with two screened collections. In the case of the additive task the first screen symbolizes the collection of six counters and the child does not need to count from one to six. Thus one would expect children at Level 3 in terms of early multiplication and division to have attained Stage 3 in terms of SEAL.

Level 4: Repeated Abstract Composite Grouping. The child at Level 4 has constructed a conceptual structure labeled an 'abstract composite unit' (Steffe and Cobb, 1988) in which the child is simultaneously aware of both the composite and unitary aspects of three for example. The child can use repeated addition to solve multiplication tasks and repeated subtraction to solve division tasks, and can do so in the absence of visible or screened items. On a multiplicative task involving six groups of three items, in which each group is separately screened, the child is aware of each group as an abstract composite unit. Construction of abstract composite units is associated with Stage 5 of SEAL. Thus, in the case of children who have significant experience with multiplication and division situations as well as addition and subtraction situations, it is likely that being at Level 4 for early multiplication and division is contemporaneous with being at Stage 5 in terms of SEAL.

Level 5: Multiplication and Division as Operations. The child at Level 5 can coordinate two composite units in the context of multiplication or division. On a task such as six threes or six groups of three, for example, the child is aware of both six and three as abstract composite units, whereas at Level 4 the child is aware of three as an abstract composite unit but is not aware of six as an abstract composite unit. Also, the child at Level 5 can immediately recall or quickly derive many of the basic facts of multiplication and division, and may use multiplication facts to derive division facts. At Level 5, the commutative principle of multiplication (for example, $5 \times 3 = 3 \times 5$) and the inverse relationship between multiplication and division are within the child's zone of proximal development. Thus, for example, the child might be aware that six threes is the same as three sixes and might use $4 \times 8 = 32$ to work out $32 \div 4$. At this level the child might also use a known fact to work out an unknown fact. For example, $4 \times 5 = 20$ is used to calculate 4×6.

The Learning Framework in Number provides a basis for assessment and teaching in Mathematics Recovery. In the next chapter we focus on the distinctive approach to assessment in the Mathematics Recovery Programme.

3
The LFIN and the Assessment Interview Schedule 1.1

Summary

In this chapter we set out how the assessment schedules relate to the Learning Framework in Number (LFIN). We explain how the key outcomes of the assessment are to elicit the child's most advanced numerical knowledge and strategies and to determine the child's stage of development in terms of Stages of Early Arithmetical Learning (SEAL). We describe the task groups in Assessment Interview Schedule 1.1 and how to administer them to arrive at levels of performance. We present the Additive and Subtractive tasks and label the strategies that we would be looking for in each task group.

We discuss the distinctive approach to assessment in the Mathematics Recovery Programme (MRP). We describe the techniques necessary for the preparation of the two assessment interviews in Part A of the LFIN and how the assessment interviews differ from a pencil and paper test. We discuss how to administer the diagnostic Assessment Interview Schedule 1.1 and how to use the models for number words and numerals to analyze the information gathered. The assessment schedules in the Mathematics Recovery Programme have been used by hundreds of teachers around the English-speaking world and this has allowed us to gather information on the types of responses children make. We present examples of these to alert the trainee and experienced interviewer to patterns of non-standard responses.

OVERVIEW

Mathematics Recovery assessment aims to provide extensive and detailed information about the child's numerical knowledge. This includes determining the child's stage and levels in terms of the Learning Framework in Number, and obtaining detailed information about the child's current numerical strategies and knowledge of number words and numerals. The key outcome of the assessment is the determination of the child's stage in terms of the Stages of Early Arithmetical Learning (SEAL). This involves eliciting the child's most advanced numerical strategies.

In order to obtain the required details of the child's numerical knowledge and strategies it is necessary to administer the assessment individually via an interview. The interview is videotaped and the outcomes of the assessment are determined by analyzing the videotape of the interview. During the assessment interview the assessor takes a somewhat flexible approach. This may involve several moves such as posing additional tasks and questions on the basis of the child's initial responses to the tasks. Because nothing needs to be written down during the course of the interview, the interviewer focuses exclusively on watching and responding to the child on the basis of their ongoing observations and decision-making.

The four parts of the LFIN give rise to six assessment interview schedules. These are set out in Table 3.1.

Table 3.1 Linking the Assessment Interview Schedules to the Learning Framework in Number

Assessment schedule	LFIN	Content
1.1 and 1.2	Part A	Early Arithmetical Strategies
		Base-Ten Arithmetical Strategies
	Part B	FNWS and Number Word After
		BNWS and Number Word Before
		Numeral Identification
2.1 and 2.2	Part C	Other Aspects of Early
		Arithmetical Learning
3.1 and 3.2	Part D	Early Multiplication and Division

THE ASSESSMENT INTERVIEW OUTCOMES

Parts A and B are assessed together by two assessment interview schedules. These are termed Assessment 1.1 and Assessment 1.2. The outcomes of the Assessment Interview 1.1 are:

▶   determination of the child's Stage of Early Arithmetical Learning in addition and subtraction within the range Stage 0 to Stage 4; and

▶   extensive information on the child's facility with number word sequences and numerals.

The outcomes of the Assessment Interview 1.2 are:

▶   determination of the child's Stage of Early Arithmetical Learning in addition and subtraction at Stage 5; and

▶   determination of the child's level of development of Base-Ten Arithmetical Strategies.

Part C has two interview schedules, 2.1 and 2.2. The outcome of the Assessment Interview 2.1 is:

▶   extensive information on the child's ability to structure numbers in the range one to ten.

The outcome of the Assessment Interview 2.2 is:

▶   extensive information on the child's ability to structure numbers in the range one to twenty.

Part D is assessed by two assessment interview schedules. These are termed 3.1 and 3.2. The outcome of the Assessment Interview 3.1 is:

▶   determination of the child's level of knowledge in the early stages of multiplication and division.

The outcome of the Assessment Interview 3.2 is:

▶   determination of the child's level of knowledge in the advanced stages of multiplication and division.

The assessment schedules differ from pencil and paper tests in several ways. They can be used with children throughout the primary phase of education. They are untimed and have been designed to be administered in their entirety or in smaller sections over a period of time. The questions are posed verbally and the assessor can interact with the child to elicit or clarify the observations and verbal information. They are quite different from standardized tests of any form.

Before we explain the detail of each assessment schedule it will be useful to consider some general principles and techniques which are universally applicable. In the following paragraphs we set out how to conduct the assessment interview, the practices needed to become skillful, and the techniques associated with presenting task items. These include re-posing and rephrasing tasks, and revisiting tasks. We also explain how to elicit the most advanced strategy, how to monitor the child's ease and comfort, the minimal use of motivation, how to introduce tasks and a technique called 'talking to the camera'.

CONDUCTING THE ASSESSMENT INTERVIEW

In order to administer the assessment interviews correctly the interviewer needs to learn the words and actions associated with presenting each kind of assessment task. It is also necessary to learn the general interview technique which involves observation and questioning in order to elicit information about the child's knowledge and strategies. The interviewing technique involves the teacher using his or her judgment during the course of the interview to pose additional questions that take account of the child's responses to the assessment tasks.

Becoming competent in administering the assessment requires extensive practice, review and reflection. Learning how to conduct the assessment should involve interviews with several children, the review of videotapes and then repeating this whole process several times. Experience has taught us that trainee assessors benefit greatly from working in pairs or trios. They can take turns to present aspects of the assessment schedule and to observe and give feedback to one another on the correct administration of the tasks and how to maintain the climate of the interview. We have found that children do not seem to be perturbed by the presence of others. Following presentation of the tasks much can be learned by the trainees working together to observe and interpret the videotaped records of children's responses. Through practice, review and reflection, the interviewer becomes very attuned to the nature and range of children's responses to the tasks and the techniques involved in posing additional questions when necessary.

Practising the Assessment Interview

Before videotaping the assessment interview, trainee assessors should practise individually and in pairs the posing of the various assessment tasks. It is recommended that the first assessment interviews with children are undertaken with more able Year 1 children. These children tend to more readily understand the tasks and are more likely to be successful, and thus it is usually easier to conduct the interview with such children. In this instance it is the assessor who is the learner and the child is the facilitator of that learning.

Re-posing and Rephrasing Tasks

Administering the assessment involves the interviewer following a prescribed schedule. It is important that the tasks are presented as described in the schedule. The interviewer should avoid presenting the task a second time, unless it is deemed necessary. The reason for this is that it can be counterproductive if the child has already started to solve the task. By continuing to speak, the interviewer can interrupt the child's thought processes. In cases where additional clarification for the child seems necessary, the interviewer may re-pose a task and repeat statements in the script. For example, this becomes particularly apparent when children are asked to provide the number word just before a number word in the backward number word sequence aspect. The children tend to give the number word after rather than the one before, reflecting their unfamiliarity with this task item. The interviewer may also rephrase or make variations to the verbal instructions, but the nature and conditions of the task should not be varied. In the initial stages of learning to administer the assessment, it is advisable to follow the scripts closely. With experience the interviewer will become more fluent and flexible in presenting the tasks, and more skillful at probing the child's initial response.

Revisiting Tasks

The interviewer must refrain from providing any verbal or non-verbal clues to the child. The tasks have the purpose of providing insight into the child's numerical thinking, and this information is equally as important as whether the child answers the task correctly. In cases where the interviewer thinks that the child may have made a random error, tasks may be re-posed at a later time during the course of the interview. The re-posing of tasks at the end of a section of items is called revisiting. It allows us to see whether the child made a slip or miscalculation or whether the original response showed a lack of knowledge. Revisiting tasks is useful if this is considered likely to provide additional information about the child's knowledge and strategies.

Eliciting the Most Advanced Strategy

The importance of closely observing the child's strategy was emphasized above. In order to elicit the child's most advanced strategy it is necessary first to understand the child's current strategy. Eliciting the child's most advanced strategy typically involves asking, 'Can you do that another way?' 'Do you have another way to check that?' Alternatively, the schedules are designed so that the interviewer might pose one or more supplementary tasks and ask the child if they can work out the problem by a different method.

Monitoring the Child's Ease and Comfort

At the beginning of the interview, the interviewer should take steps to make the child feel as comfortable as possible. As well as asking the child their name and other particulars, the interviewer should explain the purpose of the interview and tell the child what is expected of them during the interview. The interviewer should monitor and be sensitive to the child's state of ease and comfort during the course of the interview.

Use Motivation Sparingly

In most cases it is not necessary to provide ongoing encouragement and motivation to the child because, typically, children seem to gain intrinsic satisfaction from solving the tasks. Thus, as a general rule the interviewer should not routinely comment on the correctness of the child's responses. It may be appropriate to do so when, for example, the child expresses particular interest in whether they have answered correctly. Confirming that a child has correctly answered all or most of a group of tasks often seems to have a positive motivational effect on the child. In similar vein, affirming sound effort on the part of the child in attempting to solve tasks usually proves to be motivational when it is genuine and not overdone. Thus it is appropriate to use motivation and encouragement sparingly.

'Talking to the Camera'

This technique involves making a statement during the course of the interview that refers to an observation or realization concerning the child's strategy. The interviewer makes the statement for the purpose of establishing a record on the videotape of their observation or realization. If the interviewer observes that the child used their fingers in a particular way during a solution, for example, the interviewer may comment on this in a non-committal fashion, for example, 'I saw you raise four fingers.'

This technique should be used in such a way that it causes no disruption to the child and little or no interruption to the flow of the interview.

Introductory Tasks, Entry Tasks, and less and more advanced tasks

Some, but not all, of the Task Groups in the Assessment Schedules begin with an introductory task, which familiarizes the child with the new type of task. The introductory task is posed first. If the child has difficulty with the introductory task, the interviewer should explain it thoroughly and work through it with them. If necessary, a second introductory task can be presented. Then the entry task is presented. Several task items have branches which lead to less advanced or more advanced tasks. The child's performance on the entry task, or tasks, is noted and the interviewer follows one of two routes. If the child has difficulty with the entry task, the interviewer should present the less advanced tasks. If the child solves the entry task easily, the interviewer should present the more advanced tasks. In some cases it may be necessary to present the entry task, then the less advanced task and finally the more advanced tasks. Supplementary tasks are available when additional clarification of a child's strategies is required.

A summary of the interviewing techniques is presented in Table 3.2.

Table 3.2 Summary guidelines for presenting assessment tasks

1. Present the tasks in the order in which they appear in the schedule.
2. Avoid re-posing the task unless you are sure it is necessary.
3. Verbal instructions may be rephrased if it is likely to help the child understand the task.
4. Tasks may be revisited in situations where the child is thought to have made a random error.
5. Give children sufficient time to focus on solving the tasks.
6. Avoid temptations to talk to the child when they are engaged in solving a task.
7. Watch closely for lip, finger, head and body movements that might provide insight into the child's thinking.
8. As a general rule, do not comment on the correctness of the child's response.
9. Be sensitive to the child's state of ease and comfort during the course of the interview and use motivation and encouragement sparingly.
10. Use the technique of 'talking to the camera' if it is likely to be particularly useful to record an observation or realization.

THE DIAGNOSTIC ASSESSMENT INTERVIEW SCHEDULE 1.1

Having set out general guidelines let us now move to the specific. Part A and Part B are assessed together by two assessment interview schedules. The first of these is Assessment Interview Schedule 1.1. (For the second, Assessment Interview Schedule 1.2, see Chapter 6.) For convenience we will now refer to this as Assessment 1.1. The outcomes of Assessment 1.1 are, first, to determine the child's Stage of Early Arithmetical Learning in addition and subtraction within the range Stage 0 to Stage 4 and, secondly, to gain extensive information on·the child's facility with number word sequences and numerals. These are expressed as levels.

Assessment 1.1 consists of nine Task Groups (that is, groups of tasks). Table 3.3 shows the Task Groups from Assessment 1.1 and indicates for which of the models each Task Group is relevant. As can be seen in Table 3.3, Task Group 4 (Numeral Recognition) and Task Group 7 (Sequencing Numerals) do not correspond to any of the models. These are included because they can provide additional information about the child's numerical knowledge and strategies.

Table 3.3 Task Groups and associated models for Assessment 1.1

Task Groups	Model
1. Forward Number Word Sequence	FNWS
2. Number Word After	FNWS
3. Numeral Identification	Numeral Identification
4. Numeral Recognition	None
5. Backward Number Word Sequence	BNWS
6. Number Word Before	BNWS
7. Sequencing Numerals	None
8. Additive Tasks	SEAL
9. Subtractive Tasks	SEAL

OVERVIEW OF TASKS IN ASSESSMENT 1.1

As stated above, one important outcome of the assessment is the determination of the child's stage and levels. The assessment also provides extensive information about the child's numerical knowledge, including their strategies, strengths, difficulties, and so on. This kind of information is particularly useful in informing future teaching and helps teachers to gain a greater appreciation of the richness of children's numerical knowledge. Thus it is important to keep in mind that the purposes of the assessment are broader than merely determining the stages and levels. Task Groups 1 to 7 on Assessment 1.1 are mainly concerned with assessing the child's facility with number word sequences and numerals, and mainly relate to the models of FNWS, BNWS and numeral identification. Task Groups 8 and 9 are concerned with assessing the child's early numerical strategies and relate to the SEAL model.

We now present each set of task groups with explanations on how to present and analyze them. (Assessor's dialogue in italics.)

TASK GROUPS 1 AND 2: Forward Number Word Sequence and Number Word After

These two aspects are presented together in order to arrive at the child's level.

1. Forward Number Word Sequence
*Start counting from ** and I'll tell you when to stop.*

> (a) 1 (to 32) (b) 48 (to 61)
> (c) 76 (to 84) (d) 93 (to 112)

2. Number Word After
*Say the word that comes straight after ***.* Example: *Say the word that comes straight after one.*

> **(a) Entry task**
> 14   11   19   12
> 23   29   20

> **(b) Less advanced task**
> 5   9   7
> 3   6

> **(c) More advanced task**
> 59   65   32
> 70   99

Forward Number Word Sequence (FNWS) Tasks

The purpose of these tasks is to assess the child's facility with the forward number word sequence. To begin the teacher says, 'start counting from "one" please'. When the child reaches 'thirty-two' the teacher directs the child to stop. This is followed by similarly assessing parts of the number word sequence beyond the 'thirties'. For example, the teacher says, 'start counting from "forty-eight" please'. The teacher directs the child to stop on reaching 'sixty-one'. A particular purpose with this task is to assess if the child can continue beyond 'forty-nine'. Similarly, 'start counting from "seventy-six" please' (stop at 'eighty-four'). In the case of a task such as 'start counting from ninety-two' of particular interest are (a) what the child says after 'ninety-nine', and (b), if the child continues, what they say after 'one hundred and ten', and so on. We want to see if the child can cross decade numbers or whether they omit numbers or decades. Often children will keep the pattern of sound going but utter incorrect sequences. For example, 76, 77, 78, 79, forty, forty-one, *forty-two,* and so on.

Number Word After Tasks (NWA)

These tasks assess the child's ability to say the number word after a given number word. On a task such as 'what comes after seven?' we want to observe whether the child: (a) says 'eight' immediately or soon after being asked; (b) says the number word sequence forward from 'one' aloud or subvocally (referred to as a dropping-back strategy); or (c) is unable to answer. We begin these tasks with an introductory item and then proceed to the entry task by asking the word after several number words in the range 'eleven' to 'thirty'. If all are answered correctly then the more advanced tasks are presented. If more than two items are incorrect then one proceeds to the less advanced tasks. If one or two non-standard responses are made in the entry task it is advisable to revisit the items to confirm whether the child made a slip or a genuine error. Further non-standard responses direct the assessor to move to the less advanced. If the revisited item is now correct then go to the more advanced task. Of particular interest is how the child responds to words for numbers with '9' or '0' in the ones place, for example 'twenty-nine', 'fifty', 'sixty-nine'.

FNWS and NWA tasks are closely interlinked. The information from the FNWS and the NWA tasks is combined to produce a level of performance. The model for the construction of levels in FNWS and NWA is shown in Table 2.4. A shortened version is presented in Table 3.4, which relates the levels in FNWS to the items in Task Groups 1 and 2.

Table 3.4 Significant tasks for a given FNWS level

Level		Significant tasks
0:	Emergent FNWS	1(a)
1:	Initial FNWS up to 'ten'	1(a), 2(b)
2:	Intermediate FNWS up to 'ten'	1(a), 2(b)
3:	Facile with FNWSs up to 'ten'	1(a), 2(b)
4:	Facile with FNWSs up to 'thirty'	1(a), 2(a), 2(b)
5:	Facile with FNWSs up to 'one hundred'	1(a), 1(b), 1(c), 1(d), 2(a), 2(b), 2(c)

How to Determine the Child's FNWS Level

Table 3.4 lists the tasks which are significant at each of Levels 0–5 on the FNWS model. A child is assessed at Level 2, for example, if in Task 1(a) the child produces the FNWS to 'ten' at least, and answers each of the items in Task 2(a) correctly but uses the strategy of dropping back on some or all of the items in Task 2(a). Experience has shown that children's facility in terms of Task Group 1 may extend over a greater range of numbers than their facility in terms of Task Group 2. Thus children judged to be at Level 1, because they are unable to produce the number word after each of the number words in the range 'one' to 'ten', may well be able to produce the FNWS from 'one' to well beyond 'ten'. In similar vein, children judged to be at Level 4, because they are unable to, in every case, produce the number word after a given number word in the range 'one' to 'one hundred', may be successful on all of the tasks in Task Group 1.

It is useful to examine the pattern of non-standard responses in this aspect across a range of children and age groups. The information can greatly assist the person responsible for numeracy in the early years to decide where to focus attention and resources. The term 'non-standard responses' is used to include incorrect responses, for example, confusing number word after and number word before, and immature responses, for example, dropping back to one on a number word after task. Below we list examples of children's non-standard responses in Task Group 1: Forward Number Word Sequence and Task Group 2: Number Word After:

Non-standard Responses in Task Group 1: Forward Number Word Sequence

1.   Non-number words are included in an FNWS, for example, 'one, two, three, dog, cat, elephant'.
2.   An idiosyncratic FNWS is used, for example, '... eleven, twelve, sixteen, nine, four'.
3.   One or more of the number words in an FNWS are omitted, for example, '... ten, eleven, fourteen, fifteen ...'.
4.   Teen number words in an FNWS are confused with decade number words, for example, '... twelve, thirty, forty ...'.
5.   Twenty-ten is said after twenty-nine, that is, '... twenty-eight, twenty-nine, twenty-ten ...'.
6.   Decade number words are omitted from an FNWS, for example, 'fifty-eight, fifty-nine, sixty-one ...'.
7.   The incorrect decade number is used, for example, '... seventy-eight, seventy-nine, forty, forty-one ...'.
8.   Two hundred is said after one hundred and nine, that is, '... one hundred and eight, one hundred and nine, two hundred, two hundred and one ...'.

Non-standard responses in Task Group 2: Number Word After

1.   Drops back to one to work out the number word after, that is, after seven – 'one, two, three, four, five, six, seven, eight, ... eight!'
2.   Confuses number word after and number word before, for example, four after five.
3.   In the case of a decade number, says the next decade number, for example, eighty after seventy.
4.   In the case of a 'nine' number, says the incorrect decade number, for example, seventy after fifty-nine.
5.   Says a decade number instead of a teen number, for example, fifty after fourteen.

TASK GROUP 3: Numeral Identification

Numeral Identification is assessed by displaying numeral cards individually and asking the child to say the name of the numeral. There is no introductory task. Assessment begins with the entry items with double-digit numerals in the range 10 to 99.

Show each card in turn, saying, *What number is this?*

Numeral identification

(a) Entry task				
10	15	47	13	21
80	12	17	99	20	66

(b) Less advanced task					(c) More advanced task		
8	3	5	7	9	100	123	206
6	2	4	1		341	820	

The procedure is similar to the one described in the FNWS section, that is, one moves on to the more advanced tasks, three-digit numerals, if all the entry tasks are answered correctly. If more than two items are incorrect then one proceeds to the less advanced tasks. If one or two non-standard responses are made in the entry task it is advisable to revisit the items to confirm whether the child made a slip or an error. Further non-standard responses means move to the less advanced tasks.

It is useful to observe whether the child is confident and swift in responding. If there is a delayed response, observe whether the child says the FNWS from one, aloud or subvocally, in order to generate the name of the numeral. Some children may frequently confuse particular numerals. You will note that the entry tasks contain both 21 and 12. The interviewer should listen carefully to the child's articulation, especially with the numeral 20 as children often say 'twen-teen'. The three-digit numerals have been selected to provide challenging examples and an insight into the child's understanding of numerals beyond 99. We have found that non-standard responses in this task group often produce interesting patterns which provide a sound basis for understanding the child's difficulties.

The model for deriving the level of response is presented in Table 2.6. A shortened version is presented in Table 3.5, which relates the levels in numeral identification to the items in Task Group 3.

Table 3.5 Significant tasks for a given numeral identification level

Level	Significant tasks
0: Emergent Numeral Identification	3(b)
1: Numerals to '10'	3(b)
2: Numerals to '20'	3(a), 3(b)
3: Numerals to '100'	3(a), 3(b),
4: Numerals to '1000'	3(a), 3(b), 3(c)

Determining the Child's Numeral Identification Level

Table 3.5 lists the tasks which are significant at each Level on the numeral identification model. A child is assessed at Level 2, for example, if they answer correctly Task 3(a) and items in Task 3(b) involving numerals up to 20, but not some of the items in Task 3(b) involving numerals beyond 20. If the child is unsuccessful in the less advanced tasks, numeral identification 1–9, we recommend attempting the numeral recognition task.

We have noted examples of children's non-standard responses in numeral identification. They include situations where the child:

1. Identifies a two-digit numeral beyond 20 as if its digits were in the reverse order, for example '47' is identified as 'seventy-four'.
2. Has difficulty in identifying '12'.
3. Identifies '12' as 'twenty-one'.
4. Says the forward number word sequence to identify a numeral, for example, to identify '8', 'one, two . . . eight!'
5. Uses decade names for teen numbers, for example, '15' is identified as 'fifty'.

TASK GROUP 4: Numeral Recognition

Numeral recognition refers to the ability to select from a collection of numeral cards displayed in random order, the numeral card corresponding to a spoken number word.

Arrange the cards from 1 to 10 randomly. *Which number is . . . ?*

6	4	7	9	8

Some children can recognize the numerals from 1 to 5 but have difficulty with 6 to 10. Some might confuse particular numerals (for example, 6 and 9). There are no levels provided for numeral recognition.

TASK GROUPS 5 AND 6: Backward Number Word Sequence and Number Word Before

The tasks in Task Groups 5 and 6 are similar to the tasks in Task Groups 1 and 2 respectively. Thus in Task Group 5 the child is asked to say BNWSs and in Task Group 6 the child states the number word before a given number word within a particular range. Task Groups 5 and 6 provide assessment information for determining the level of BNWS development. The BNWS tasks (Task Groups 5 and 6) are not presented immediately after FNWS tasks (Task Groups 5 and 6). This serves to reduce the possibility of the child confusing forward and backward number word tasks, that is, confusing number word after with number word before or confusing FNWSs with BNWSs.

5. Backward Number Word Sequence
Example: *Count backwards from 3. Three, two, one.*
*Now count backwards from ** and keep going until I say stop.*

(a) 10 (down to 1)	(b) 15 (down to 10)
(c) 23 (down to 16)	(d) 34 (down to 27)
(e) 72 (down to 67)	

6. Number Word Before
*Say the number word that comes just before ***. Example: Say the number just before 2.*

(a) Entry task

24	17	20	11
13	21	14	30

(b) Less advanced task

7	10	4
8	3	

(c) More advanced task

67	50	38	100
83	41	99	

Backward Number Word Sequence Tasks

We begin by asking the child to count from 'ten' back to 'one'. This is followed by 'fifteen' back to 'ten' and 'twenty-three' back to 'sixteen' and 'thirty-four' back to 'twenty-seven'. For many children, all but the first of these will be difficult, or impossible. Some children are able to respond to these but do so slowly and with what appears to be a good deal of mental effort. The interviewer needs to observe carefully for signs of fatigue or distress in the child. The ability to say BNWSs in the teens is usually more difficult for children than FNWSs in the teens. Children quite frequently use a dropping back strategy (subvocally or aloud) to determine a particular number word. For example, a child might say the FNWS from ten to figure out what comes before 'thirteen'. As in the case of the forward number word sequence, backward sequences in the range 'thirty' to 'one hundred' are also assessed. Here we often find that there are two relatively common non-standard responses. The first is to omit the decade number (for example, 'forty-one, thirty-nine, thirty-eight, and so on.'). The second is to say the decade number which is ten less than the correct decade number (for example, 'forty-one, thirty, thirty-nine, thirty-eight, and so on').

Number Word Before Tasks

These tasks assess the child's ability to say the number word before a given number word. On a task such as 'What comes before nine?' we want to observe whether the child: (a) says 'eight' immediately or soon after being asked; (b) says the number word sequence forward from 'one' aloud or subvocally (referred to as a dropping-back strategy); or (c) is unable to answer. We begin these tasks by asking the word before several number words in the range 'one' to 'ten', presented in a random order, and then similarly in the ranges 'eleven' to 'thirty'; and 'thirty' to 'one hundred'. Of particular interest are words for numbers with '0' or '1' in the ones' place, for example, 'sixty', 'thirty-one'.

The model for deriving the level of response is presented in Table 2.5. A shortened version is presented in Table 3.6, which relates the levels in BNWS to the items in Task Groups 5 and 6.

Table 3.6 Significant tasks for a given BNWS level

Level	Significant tasks
0: Emergent BNWS	5(a)
1: Initial BNWS up to 'ten'	5(a), 6(b)
2: Intermediate BNWS up to 'ten'	5(a), 6(b)
3: Facile with BNWSs up to 'ten'	5(a), 6(b)
4: Facile with BNWSs up to 'thirty'	5(a), 5(b), 5(c), 5(d), 6(a), 6(b)
5: Facile with BNWSs up to 'one hundred'	5(a), 5(b), 5(c), 5(d), 5(e), 5(f), 6(a), 6(b), 6(c)

Determining the Child's BNWS Level

Table 3.6 lists the tasks which are signif.cant at each of Levels 0–5 on the BNWS model. A child is assessed at Level 4, for example, if they answer correctly Tasks 5(a), 5(b), 5(c), that part of 5(d) involving numbers in the range 1 to 30 and each of the items in 6(a) and 6(b) without using the strategy of dropping back, and do not answer correctly one of the following: 5(e), 5(f), that part of 5(d) involving numbers beyond 30, or one or more of the items in Task 6(c).

Children do have difficulty with the BNWS and we list the common non-standard responses.

Examples of Children's Non-standard Responses in Backward Number Word Sequence

1.   One or more of the number words in a BNWS are omitted, for example, 'fifteen, fourteen, twelve, eleven . . .'.

2. Decade number words in a BNWS are omitted, for example, ' . . . thirty-four, thirty-three, thirty-two, thirty-one, twenty-nine, . . . ' .
3. Goes back eleven when reaching the decade, for example, 'seventy-two, seventy-one, sixty, sixty-nine, sixty-eight, sixty-seven'.

Examples of Children's Non-standard Responses in Number Word Before

1. Drops back to one to work out the number word before, for example before 'seven', 'one, two, . . . six, seven, six!'
2. Confuses number word before and number word after, for example, nine before eight.
3. In the case of a decade number, says the next decade number, for example, twenty before thirty.
4. Says a decade number instead of a teen number, for example, sixty before seventeen.

TASK GROUP 7: Sequencing Numerals

Task Group 7 assesses the child's ability to correctly sequence a set of numeral cards. Children's solutions of sequencing numeral tasks are likely to draw on their FNWS knowledge as well as their numeral identification knowledge. Therefore, these tasks can provide interesting additional insights into these aspects of children's numerical knowledge. Tasks Group 7 is not directly concerned with determining the child's stage or levels.

7. Sequencing Numerals

Show the ten numbered cards face up in random order, asking the child to identify each number as you put it out. Then say *Can you place the cards in order? Start by putting the smallest down here.*

(a) Entry task	(b) Less advanced task
Cards from 46 to 55	Cards from 1 to 10

Ensure there is sufficient table space to allow the cards to be placed in a single line. The assessor should observe how the child puts the cards in sequence. This can provide interesting insights into children's knowledge and ways of thinking. Sequences which cross the decades are much harder than those within the decades. It is not unusual in the above task, 46 – 55, for some children to sequence numerals according to the right hand digit only. Thus the numerals might read 50, 51, 52, 53, 54, 55, 46, 47, 48, 49. If this happens the child is asked to read the numerals to see if they can detect an error. The spatial arrangement of the cards also provides clues to the child's understanding. It is important to observe whether the child places a numeral in a particular spatial relationship to another card. For example, does the child leave space between cards for the insertion of one or more numerals. It is sensible to provide sufficient time for the child to think hard as the task may involve the child identifying numerals, then thinking about the corresponding FNWS, in order to sequence the numerals.

The above task groups, 1 to 7, have been concerned with the Number Words and Numerals Strand. We now turn to the assessment of additive and subtractive strategies in the Counting Strand which in turn will introduce us to the important area of the Stages of Early Arithmetical Learning (SEAL).

TASK GROUPS 8 AND 9: Additive Tasks and Subtractive Tasks

Overview

Task Groups 8 and 9 focus on the child's strategies when solving additive and subtractive tasks. Because the assessor has to try and detect the child's strategy it is important to be aware of certain steps when administering the task item. Figure 3.1 sets out the list of steps. The first step is to ensure that the child understands the task item. If they attempt the item and produce an incorrect response it is advisable not to comment but simply to re-present the task. If the child produces a correct response, the assessor has to decide whether they have sufficient evidence to detect the strategy employed. If not, it is useful to probe the child's thinking before finally allowing the child to check the result.

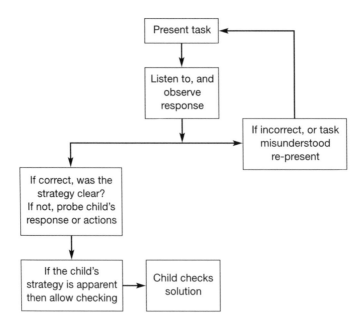

Figure 3.1 Diagrammatic representation of task administration

The key task is to understand the child's solution strategies. Thus, as a general rule, the interviewer should ask the child how they are solving these tasks. This is referred to as probing. However, there are certain provisos to this. For example, children are sometimes apparently unable to explain their strategy. Some children may knowingly, or unwittingly, describe a strategy that differs from their original strategy. For example, after solving the additive task of 3 + 2 the child might say, 'I counted one, two, three and then four, five', when they actually may have counted-on from three. One must also be aware that questioning the child too frequently about their solution process can become routine and tedious because the child may tend to respond in a non-reflective way. Thus repeatedly asking the child 'How did you do that?' may be counterproductive. Questions should be as open as possible, for example, 'I saw you moving your lips and your head, what words were you saying?' Try to avoid dichotomous questions such as 'Did you count? Did you start from seven?', and questions that embody unwarranted assumptions, for example, 'Where did you count from?'

Judicious questioning of children about their strategies is one of the more challenging requirements of the interview process. Close attention to and observation of the child's problem-solving procedures can greatly reduce reliance on their explanations, in order to understand their strategies. Finally, it is often the case that the child's strategy becomes apparent only during the video analysis phase, that is, after the interview has been completed. Summary guidelines for the presentation of additive and subtractive tasks are presented in Table 3.7.

Table 3.7 Summary guidelines for the presentation of additive and subtractive tasks

1. Keep firmly in mind the goal of gaining insight into the child's strategy.
2. Observe the child's solution strategy as closely as possible.
3. When the child has completed their solution, question the child about their strategy. Questions should be tailored as closely as possible to the child's observed strategy.
4. Be careful not to overdo the technique of asking the child how they solved the task.
5. Avoid questions that embody unwarranted assumptions about the child's strategy and, as a general rule, avoid dichotomous questions.
6. Remember that children frequently use strategies that are less sophisticated than those of which they are capable.

TASK GROUP 8: Additive Tasks

Because of the perceived novelty of the additive tasks we begin with an introductory item before proceeding to the entry task. It is not necessary to probe the child's responses to the introductory task, 3 + 1, as this is more to familiarize them with the fact that the items are screened, the counters are of two colours and that they can check the results.

Posing additive screened tasks

Additive Tasks (screened, use counters of two colours)

Introductory task:
There are three red counters under here, and one yellow counter under here. How many counters are there altogether?

| 3 | + | 1 |

Entry Tasks

Two tasks are presented in the entry task, (a), one within the finger range and one beyond. Two additional items, both using numerals beyond the finger range, are provided in section (e) should further evidence be required to ensure that one has detected the child's solution strategy.

(a) Entry tasks (both collections screened)

| 5 | + | 4 | | 9 | + | 6 |

(e) Supplementary additive tasks to (a) (both screened, use counters of two colours)

| 8 | + | 5 | | 9 | + | 3 |

Posing partially screened tasks

The responses to questions (a) and (e) dictate which one of two routes to follow through the assessment. If the child gets both questions correct in (a) then the supplementaries in (e) can be presented before tackling the Missing Addend Tasks (f). However, if the child makes one or more errors it is necessary to present the task items in 8(b). These are termed Less Advanced Additive tasks. These are less advanced because only one collection is screened. This is always the larger number. The items range through the finger range to beyond and are presented below.

(b) Less advanced task (first collection screened)

| 5 | + 2 | | 7 | + 3 | | 9 | + 4 |

Checking the answer

If the child responds correctly to all three items then one can attempt subtractive tasks beginning with Removed Items 9(c). Should the child fail on any one of the less advanced tasks it is advisable to move to the tasks in 8(c). These tasks use the same questions as above but are presented unscreened.

(c) Perceptual counting: two collections

    5 + 2   7 + 3   9 + 4

Finally, if the child continues to make errors, or is not able to respond, then two counting tasks, each involving one collection only, are presented. These are shown in (d). The assessor places 13 counters of one colour out in a serpentine row and the child is asked to count them. A second

---

(d) Perceptual counting: one collection
Would you count to see how many counters there are altogether in this group?

Place out 13 counters.   Place out 18 counters

Perceptual Counting: one collection

task is presented using 18 counters.

It is recommended that the assessment be curtailed if a child has not completed the perceptual counting tasks correctly.

In the above sections we explained the administrative route for a child who had difficulties on the entry tasks (a). Now let us turn to the situation if the child had been successful with tasks (a) and (e). He or she will have demonstrated that they have strategies for additive tasks. Task Group (f) will allow us to see if their strategy can be applied to a different problem, that of the missing addend.

Missing Addend

In first part of this task, 4 is the known addend, 2 is the missing addend and 6 is the known sum. In the second and third parts the missing addend is kept below 5. This can facilitate the use of a counting-up-to strategy.

Only one screen is needed but it is important to use two colours of counters to preserve the distinctiveness of the two addends. In the first task four counters are shown to the child being placed under the screen. Thus 4 is the known addend. They are requested to look away. The assessor then places an additional quantity of different coloured counters under the screen, the missing addend. When the child looks back they are told how many counters there are in total, the known sum and asked to solve how many additional ones were placed. The question for the assessor is to detect the strategy. Will the child use the counting-up-to, which is also known as

---

(f) Missing addends

Here are four red counters. Now look away. While you were looking away I put some more yellow counters under here. Now there are 6 counters altogether. How many yellow counters did I put under here?

Introductory task $4 + [\ ] = 6$

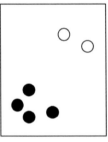

Tasks $7 + [\ ] = 10$ $12 + [\ ] = 15$

---

the count-on strategy, or use subtraction to determine the missing addend?

This completes the additive tasks. We now turn our attention to the assessment of subtractive tasks.

Posing a missing addend task

Observing and listening to the response

Probing the solution strategy

TASK GROUP 9: Subtractive Tasks

Task Group 9 focuses on the child's strategies when solving three different kinds of subtractive tasks. The subtractive tasks start with the hardest, these are Subtraction sentences, (a), then move to less difficult, missing subtrahends, (b) and finally to the easiest, removed items (c).

This information on subtraction contributes to determining the child's stage (that is, in terms of SEAL). The tasks are presented below. For detailed discussion of the strategies and their relationship to SEAL see Chapter 4.

(a) Subtraction sentences
Present the tasks as a written number sentence on card. Say to the child, *What does this say? Do you have a way to work out what the answer is?*

Entry task	Supplementary task
16 – 12	17 – 14

The first task involves presenting '16 – 12' in written form on a card. This task is relatively advanced and is likely to be the most difficult of the subtractive tasks. The task is presented in order to provide a situation where the child may exhibit an advanced strategy, for example, a part, or parts, of the strategy may involve other than counting-by-ones. The task is presented before the other subtractive tasks because, during the course of an interview, children are likely to continue using strategies that are successful. Thus if the task of '16 – 12' is placed later in the interview, a child who has used counting-by-ones successfully, to solve an earlier subtractive task might use counting-by-ones out of habit almost, rather than a more advanced strategy, to solve '16 – 12'.

Missing Subtrahend

A purpose of the missing subtrahend tasks is to elicit the strategy of 'counting-down-to'. The task involves displaying and screening a collection and while the child is looking away to reduce that collection to a certain amount. The child has to calculate by how many the set was reduced, that is, the missing subtrahend. This is a challenging task for most young children so an introductory item is provided, followed by two entry tasks. If the child gets both correct a more advanced item is available.

(b) Missing subtrahend
Here are five counters. (Ask the child to look away. Remove and screen two counters.) *There were five counters. While you were looking away I took some away. Now there are only three. How many did I take away?*

(i) Introductory task	5 to 3	$\{5 - [\ ] = 3\}$
(ii) Entry tasks	10 to 6	$\{10 - [\ ] = 6\}$
	12 to 9	$\{12 - [\ ] = 9\}$
(iii) More advanced task	15 to 11	$\{15 - [\ ] = 11\}$

Removed Items

The purpose of the removed items tasks is to elicit the strategy of 'counting-down-from'. As with all of the assessment tasks it is important for the interviewer to maintain an open frame of mind about the types of strategies the children use to solve these subtractive tasks. The task is simple to administer because the assessor reduces the first screened collection by a stated amount and asks the child how many will remain under the screen. The removed quantity is briefly displayed to the child and then screened. As above there is an introductory task followed by entry and advanced tasks.

(c) Removed items
Here are three counters (briefly display, then screen). If I take away one, (remove one counter, display briefly, then re-screen) *how many are left under here?* (Indicate the first screen.)

(i)	Introductory task	3 – 1		
(ii)	Entry tasks	6 – 2	9 – 4	15 – 3
(iii)	More advanced task	27 – 4		

Earlier, when we presented partially screened, additive tasks, 8(b) we indicated that if a child responded correctly to all three items then the assessor could present the subtractive tasks but commencing with removed items, 9(c). It is anticipated that such children would have difficulty with the subtractive tasks beyond removed items.

In the next chapter we explain and exemplify the Stages of Early Arithmetical Learning.

4

The Stages of Early Arithmetical Learning (SEAL)

Summary

The Stages of Early Arithmetical Learning are defined and illustrated by profiles of typical children. These are explained further by the presentation of scenarios taken from assessment and teaching sessions. Additional guidance is provided to analyze what might be termed 'difficult cases'.

INTRODUCTION

In the previous chapter we showed how to administer the Assessment Interview 1.1. We presented information and models for the analysis and allocation of levels for the Number Words and Numerals Strand of the LFIN and explained how to administer the additive and subtractive tasks. In this chapter we focus on the analysis of the child's performance on these tasks by explaining and exemplifying the five Stages of Early Arithmetical Learning (SEAL). Table 4.1 show the significant task groups in Assessment Schedule 1.1 for a given Stage of Early Arithmetical Learning. Assessment 1.1 will place a child in one of six Stages. More detailed information on whether a child is Stage 5 can be gleaned by the application of Assessment Interview 1.2, Task Group 3: Non-Count-by-Ones Strategies which is explained in Chapter 6.

Table 4.1 Significant tasks for a given Stage of Early Arithmetical Learning

Stage		Significant tasks	
0:	Emergent Counting	8	Additive tasks
1:	Perceptual Counting	8	Additive tasks
2:	Figurative Counting	8	Additive tasks
3:	Initial Number Sequence	8, 9	Additive and Subtractive tasks
4:	Intermediate Number Sequence	8, 9	Additive and Subtractive tasks
5:	Facile Number Sequence	8, 9,	Additive and Subtractive tasks and Task Group 3, Non-Count-by-Ones Strategies, Assessment Interview 1.2

Progression across the stages involves the child using counting in increasingly sophisticated ways to solve additive and subtractive tasks. For each of the stages, we present two examples of children's solution attempts. Each example consists of an objective description of the child's solution of one or more problems, and a discussion of the strategies used by the child in terms of SEAL.

The model of the Stages of Early Arithmetical Learning was introduced in Chapter 2. The Stage model constitutes the primary and most important aspect of the Learning Framework in Number, and provides a model of increasingly advanced numerical strategies used by children in situations that involve counting, adding or subtracting. In this chapter the origin and background of SEAL is explained. This presentation includes an introduction to the particular sense in which the term 'counting' is used in SEAL, and explanations of the terms 'stages' and 'levels', together with a discussion of the means by which children's numerical strategies may be observed. This is followed by a detailed description of each of the stages. Included in the description of each stage are two examples of children's problem-solving activity relevant to the stage. These examples take the form of video excerpts, that is, objective descriptions of the child's problem-solving activity from real classroom situations. Each video excerpt is followed by a discussion of the problem-solving activity portrayed in the excerpt.

Overview of SEAL

The model of the Stages of Early Arithmetical Learning is based on a coherent body of research into young children's number learning undertaken by Steffe (Steffe, 1992a; Steffe and Cobb, 1988; Steffe et al., 1983) and related research by Wright (1989; 1991a). This research involved longitudinal studies in which children were taught several times per week during teaching cycles of up to 20 weeks' duration, in their first and/or second years of school. An important focus of this research was the ways in which children's numerical strategies arose during enquiry-based teaching, and how these strategies developed and changed over the course of one or two years of school.

Teachers who have learned about and applied SEAL have found that it provides crucial directionality to their teaching. By applying SEAL in the observation and assessment of children these teachers have a sound knowledge of the child's current level in terms of the development of early arithmetical strategies. This is very important when teachers are being required to have enhanced assessment skills in deciding standards of performance. Also, SEAL provides a clear framework for determining teaching activities that are optimal in the sense of leading to advancement. By this we mean advancements in which children reorganize their numerical thinking and construct novel strategies that, in a mathematical sense, are more sophisticated than their previous strategies. For a full discussion of how SEAL relates to teaching see Wright et al. (2002).

COUNTING

Steffe et al. (1983) make a crucial distinction between counting and the mere utterance of number words in sequence. Counting in the terms of Steffe et al., arises in problem-solving contexts, for example, additive or subtractive situations. In these situations it is assumed that the child has a goal, for example, figuring out how many counters there are in two screened collections or how may counters remain under the screen when some have been removed. In the terms of Steffe et al. (1983) counting involves the coordination of each uttered number word with the conceptual production of a 'unit item'. The nature of this unit item changes according to the child's stage in SEAL. Steffe's notion of 'unit item' is particularly useful for observing and understanding the counting behavior of children who are in Stage 2. This is discussed later in this chapter.

STAGES AND LEVELS

In the work of Steffe et al. (1983) the term 'stage' is used in a formal and theoretical sense to encompass four characteristics:

1.   A characteristic remains constant for a period of time.
2.   The stages form an invariant sequence.

3.   Each stage builds on and incorporates the previous stage.
4.   Each new stage involves a significant conceptual reorganization.

A level is regarded as a point in time rather than a period of time. The child has attained a level when he or she satisfies specific performance criteria for that level. This distinction between stage and level is explained in detail by von Glasersfeld and Kelley (1982). In the Learning Framework in Number, the term 'level' is used in the models which focus on the development of number word sequences, numeral identification and knowledge of tens and ones, and the term 'stage' is used in the SEAL model, which is the focus of this chapter.

OBSERVING CHILDREN'S STRATEGIES

Fundamental to the research on which SEAL is based is the notion that, in order to understand children's mathematical learning, it is necessary to closely observe their behavior in problem-solving situations. In studying children's early numerical learning in particular, this observation focuses on children's verbal and non-verbal responses in situations in which they solve problems involving counting, addition or subtraction. These problems typically involve presenting children with a range of tasks involving counters that may be displayed or screened. These types of situations, that is, involving what adults might regard as trivial number problems, have been found to be extremely useful for the purpose of studying children's early numerical learning.

EXPLAINING THE STAGES

In the remainder of this chapter, each of the Stages of Early Arithmetical Learning is explained. First we present the definition of the Stage and then a profile of a typical child at each stage and how this relates the models in Part A and Part B of the LFIN. We use the profile of a typical child for convenience here to exemplify the stage. Of course, knowing that a child is at a given stage in terms of SEAL does not necessarily determine the child's levels of the other models of early number knowledge. Nevertheless, it is feasible to assume levels on the other models that frequently appear for a child at a given stage. The numerical profile, derived from the models, is further fleshed out by describing the behaviors of a typical child at each stage and how their performance can be linked to the assessment schedules. Two illustrations of child problem-solving behavior, each in the form of an objective description of an excerpt from a videotape of an assessment or teaching session, are presented. Each excerpt is followed by a discussion. In writing the discussion the author takes account of the videotape excerpt *per se*, rather than the description. Ten of the excerpts are based on Mathematics Recovery assessment sessions and two on MR teaching sessions. For purposes of clarification, this is stated at the beginning of the excerpt in the case of the two teaching sessions.

STAGE 0: EMERGENT COUNTING

> **Stage 0: Emergent Counting.** The child cannot count visible items. The child either does not know the number words or cannot coordinate the number words with items.

The work of Steffe et al. (1983) and Steffe and Cobb (1988) resulted in a five-stage model of the development of early arithmetical strategies, that is, strategies for counting, adding and subtracting. The first of these stages is given the label of 'perceptual'. In research projects conducted by Wright (1991b; 1994) prior to MR, it became apparent that among children in the first two years of school, there are a significant number who are not able to count a visible collection, for example, a collection of, 12, 15 or 18 counters. In MR the label 'emergent' was adopted for such children. The label 'Stage O' is used to indicate children at this emergent level.

The Typical Emergent Child

In Table 4.2 we set out the stage and indicative levels for the emergent child on the models pertaining to FNWSs, BNWSs, numeral identification and tens and ones.

Table 4.2 Stage and levels of a typical emergent child

Model	Stage/level
Stage of Early Arithmetical Learning (SEAL)	0
Level of Forward Number Word Sequences (FNWSs)	1
Level of Backward Number Word Sequences (BNWSs)	0
Level of Numeral Identification	0
Level of Tens and Ones Knowledge	0

Stage of Early Arithmetical Learning

The child at the Emergent Stage (Stage 0) is not able to count a collection of counters, for example 13 or 18 counters. The child might not know the forward number word sequence from one to ten or beyond ten. Alternatively the child might know the number words but not be able to correctly coordinate a number word with each counter. This might involve omitting one or more counters, or perhaps pointing to one or more counters twice during counting. More frequently the child simply lacks the ability to coordinate each spoken number word with each item to be counted. In many cases the child's pointing actions seem to outpace their production of the number words in turn. The child might be able to count the counters in smaller collections, for example, collections up to 10. Some emergent children seem to interpret questions such as, 'How many counters are there?' literally as an instruction to say the number word sequence from one. It is as if the literal meaning for the child is to say the words 'one, two, three and so on' while pointing at the collection of items in question. This might involve pointing generally in the direction of the collection, rather than pointing at each item in turn.

FNWSs, BNWSs and Numeral Identification

The emergent child might well be able to say the forward number word sequence from one to beyond ten, nevertheless they probably will not be able to say, immediately, the number word after a given number word in the range one to ten. Also, they probably will not be able to use a dropping back strategy, to say the number word after a given number word, for each of the numbers in the range one to ten. The emergent child typically has difficulty with saying backward number word sequences. For example, the child might not be able to say the words from ten to one, and might even have difficulty in saying the words from three to one. As well, the child typically cannot say the number word before a given number word, even permitting use of the dropping back strategy. The emergent child can typically name some, but not all, of the numerals in the range one to ten. They might be able to recognize most of the numerals in the range 1 to 5, but might be unable to name numerals beyond five, or might confuse numerals such as 6 and 8 or 6 and 9.

Spatial Patterns and Finger Patterns

The emergent child might be able to recognize some but not all of the regular spatial patterns (for example, the domino patterns) in the range 2 to 6. In many cases they will try to count the dots in a spatial pattern rather than immediately assign a number name to the pattern. The emergent child might be able to make finger patterns corresponding to the numbers from one to five. This typically will involve looking at the fingers and raising them slowly and sequentially, for example, the child might slowly raise three fingers sequentially, in response to a request to show three fingers. The emergent child might be able to copy or count temporal sequences of two or three but no larger (for example, on hearing a sequence of three sounds the child could tap a similar sequence).

Two illustrations of the problem-solving behavior of a child at Stage 0 now follow, each in the form of an objective description of an excerpt from a videotape of an assessment or teaching session. Each excerpt is followed by a discussion.

Video Excerpt 0.1: Heather and Larry

H: (Places out five red counters and screens them. Then places out four blue counters and screens them.) Five red counters and four blue counters. Can you tell me how many I have altogether this time?

L: (Immediately.) Six.

H: Are you thinking? Five and four more. (Points to the screens in turn.)

L: (Thinks for a few seconds, looking up.) Umm.

H: How are you going to work out how many that makes?

L: (Sequentially raises the five fingers of his left hand. Then looks at his right hand while raising one finger.) How many is that?

H: Five on this one and four on this one. (Points to the screens in turn as before.)

L: (Sequentially raises four fingers on his right hand and then looks at his left hand.) One, two, three, four (wagging a finger in coordination with each count. Now looks at his right hand.) Five. (Pauses.) Five, six, seven, eight! (Again wagging fingers in turn.)

H: (Removes both screens.) Have a look.

L: (Looks at the collection of five counters.) One, two, three, four. (In co-ordination with four points over the collection of five counters. Now looks at the collection of four counters. Points at one counter.) Five. (Pauses.) Five, six, seven, eight! (In coordination with four points over the collection of four counters.)

H: (Places out 13 counters.) Can you tell me how many counters there are there altogether?

L: One, two, three . . . twelve. (Moves each of the 13 counters in turn but makes an error in coordinating his counts with his points.)

Discussion of Video Excerpt 0.1

Significant in the above excerpt is that, on three occasions, Larry does not correctly count visible items. When the screened collections of five and four are unscreened Larry counts 'eight' rather than 'nine'. When counting the collection of 13 counters, Larry counts 'twelve'. Additionally, Larry counts eight when counting his raised fingers, that is five on one hand and four on the other. On each of the three occasions Larry is unable to properly coordinate his counts with the perceptual items, that is counters. Counting behavior of this kind is illustrative of the child at the Emergent Stage, Stage 0.

Video Excerpt 0.2: Terry and Rita

T: What's three plus two? (Points to three unscreened counters and then to two unscreened counters.) How many would that be?

R: (Looks at Terry.) Equals.

T: What does it equal?

R: (Immediately.) Equals nine.

T: Nine do you think? (Points to both collections.) Do you think there are nine counters there?

R: Uhh, yeh!

T: I'm going to give you a group of counters Rita. (Places out 13 counters.) Can you tell me how many counters there are?

R: One, two, three . . . eleven. (Coordinates a number word with each count but omits to point at two of the counters.)

Discussion of Video Excerpt 0.2

In the above protocol Rita is presented with the task of 3 counters plus 2 counters with both collections unscreened. It is interesting to observe that Rita does not use a counting strategy to figure out how many counters altogether. She answers 'equals nine' but does not count. She does not spontaneously count the counters in this particular situation, that is, with two separate collections – even though they are very small collections – 3 and 2. She does not seem to have this strategy available, that is, she does not seem able to conceive of the counters as forming or being reformed into one collection, for the purposes of establishing how many altogether. At this point Terry places out 13 counters and asks Rita to tell her how many counters there are. Rita counts from 'one' but does not correctly coordinate the number words with the counters. For this reason Rita is classified as Stage O: Emergent Counting.

Children who are classified at Stage O are those who are not able to count perceptual items, that is they cannot coordinate number words with items when they count. When attempting to count 13 counters Larry points 13 times while saying the words from one to twelve. Larry's error is one of not coordinating his number words with his points. By way of contrast Rita correctly coordinates her number words with her points but omits two of the counters. A child may also be classified as Stage 0 if they cannot say the forward number word sequence, for example, the child cannot count 13 counters because they do not know the number word sequence from one to thirteen. Rita's difficulty on the first task, that is, not having a strategy to establish the numerosity of two collections, for example, not counting the collections, has been observed among children classified as being at Stage 0 (and also some children at Stage 1). Their lack of counting to solve these tasks is possibly attributable to an inability to conceptualize that two collections can alternatively be regarded as one collection.

STAGE 1: PERCEPTUAL COUNTING

Stage 1: Perceptual Counting. Can count perceived items but not those in screened (that is concealed) collections. This may involve seeing, hearing or feeling items.

Children at Stage 1: Perceptual Counting are able to solve additive tasks involving material (for example, counters) which is perceptually available (for example, visible), that is, tasks involving one collection or two collections of counters that are displayed rather than screened (Steffe et al., 1983, pp. 22–3). Children at Stage 1 are unable to solve additive or subtractive tasks involving screened items. Children at Stage 1 are said to count 'perceptual unit items'.

Table 4.3 sets out the stage and indicative levels for the perceptual child on the models pertaining to FNWSs, BNWSs, numeral identification and tens and ones.

Table 4.3 Stage and levels of a typical perceptual child

Model	Stage/level
Stage of Early Arithmetical Learning (SEAL)	1
Level of Forward Number Word Sequences (FNWSs)	3
Level of Backward Number Word Sequences (BNWSs)	1
Level of Numeral Identification	1
Level of Tens and Ones Knowledge	0

The Typical Perceptual Child

The child at the Perceptual Stage is able to count a collection of counters, for example, 13 or 18 counters, but is not able to solve additive tasks involving two collections in cases where one or both of the collections are screened. Some children at this stage seem to have difficulty establishing the numerosity of two unscreened collections taken together. In the case of a task such as establishing the numerosity of a single collection, for example, a collection of 18 counters, the child can correctly count the counters by ones from one to 18. In the case of two separate collections, for example a collection of 9 red counters and a collection of 6 blue counters, some perceptual children do not seem to alternatively regard the two collections as one for the purposes of establishing the overall numerosity. This difficulty has been observed to arise even in cases involving very small numbers of counters (for example, five and two). Thus, when asked how many counters in all the child answers 'five' or 'two', but does not seem to realize that they can make one count from one, to count the counters in both collections. As well, in the situation just described (that is, a collection of 5 counters and a collection of 2 counters — labeled verbally with the number words 'five' and 'two' respectively), some children seem to regard the numbers 5 and 2, as constituting a 2-digit number, that is '52'. The latter behavior can result from premature teaching of place value ideas.

FNWSs and BNWSs and Numeral Identification

The child at the Perceptual Stage typically has good facility with FNWS in the range 1 to 10. As well, the child might be able to say the FNWS into the twenties, sometimes stopping at 29 or might say the number word sequence beyond 30. Nevertheless the child might well have difficulty with tasks involving saying immediately the number word after a number beyond 10 (for example, say the number word after 13). Thus the child might use a dropping back strategy or not be able to solve the task at all. In the case of BNWS the child typically will be able to say the number words from 10 to 1, but might have difficulty with tasks involving saying immediately the number word before a number in the range one to ten. Again, the child might not be able to solve the task at all, or might use a dropping back strategy.

Children at this stage typically can recognize and identify numerals in the range 1 to 10, but might not be able to do so with numerals in the teens. They might incorrectly identify '12' as 'twenty' or 'twenty-one', or a numeral in the range '13' to '19' as the corresponding decade number (for example, '17' is named as 'seventy'). If asked to write a teen numeral, for example, '16', the child might first write the digit '6' and then write the digit '1' to the left of the '6'. The likely explanation for this is that, rather than form a mental image of the numeral prior to writing, the child determines each of the digits '6' and '1' from the sound image of the number word (that is, 'six – teen'), first writes the digit '6' and only then realizes that the digit '1' should be placed to the left of the digit '6'.

Spatial Patterns and Finger Patterns

Children at this stage typically can subitize in the range one to four, that is, they can correctly ascribe number to spatial patterns, particularly regular patterns in the range one to four, and typically do not count from one when doing so. Some children at this stage have facile finger patterns for numbers in the range 1 to 5, and might use their finger patterns to solve additive tasks in cases where both numbers are in the range 1 to 5. This frequently occurring strategy involves making a finger pattern on one hand to correspond with the first addend and similarly making a finger pattern on the other hand for the second addend. The child then counts their raised fingers from one to obtain the answer. Establishing the finger patterns might involve sequentially raising fingers in coordination with counting to the number of the corresponding addend. Children with more facile finger patterns will raise fingers simultaneously to correspond to an addend, and do not count from one when doing so. At the same time these children typically will not have facile finger patterns for the numbers in the range 6 to 10. Thus if asked to show 7 on their fingers they will raise seven fingers sequentially while counting from one to seven.

In Video Excerpt 1.1, Amy solves tasks in which the counters are displayed but is generally unsuccessful on tasks in which counters are screened.

Video Excerpt 1.1: Mary and Amy

M: (Places out five blue counters and screens them.) Five counters there. (Places out two red counters leaving them unscreened.) And two counters there. How many altogether?

A: (Quickly.) Five! Eight.

M: (Removes the screen covering the five blue counters.) Want to check?

A: (Looks steadily at the desk on which counters are placed for five seconds and then looks up.) One.

M: (Waves hand over the counters.) How many altogether?

A: (Immediately.) Three.

M: Would you like to count them up?

A: (Points at one blue counter.) One. (Pauses and then moves the collection of two red counters adjacent to the collection of five blue counters.) One, two . . . seven. (Counts quickly while pointing to each counter in turn.)

M: This time, there are four counters there. (Places out four red counters and screens them.) And four counters there. (Places out a second collection of four red counters and leaves them unscreened.) How many altogether?

A: (Looks at the unscreened collection for five seconds.) One.

M: (Places her hand on the screen.) How many are under here?

A: (Immediately.) Four.

M: (Waves her hand over the unscreened collection.) How many here?

A: (Immediately.) Four.

M: (Waves her hand over both collections.) How many altogether?

A: (Looks at the desk for three seconds.) Eight.

M: (Removes the screen.)

A: (Moves one collection adjacent to the other and begins to count while pointing at each counter in turn.) One, two. (Moves a counter which is on top of another counter and then restarts her count, pointing at each counter in turn.) One, two . . . eight.

M: (Places out seven blue counters and screens them.) This time Amy there are seven under there. (Places out five red counters and does not screen them.) And five there.

A: (Immediately.) Umm – six!

M: (Points to the screened collection.) How many under here?

A: (Looks at the screen for seven seconds.) Eight.

M: Seven.

A: Seven. (After 13 seconds.) Six!

M: (Removes the screen.)

A: (Moves one collection adjacent to the other and then points at each counter in turn.) One, two . . . twelve.

Discussion of Video Excerpt 1.1

In the first task Amy answers quickly 'five' and then 'eight'. She does not appear to have a strategy involving counting. When Mary removes the screen Amy correctly counts the seven counters. In the second task Amy looks at the unscreened counters for five seconds and then answers 'one'. Mary re-poses the task and Amy on this occasion answers 'eight' but no counting strategy is apparent. It seems that Amy recalls that 4 + 4 make 8 and hence is able to answer correctly on this occasion. On the third task Amy again does not have a counting strategy and her answers seem to be no more than guesses. When the screen is removed Amy seems to be immediately aware of what she is expected to do. She pushes the two collections together and correctly counts the 12 counters. Amy's act of pushing all the counters together seems to be of cognitive significance for her. It seems that, from her point of view, it now makes sense to count a collection whereas, when the counters were in two collections, regarding all of the counters as a collection, that is, including the screened and unscreened counters, did not make sense. In summary, Amy does not have a strategy for solving additive tasks involving two collections, one of which is screened. This is characteristic of children classified as Stage 1: Perceptual Counting.

Video Excerpt 1.2: Heather and William

H: (Places out three red counters and screens them.) Three red counters, William. I'm going to put them under there. (Places out two blue counters and screens them.) Two blue counters and I'm going to put them under there. How many counters is that altogether?

W: (Immediately.) Four.

H: Would you like to look and check?

W: (Raises screen and points to three counters in turn.) One, two, three. (Raises the other screen and points to two counters in turn.) Four, five!

H: Were you right?

W: (Shakes his head indicating that he was not correct.)

H: We'll try another one. I'll make it five red counters this time. (Places out two more red counters and screens them.) And four blue counters. (Places out two more blue counters and screens them.) How many does that make altogether?

W: (Immediately.) Eleven.

H: Eleven. How did you work that out?

W: I just knew.
H: (Removes both screens.) Would you like to check and see?
W: (Points to the nine counters in turn.) One, two . . . nine.

Heather then presented a similar task involving a screened collection of nine red counters and a screened collection of six blue counters. William immediately answered 'forty-one'.

Discussion of Video Excerpt 1.2

Like Amy, William does not seem to have a counting strategy. Rather, on each of the three tasks he seems to immediately guess. When questioned about his response to the second task William did not seem to reflect on his strategy. His statement 'I just knew' seemed mostly motivated by a desire to say something to satisfy the teacher. It is not uncommon for children to respond in this way when questioned about their strategy, and in such situations it may be unproductive to continue to question the child. Close observation is often more informative than engaging the child in a discussion about their solution. In the previous protocol the tasks presented to Amy involved a screened and an unscreened collection, whereas the tasks presented to William involved two screened collections. Nevertheless, William, like Amy, does not count to find how many in all and seems to have no strategy other than guessing. When the counters are unscreened, William, like Amy, can count to find how many in all. This is typical of Stage 1: Perceptual Counting.

STAGE 2: FIGURATIVE COUNTING

Stage 2: Figurative Counting. Can count the items in a screened collection but counting typically includes what adults might regard as redundant activity. For example, when presented with two screened collections, told how many in each collection, and asked how many counters in all, the child will count from 'one' instead of counting on.

Table 4.4 sets out the stage and indicative levels for the perceptual child on the models pertaining to FNWSs, BNWSs, numeral identification and tens and ones.

Table 4.4 Stage and levels of a typical figurative child

Model	Stage/level
Stage of Early Arithmetical Learning (SEAL)	2
Level of Forward Number Word Sequences (FNWSs)	4
Level of Backward Number Word Sequences (BNWSs)	3
Level of Numeral Identification	2
Level of Tens and Ones Knowledge	0

The Typical Figurative Child

The child at the Figurative Stage can solve additive tasks involving two screened collections, and when doing so, counts from one. Thus on an additive task such as a collection of 5 red counters and a collection of 4 yellow counters, both of which are screened, the child might count from one to five to count the counters in the first collection, and then continue counting from six to nine to count the counters in the second collection. From a cognitive perspective it seems necessary for the child to count from one in order to give meaning to six, that is, the number of counters in the first collection. Also, the child typically cannot make sense of subtractive tasks such as Missing Addend, Missing Subtrahend or Comparison tasks.

FNWSs, BNWSs and Numeral Identification

Children at this stage typically are facile with FNWSs in the range 1 to 30 but might not know the FNWS to 100. They might not be able to say the number word after some of the numbers beyond 30, for example, 49 or 80. Typically these children are facile with BNWSs to 10, but might have difficulty in producing the BNWS from 23 to 16 and from 15 to 10. In similar vein they might have difficulty saying the word before number words such as 12, 15, 20, 21 and 30, or might use a dropping back strategy to work out the number word before a given number word. Some children at this stage say an incorrect decade number when saying BNWSs, for example, '52, 51, 40, 49, 48'. Children at this stage typically can recognize and identify one-digit numerals and numerals in the teens, although the numeral '12' might be incorrectly identified as 'twenty' or 'twenty-one'. Also common at this stage is the error of 'digit reversal' when identifying two-digit numbers. Thus, for example, '27' is named as 'seventy-two'.

Spatial Patterns and Finger Patterns

Children at this stage typically will have facile finger patterns for numbers in the range 1 to 5 and some children will also have finger patterns for numbers in the range 6 to 10. Children may also have sound knowledge relating to spatial patterns (for example, pair-wise patterns for the numbers from 1 to 10) and are able to subitize random arrays of up to 5 items. They can regard a pattern for 6 for example, alternatively as 3 twos or 2 threes, and a pattern for 8, as 2 fours or as 5 and 3.

Figural, Motor and Verbal Counting

Children at Stage 2 have been observed to use one or more of three types of counting, that is, figural, motor or verbal. Alternatively, one could say the child counts figural, motor or verbal unit items (as discussed earlier in this chapter). Typically these types of counting arise when the child is counting the second, screened collection. In the case of figural unit items, visualized items (for example, counters) are regarded as being significant for the child when counting. Thus, in solving the above task, the child may be observed to be apparently visualizing a collection of four counters. In the case of motor unit items, movements (for example, sequentially raising fingers) are regarded as significant because the child utters the corresponding number word after making each movement. Finally, in the case of verbal unit items, the uttered number words are regarded as significant. For example, in solving the above task the child will use double counting. Thus after counting from one to eight, the child may say 'one more is nine', and so on, and thereby keep track of the four counters in the second screened collection.

The label of 'figurative' is applied collectively to figural, motor and verbal counting because each involves counting based on re-presentation (like a mental replay) of sensory-motor material, rather than direct perception of sensory-motor material which occurs at Stage 1. Figural is regarded as the least advanced of these and verbal is regarded as the most advanced, and advancement from figural to motor and motor to verbal involve progressively less dependence on re-presented sensory material. Thus the child whose most advanced strategy involves counting figural unit items is referred to as 'early Stage 2' and the child whose most advanced strategy involves counting verbal unit items is referred to as 'late Stage 2'.

Video Excerpt 2.1: Jane and Shirley

The following video excerpt is taken from an MR teaching session.

J: (Briefly displays and then screens three counters. Then screens two counters.) And two here. How many have I got altogether? Three and two?

S: (Looks at the screen covering three counters and makes three points in coordination with counting.) One, two, three (turns to the other screen and make two points in coordination with counting), four, five.

J: (Removes both screens.) Show me.

S: (Points at each counter in turn.) One, two, three – four, five.

J: Right. What about if I put five here (screens five counters) and three here? (Screens three counters.)

S: (Looks at the screen covering three counters and makes three points in coordination with counting.) One, two, three (looks at the other screen and again coordinates a point with each number word), four, five, six, seven (pauses and looks up), eight!

J: (Removes both screens.) Show me.

S: (Points at each counter in turn.) One, two, three – four, five, six, seven, eight!

J: What about if I put ten here (screens ten counters) and three here (screens three counters).

S: (Looks at the screen covering three counters and makes three points in coordination with counting.) One, two, three (looks at the other screen and again coordinates a point with each number word) four, five, six, seven, eight, nine (pauses and looks up) – ten – eleven, twelve?

J: Have another think. (Places her hand on the screen covering ten counters.) Start with this side. How many here?

S: Ten.

J: Right. Start with this side.

S: (Looking up) One, two, three, four (in coordination with four points), five, six (looks at the screen and appears to feel the counters).

J: (Interrupting.) No, don't feel them. How many are here?

S: (Places left hand on the screen covering ten counters.) Ten there –.

J: Alright and three there.

S: (Places right hand on other screen.) Three there. (Looks at the screen covering ten counters and coordinates a point with each number word.) One, two, three, four, five, six (looks at the second screen) seven –.

J: (Interrupting) No, ten here (points to the screen).

S: Ten, three (places a hand on each screen).

J: Start at ten and count these ones on (points to each screen in turn).

S: (Looks at the screen covering ten counters and then touches the screen four times in coordination with counting). One, two, three, four.

J: (Interrupting) No, don't touch them. We know how many are there. How many are there? (Removes the screen.) You count them.

S: (Points to each counter in turn.) One, two . . . ten.

J: (Rescreens the counters.) Now do we have to count them again? How many are there?

S: Ten.

J: Now let's just say ten.

J: (Points to the screen covering three counters.)

S: Three!

J: (Points to the screen covering ten counters.) Ten –. (Points to the screen covering three counters.)

S: Three.

J: (Points to the screen covering ten counters.) Ten –. How many altogether? (Points again to the screen covering ten counters.) Ten –.

S: (Looks at Jane and then looks at the screen covering ten counters and makes ten points in coordination with counting.) One, two . . . ten (looks at the second screen and continues to make points in coordination with counting), eleven, twelve, thirteen!

Discussion of Video Excerpt 2.1

In the first task (3 and 2) Shirley counts aloud from one and keeps track of the second collection (that is, two counters). In the second task (5 and 3) Shirley counts from one, first counting the collection of three counters and then the collection of five. Thus her solution involves keeping track of five counts. Because Shirley solves tasks involving screened collections and, in doing so, counts from one she is classified as Stage 2: Figurative Counting. Shirley's strategy seems to involve visualizing, that is, figural counting or counting figural unit items. She seems to visualize the second collection to keep track of the items to be counted. Although her strategy involves movements, that is, pointing at the counters, her visualizing seems to be the most significant aspect of her counting. In the last task (10 and 3) we see that Shirley seems necessarily to have to count from 'one' and doing so provides meaning to 'ten' for Shirley. This is typical of children at Stage 2. As in the earlier tasks, Shirley's strategy seems to involve visualizing the second collection when continuing after counting to 'ten'.

Video Excerpt 2.2: Molly and Tom

M: (Places out five red counters and screens them and then places out four blue counters and screens them.) Now if I've got five counters there Tom and I cover them up and four counters here and I cover them up, how many counters would I have altogether there?

T: (Smiles and shifts in his seat.) These are the hard ones. (Thinks for three seconds.) Umm.

M: (Nods and points at each collection in turn.) Five and four?

T: (Looks momentarily at the screens and then looks up and to his right. Then counts subvocally for seven seconds.) Nine!

M: Why do you think it's nine?

T: Because I counted through them.

M: Did you? How did you count? Could you just tell me?

T: I went one, two, three, four, five (points at the screen covering five counters and then looks at the second screen), and then one, two, three, four. (Pauses.) So it's seven. I can tell that's seven –

M: (M interrupts Tom's thinking and removes the screens.) Umm.

T: So I went – (counts subvocally from one to nine in coordination with moving each counter in turn). Yes!

M: (Places out seven red counters and screens them and then places out five blue counters and screens them.) Seven red ones and five blue ones. Seven and five. How many would that be altogether?

T: (Looks at the screen covering seven red counters and counts subvocally. Then looks at the second screen and continues to count subvocally.) Twelve!

M: (Removes the screens.) Want to check to see if you are right?

T: (Moves each counter in coordination with counting.) One, two . . . twelve!

Discussion of Video Excerpt 2.2

In each of the two tasks Tom's strategy is to count subvocally. Nevertheless, it is reasonably apparent that he is counting from 'one' and this is confirmed in his explanation of his solution to the first task. In both tasks, when continuing after counting the first collection Tom seems to focus on the number words themselves. Thus, in the first task, for example, although he does not explicitly double count, he seems to focus on the words from 'six' to 'nine' in order to keep track of making four counts, rather than visualize as in the case of Shirley. As discussed above this is referred to as verbal counting or counting verbal unit items.

STAGE 3: INITIAL NUMBER SEQUENCE

Stage 3: Initial Number Sequence. Child uses counting-on rather than counting from 'one', to solve addition or missing addend tasks (for example, $6 + x = 9$). The child may use a count-down-from strategy to solve removed items tasks (for example, $17 - 3$ as 16, 15, 14 – answer 14) but not count-down-to strategies to solve missing subtrahend tasks (for example, $17 - 14$ as 16, 15, 14 – answer 3).

Children at Stage 3 use counting-on to solve additive and missing addend tasks and may also use counting-down-from to solve removed items tasks. When solving an additive task such as 8 and 4, for example, presented as two screened collections, the child seems to be aware that, when counting-on, the number word 'eight' signifies the act of having counted the first collection from 'one' to 'eight'.

Table 4.5 sets out the stage and indicative levels for the counting-on child on the models pertaining to FNWSs, BNWSs, numeral identification and tens and ones.

Table 4.5 Stage and levels of a typical initial number sequence child

Model	Stage/level
Stage of Early Arithmetical Learning (SEAL)	3
Level of Forward Number Word Sequences (FNWSs)	5
Level of Backward Number Word Sequences (BNWSs)	4
Level of Numeral Identification	3
Level of Tens and Ones Knowledge	1
Level of Early Multiplication and Division Knowledge	1

The Typical Initial Number Sequence Child

The child at the Initial Number Sequence Stage (Stage 3) has developed one or more of the **advanced counting-by-ones strategies** of **counting-up-from**, counting-up-to, and counting-down-from. Thus children at these stages will solve additive tasks by counting-up-from, and typically counts-up-from the first mentioned or larger addend. On additive tasks involving two covered collections children are able to keep track of six or more counts, when counting the second collection. In many cases children are able to use these counting-on strategies in the range 1 to 100. Eighty-seven and five for example, is solved by counting-on five from 87. The child knows to stop at 'ninety-two' because they realize they have made five counts. Thus prior to commencing the count from 87, the child anticipates that they can keep track of the number of counts. This anticipation and capacity to keep track of the number of counts is the hallmark of this stage.

Counting-up-to and Counting-down-from

The counting-up-from strategy described in the previous paragraph is also referred to simply as counting-on. Counting-on also includes counting-up-to which typically arises when solving tasks involving a small unknown addend, for example, $7 + x = 10$, presented using counters of two colours and referred to as missing addend tasks. Some children who count-on to solve additive tasks might not have developed the counting-up-to strategy. They might be unfamiliar with missing addend tasks, and it is common for children to misinterpret a missing addend task as an additive task (for example, in the task just described they might attempt to start from seven and count-on ten). In the case of most children though, counting-up-to emerges at the same time as, or soon after, counting-up-from. At around the same period children learn to use counting-down-from to solve subtractive tasks with small known differences (referred to as removed items tasks). Thus on a task such as removing three counters from a collection of 15 (with the counters concealed), the child will count down three from 15. As before, the child anticipates that they can keep track of the number of counts, and thus stops after three counts.

FNWSs, BNWSs and Numeral Identification

It is typical for the child at this stage to be facile with FNWSs to 100 and beyond. In the case of BNWSs children might be facile to beyond 30 but not necessarily to 100. A reasonably common mistake in the case of saying BNWSs is the following: when saying the words backward from 53 for example, the child says '53, 52, 51, 40, 49, 48 . . .'. This kind of mistake occurs at any decade number and a likely explanation is that the child counts backwards by ten from the decade number in order to determine the next decade (for example, counts '50, 40' to figure out the decade number before the fifties). Children at this stage typically can recognize and identify most or all of the numerals in the range 1 to 100 and beyond although some digit reversal errors (for example, '27' is named as 'seventy-two') may persist. Children might also be able to name some 3-digit numerals. The 3-digit numerals with a zero in the ones or tens (for example, 620, 407) are less likely to be correctly identified.

Tens and Ones

The child at this stage typically has made little progress in developing knowledge of tens and ones. They are likely to be able to count forwards and backwards by tens on the decade (10, 20,

30, and so on) but not off the decade (2, 12, 22, and so on). On tasks involving tens and ones materials (for example, bundling sticks) they might increment by tens in the case of whole tens and no ones (for example, 10, 20, 30, and so on), but often this amounts to no more than recognition of the familiar sequence of the decade number words (ten, twenty, and so on). In cases involving incrementing by tens off the decade or incrementing by tens and ones, these children typically resort to counting-on by ones, or they incorrectly count ones as tens etc.

Early Multiplication and Division

The child at this stage might also have developed initial multiplication and division knowledge relating to equal groups, equal shares and arrays, for example, combining equal groups and finding the total, sharing equally and finding the number in one share, making an array, or determining how many dots in an array.

The assessment of knowledge and strategies used in the solving of tasks in tens and ones is discussed in detail in Chapter 6 and Early and Advanced Multiplication and Division in Chapter 8.

Video Excerpt 3.1: Julie and Tania

J: I've got five under there (points to a screen), and four under there (points to a second screen).
T: (Counts subvocally in coordination with pointing in turn at four fingers on her left hand.) Nine.
J: How did you work that out?
T: Counted on my fingers.
J: What numbers did you count?
T: (Points to her one finger.) Six – (pauses), five, six, seven, eight, nine. (Coordinates the last four number words with pointing to each finger in turn.)
J: I've got nine under there and six under there. How many altogether?
T: Nine, ten . . . fifteen (points in turn at the five fingers on her left hand and one finger on her right hand).

Discussion of Video Excerpt 3.1

Tania's strategy for solving these tasks involves counting-on and using her fingers to keep track of the number of her counts, that is, when counting the second collection. In the first task, for example, she does not raise her four fingers prior to commencing to count, that is, it is not necessary for her to raise four fingers in advance in order to keep track of counting-on. Rather, her strategy involves recognizing when she has raised four fingers to keep track of the second collection. In the second task, in similar vein, Tania knows when she has raised six fingers to keep track. Her counting-on strategy includes a quite facile (that is, skillful) use of finger patterns.

Video Excerpt 3.2: Jane and Shirley

The following video excerpt is taken from an MR teaching session.

J: (Points to a screen and then covers four counters with a second screen.) Twelve, and I've got four more under here?
S: (Places her hand on the first screen and looks ahead.) Twelve. (Moves her hand to the second screen. After three seconds during which time she moves her fingers over the second screen.) Sixteen!

J: Alright. Maybe we can just pretend. (Places a screen on the desk.) If I say, under here I've got – I'm pretending there's twenty-four. Twenty-four (places out and screens three counters), and three more?

S: Twenty-four (points to the second screen and answers almost immediately), twenty-seven.

J: Great work. (Places out a screen.) Let's pretend there's forty-five under here. Forty-five (places out a screen covering four counters), and four more.

S: (Places her hand on the first screen.) Forty-five (moves her hand over the second screen and counts subvocally), forty-nine!

J: (Places out a screen.) Let's pretend there's fifty-eight under here. Fifty-eight (places out a screen covering three counters), and three more.

S: (Places her hand on the first screen. Then moves her hand to the second screen and counts subvocally while moving her fingers.) Sixty-two!

J: No, have a think. (Places her hand on the first screen) fifty-eight – (moves her hand to the second screen).

S: (Looks at the second screen for two seconds.) Sixty-one.

J: (Places her hand on the first screen.) What about if I've got eighty-two under there? (Briefly displays and then screens five counters.) Eighty-two and five more?

S: (Looks at the second screen momentarily and then looks up and to her left. Counts subvocally for six seconds.) Eighty-seven.

Discussion of Video Excerpt 3.2

In this excerpt Shirley solves five additive tasks – 12 and 4, 24 and 3, 45 and 4, 58 and 3, 82 and 5 – by counting-on. One can hypothesize about the means by which Shirley keeps track of the second collection. Shirley does not appear to explicitly double count. Nevertheless she appears to focus on her number words when counting-on. A plausible explanation is that Shirley uses patterns for counting-on a given number of counts and that these patterns are temporal sequences of counts that she can apply irrespective of the particular number words. Prior to commencing her count, Shirley seems to anticipate that she can count-on the given number of counts. In summary, Shirley has a facile and spontaneous counting-on strategy which is indicative of a child at Stage 3: Initial Number Sequence.

STAGE 4: INTERMEDIATE NUMBER SEQUENCE

> **Stage 4: Intermediate Number Sequence.** The child counts-down-to to solve missing subtrahend tasks (for example, 17 – 14 as 16, 15, 14 – answer 3). The child can choose the more efficient of count-down-from and count-down-to strategies.

The child at Stage 4 has developed counting-down-to as well as the other advanced counting-by-ones strategies. Counting-down-to is not easy to detect and it is useful to discuss this strategy in more detail. The tasks involve small, unknown subtrahends, for example remove some counters from a collection of eleven to leave eight (11 – [ ] = 8), known as missing subtrahend tasks. Tasks of this kind can evoke the counting-down-to strategy. Thus the child counts back from 11 until they reach 8, and keeps track of the number of counts after saying 'eleven', that is, three counts. In the terms of the Learning Framework in Number counting-down-to is regarded as more sophisticated than the other advanced counting-by-ones strategies. Thus it is not surprising to find children who can solve additive, missing addend and removed items tasks like those described above, but cannot solve missing subtrahend tasks of the kind described, that is, they cannot use a counting-down-to strategy.

Table 4.6 sets out the stage and indicative levels for the intermediate number sequence child on the models pertaining to FNWSs, BNWSs, numeral identification and tens and ones.

Table 4.6 Stage and levels of a typical intermediate number sequence child

Model	Stage/level
Stage of Early Arithmetical Learning (SEAL)	4
Level of Forward Number Word Sequences (FNWSs)	5
Level of Backward Number Word Sequences (BNWSs)	4
Level of Numeral Identification	3
Level of Tens and Ones Knowledge	1
Level of Early Multiplication and Division Knowledge	1

The Typical Initial Number Sequence Child

The typical behaviors are similar to those for the stage 3 child described above.

Video Excerpt 4.1: Libby and Kelley

L: (Places out '10 – 7 =', using plastic digits and signs.) This time, ten take seven away?

K: Ten. (Raises ten fingers directly in front of her. Looks at her right hand and then her left. Lowers two fingers on her left hand and then all five on her right. Picks up the plastic digit for '3' and places it beside the equals sign.)

L: Right. Okay, now try this one. (Places out '16 – 12 =') Sixteen take twelve away?

K: (After 20 seconds, raises her thumb and index finger. Then lowers both her thumb and index finger.) Umm fifteen (raises her thumb and then pauses), fourteen, thirteen (in coordination with raising two fingers in turn. Pauses, then raises her third finger and utters uncertainly), twelve. (Looks at her fingers, then simultaneously raises her little finger and lowers her thumb.) Four!

Discussion of Video Excerpt 4.1

In the first task, 10 – 7, presented with plastic numerals, Kelley uses a strategy that we might suppose is convenient for her. She simultaneously raises 10 fingers and then looks carefully at her fingers and after a little while lowers 2 fingers on her left hand and then the 5 fingers on her right hand. A plausible explanation is that, at this point she has established a finger pattern that stands for 7 for her, that is, for the 7 being taken away. She immediately knows that now she has 3 fingers remaining, that is, she recognizes a finger pattern for three and it is not necessary for her to count from one. In summary, Kelley knows the patterns for 10 and 3, and she builds a pattern for 7 by lowering two fingers on one hand and then five on the other. Kelley's strategy on this task involves facile use of finger patterns. Thus her solution in the first task does not provide an indication of whether she might use advanced counting strategies in some tasks.

The second task involves 16 – 12 and is presented with plastic numerals. It seems reasonable to suggest that Kelley cannot use finger patterns on this task because she cannot readily make a pattern to signify 16. In other words, 16 is 'beyond the finger range' in terms of signifying numbers in the same way as done in the task of 10 – 7. Kelley seems to spend around 20 seconds focusing on trying to solve the problem after which she seems to suddenly become aware of a strategy that she can use. Kelley uses a counting-down-to strategy to solve the task. She begins at 16 and then keeps track of the number of counts until she gets to 12 and stops, and she uses her fingers on her right hand to keep track. A plausible explanation is that, prior to beginning to count down, Kelley was aware of the 12 as being a part of the 16. She was aware of 12 as a whole, or as a unit within the larger unit of 16. It is this kind of thinking that is the hallmark of Stage 4. She is able to conceptualize the smaller unit within the larger unit prior to commencing her count. It is also interesting to see that she raises her thumb and 3 fingers and then deftly switches the pattern by lowering her thumb and raising her little finger. She then recognizes immediately her finger pattern for 4. She does not have to count from 'one' to 'four'. In summary, Kelley uses counting-down-to and in doing so uses her fingers to keep track of four counts. For this reason Kelley is classified as Stage 4: Intermediate Number Sequence.

Video Excerpt 4.2: Terry and Sarah

T: There's eight there, okay? (Places eight counters under a screen.) I'm taking some away (reaches under the screen and removes two counters without displaying them), and I've got six left (momentarily displays the remaining six counters). How many did I take away?

S: (Immediately.) Two.

T: How did you do that so quickly?

S: (Shrugging her shoulders.) I don't know.

T: Twelve, okay? There's twelve there this time. (Places twelve counters under a screen.) I am going to take some away (reaches under the screen and removes three counters without displaying them), and there are nine left (momentarily displays the remaining nine counters).

S: (Sequentially raises three fingers.) Three?

T: Okay, now what numbers were you saying to yourself to get those three?

S: I was saying twelve, and I took away some and then I counted to nine, so I went, twelve, eleven, ten (in coordination with raising three fingers), and that was nine (moves her fourth finger), so I put that down and then I worked it out.

Discussion of Video Excerpt 4.2

In the first task, Terry's questioning of Sarah about her strategy seems most appropriate, in that she does not continue questioning after Sarah says 'I don't know'. A reasonable explanation of this is that Sarah knows the answer to 8 – 6 and does not use a strategy to obtain the answer. Continuing to question a child about their strategy in this kind of situation can be somewhat disconcerting for the child. The second task is apparently more challenging for Sarah. In her explanation it becomes apparent that Sarah indeed has counted backwards. She has used a counting-down-to strategy to solve this Missing Subtrahend task. She raised 3 fingers to keep track of counting down. After completing her counting down, she recognizes the finger-pattern for 3. Terry once again very skillfully questions without leading, and without presupposition or presumption, and Sarah's strategy unfolds. This is another excellent example of a count-down-to strategy that is characteristic of Stage 4.

STAGE 5: FACILE NUMBER SEQUENCE

> **Stage 5: Facile Number Sequence.** The child uses a range of what are referred to as non-count-by-ones strategies. These strategies involve procedures other than counting-by-ones but may also involve some counting-by-ones. Thus in additive and subtractive situations the child uses strategies such as compensation, using a known result, adding to ten, commutativity, subtraction as the inverse of addition and awareness of the 'ten' in a teen number.

This section provides an overview of a typical child at the Facile Stage, that is at Stage 5 of the Stages of Early Arithmetical Learning. Table 4.7 sets out the stage and indicative levels for the counting-on child on the models pertaining to FNWSs, BNWSs, numeral identification, tens and ones, and multiplication and division. The overview discusses the six aspects of early number knowledge listed in Table 4.7 and grouping by fives and tens.

Table 4.7 Stage and levels of a typical facile child

Model	Stage/level
Stage of Early Arithmetical Learning (SEAL)	5
Level of Forward Number Word Sequences (FNWSs)	5
Level of Backward Number Word Sequences (BNWSs)	5
Level of Numeral Identification	4
Level of Tens and Ones Knowledge	2
Level of Early Multiplication and Division Knowledge	3

The Typical Facile Child

The child at the Facile Stage typically has developed strong facility in a range of aspects of the Learning Framework in Number. Facile arithmetical strategies might include knowing a range of doubles and using doubles to work out other facts, for example, using 5 + 5 to work out 4 + 5. These strategies can also incorporate knowledge of the numbers in the teens in terms of a ten and ones, for example, the child uses knowledge of 3 + 3 to work out 13 + 3. Understanding of the inverse relationship between addition and subtraction is also common at this stage. Thus the child might use knowledge of 9 + 3 to work out 12 – 3, or knowledge of 10 + 5 to work out 15 – 11.

Grouping by Fives and Tens

The child at this stage might use grouping by fives and tens when adding or subtracting in the range 1 to 20 (for example, 4 + 3 is found by partitioning 3 into 1 and 2, and then adding 2 to 5, and 13 – 8 is found by partitioning 8 into 3 and 5, and then subtracting 5 from 10). As well, they might solve without counting by ones, additions such as 40 + 8 and subtractions such as 28 + x = 30, 87 – x = 80, and 30 – 2. Finally, the child might use the strategy of adding to 10, for addition (for example, 18 + 6 is found by finding the complement of 8 in 10, that is, 2, then partitioning 6 into 2 and 4, and then adding 4 to 20), and subtracting to 10 for subtraction (for example, 42 – 6 is found by partitioning 6 into 2 and 4, and then subtracting 4 from 40).

FNWSs, BNWSs and Numeral Identification

The child at this stage typically is facile with FNWSs and BNWSs in the range 1 to 100 and beyond, and can count forwards and backwards by 2s, 10s, 5s, 3s and 4s. Also, the child can recognize and identify numerals in the range 1 to 100. In many cases the child can also recognize and identify many three-digit numerals as well, although numerals with the digit '0' in the right-hand or middle place (for example, 602, 808) are likely to be more difficult.

Tens and Ones

The child at this stage is likely to be able to increment and decrement in the range 1 to 100, by tens on and off the decade (for example, 40 and 10, 70 less 10, 32 and 10, 88 less 10), and by tens and ones on and off the decade (for example, 32 and 2 tens and 3 ones, 87 less 2 tens less 2 ones).

Early Multiplication and Division

The child at this stage is likely to be able to use skip counting and repeated addition or subtraction to solve multiplicative and divisional tasks involving screened equal groups and screened arrays. Examples of these tasks are, determining the number of items altogether in equal groups or an array and, given the number of items altogether determining the number of groups, the number in each group or the number in each row of an array.

Video Excerpt 5.1: Robin and Allan

R: (Places 12 counters under a screen.) There were twelve counters and I took away some (removes and screens three counters), and I have nine left. How many did I take away?
A: (Looks at Robin.) Three.
R: How did you work that out?
A: Nine plus three is twelve, and then you take away, it's nine.
R: (Places 15 counters under a screen and then removes and screens four counters.) This time I had fifteen counters, I took some away and I have eleven left. Fifteen, took some away and I've got eleven left.
A: (Looks ahead for nine seconds.) Four!
R: Tell me how you did that one.
A: Umm, you had fifteen and took some away to make eleven because you just take away four, 'cause if you took away five it would be ten and you just plus it on.
R: (Places counters under a screen.) What if I start off with fifteen under there (removes, displays and then screens three counters), take three out, how many are left under there?
A: Twelve.
R: Hmm, how did you do that one?
A: Because five take away three is two, and then you just, 'cause there was fifteen so you just take away three and it's twelve.

Discussion of Video Excerpt 5.1

Allan shows a good number of non-count-by-ones strategies on these tasks. In the case of the first task – 12 take-away some, now I have 9, how many did I take away? – it becomes apparent in Allan's explanation that he worked this Missing Subtrahend task out by thinking of the addition '9 and 3 are 12'. This is a very advanced strategy for a 6-year-old and is an excellent example of a non-count-by-ones strategy. Strategies such as this are commonly referred to as thinking strategies for the basic facts, that is, using addition to work out subtraction, or exploiting knowledge that subtraction and addition are inverse operations. Allan's solution of the second task involves knowledge of the tens and ones structure of the number 15. Allan realizes that 15 is 10 and 5. Again this is very advanced for a 6-year-old and not typical of children lower than Stage 5. Allan also uses what is commonly referred to as a compensation strategy – if 5 are taken from 15 the answer is 10, thus, if the answer is 11, only 4 are taken away. These strategies are very advanced and are referred to as non-count-by-ones strategies.

In the final task in this excerpt, 15 take away 3, Allan in explanation indicates that he has worked the task out by thinking of 5 take away 3. As with the above strategies, this is an example of a non-count-by-ones strategy. He seems to be aware of a correspondence of the relationship between 5 and 15, on the one hand, with the relationship between 2 and 12, on the other hand, that is, in both cases the second number is 10 more than the first. Given the problem of the names of these numbers, for example 'twelve', which does not give any clue of the relationship between 2 and 12, it seems plausible to suggest that Allan is thinking in terms of written symbols perhaps even written symbols arranged in columns. This corresponds with how we might expect an advanced child, or a child beyond Year 1, to work such a subtraction. Whatever the precise nature of Allan's thinking, it is quite advanced. In Allan's solutions we see strategies well beyond counting-by-ones. His strategies, considered across all of these tasks, are characteristic of Stage 5: Facile Number Sequence, where non-count-by-ones strategies are used spontaneously.

Video Excerpt 5.2: Kathryn and Loretta

K: If we have five under there (places five counters under a screen) and four under there (places four counters under a second screen), how many would we have?
L: (Immediately.) Five and four more is nine.
K: And how do you know that?
L: Well, five and three more is eight and so one more is nine.

Discussion of Video Excerpt 5.2

Loretta, in explanation, reveals a strategy where 5 plus 4 is worked out from 5 plus 3. This kind of strategy, that is, using a known fact to work out an unknown and making an appropriate adjustment – one more in this case – is well known and is referred to as a 'thinking strategy' for the basic facts. Because Loretta uses a strategy that has features other than counting-by-ones she is classified as Stage 5: Facile Number Sequence.

CONCLUSION

The model of the Stages of Early Arithmetical Learning presented in this chapter provides a means of understanding the progression of children's early number learning from perceptual counting strategies in which children are reliant on seeing materials to the point where children have a relatively sophisticated knowledge of addition and subtraction, in the range 1 to 100 and beyond. Children at the Perceptual Stage (Stage 1) can solve problems involving visible items, whereas children at the Figurative Stage (Stage 2) can solve problems involving hidden items but count from one when doing so. Children at the stage of the Initial Number Sequence (Stage 3) use counting-on to solve additive and/or missing addend tasks, and may use counting-down-from to solve removed items tasks, while children at the stage of the Intermediate Number Sequence (Stage 4) use counting-down-to to solve missing subtrahend tasks. Finally, children at the stage of Facile Number Sequence (Stage 5) use a range of strategies other than counting-by-ones to solve additive and subtractive tasks.

Two examples of children's attainment were presented to further exemplify the stages. We are aware, however, that more experience and practice may be necessary before one is confident to recognize the stages. Therefore, we now provide two support mechanisms. First, we conclude this chapter by presenting a discussion of the common difficulties which trainee assessors face when trying to allocate a stage. Secondly, in Chapter 5 we present twelve scenarios, two for each of the Stages 0–5 but not in any defined order. We challenge you to identify the stages. The answer for each scenario is given at the end of the chapter with an explanation why each child is placed at a particular stage.

Determining the Child's Stage: Judging on the Basis of the Most Advanced Strategy

When determining the child's stage it is important to remember that the child is judged on the basis of the most advanced strategy they use. In all the additive and subtractive tasks, the interviewer should attempt to elicit the most advanced strategies. In the discussions in the following paragraphs the term 'at least' is often used as a qualifier, for example, 'the child who correctly counts these [visible] collections is judged to be at Stage 1 at least' and 'the child who counts-down-to to solve missing subtrahend tasks is judged to be at Stage 4 at least'. A child might count-down-to on missing subtrahend tasks and use Stage 5 strategies on other tasks. In this case the child is judged to be Stage 5. In similar vein, the child who counts from one to solve additive tasks, counts-on to solve missing addend and counts-down-from to solve removed items is judged to be at Stage 3 (assuming they do not use Stage 4 or Stage 5 strategies).

Stage 0 or Stage 1?

The need to distinguish between Stage 0 and Stage 1 is likely to arise in cases where the interviewer has presented the two items in Assessment Interview 1.1, Task Group 8(d), perceptual counting, that involve counting unscreened collections of 13 and 18 counters. The child who is unable to count these collections because they omit some of the counters, or do not correctly coordinate the number words with the counters, or because they apparently do not know the FNWS, is judged to be at Stage 0. The child who correctly counts these collections is judged to be at Stage 1 at least. In most cases, because the interviewer decided to present these tasks on the basis of their performance on the Entry Tasks, the child is no more advanced than Stage 1.

Stage 1 or Stage 2?

The need to distinguish between Stage 1 and Stage 2 arises when the child uses particular finger patterns to solve the additive tasks of 3 and 2 (that is, the introductory example) and 5 and 4, and unsuccessfully attempts to use finger patterns to solve tasks such as 9 and 6, 8 and 5, 9 + 3 (1.1:8(a) and 8(e). Matthew in Chapter 5 exemplifies this case. His raised fingers constitute perceptual replacements for the screened counters and he establishes his finger patterns prior to commencing to count both collections. In this case the child is classified at Stage 1 only. Distinguishing between Stage 1 and Stage 2 also arises in cases where the child solves tasks involving one screened collection 1.1:8(a) and one unscreened collection 1.1: 8(b). If the child counts the unscreened collection first, and then keeps track while continuing in order to count the screened collection, the child is judged to be at Stage 2, with the proviso that the child's use of this strategy is not limited to the first, partially screened, additive task of 5 and 2. Thus it is necessary that the child use this strategy on one or both of the tasks of 7 and 3 and 9 and 4. In the case where the child counts the screened collection first and then continues in order to count the unscreened collection, the child is judged to be at Stage 1. In this case the means by which the child has counted the screened collection does not constitute figurative counting.

Stage 2 or Stage 3?

Distinguishing between Stage 2 and Stage 3 is usually unproblematic. In the case where the child counts-on to solve additive tasks but does not seem to understand the missing addend tasks, 1.1:8(f), the child is judged to be at Stage 3 'at least'. Thus, it is sufficient to use counting-on to solve additive tasks only. In many cases, children who do not seem to understand missing addend tasks will count-down-from on the removed items tasks, 1.1:9(c), as well as count-on for additive tasks.

Stage 3 or Stage 4?

The child who counts-down-to to solve missing subtrahend tasks (1.1:9(b) is judged to be at Stage 4 at least. Counting-down-to to solve the written task of 16 – 12 (Task Group 9) is also indicative of Stage 4. Attempting to solve missing subtrahend tasks or the written task of 16 – 12 by counting-down-from is not indicative of Stage 4, for example, the child attempts to count down 12 counts from 16. Children may count-up-to to solve missing subtrahend tasks although this is not a common occurrence. One might say these children interpret a missing subtrahend task as they might interpret a missing addend task. In such cases the child is judged to be at least at Stage 4. Their ability to conceptualize the task in this way is regarded as indicative of Stage 4 rather than Stage 3.

We recognize that additional exemplification and practice may be necessary in order to become skilled in analysis, and this is provided next, in Chapters 5 and 6.

5

Identifying the Stages of Early Arithmetical Learning

Summary

Through careful observation of a child's problem-solving activity during the assessment interview, teachers can determine the child's stage in terms of the SEAL model. This is based on determining the most advanced strategy available to the child. In this chapter we present scenarios similar to the examples in Chapter 4 and challenge you to determine the stage of SEAL for each example. The chapter provides the answer for each example and an explanation of why each child is placed at a particular stage.

Analysis of Mathematics Recovery assessments involves a good deal of learning on the part of teachers. This learning is best undertaken through practice, reflection and discussion, and this chapter introduces the reader to this process. Twelve scenarios of children's problem-solving activity in early number are presented. These scenarios are based on actual assessments by MR teachers, and focus specifically on Task Groups 8 and 9 of Assessment Interview Schedule 1.1, that is, additive and subtractive tasks. The exercise for the reader is to study carefully each scenario in order to determine the child's stage in terms of the SEAL model. This exercise serves several purposes. As well as providing important practice for the reader in analyzing children's problem-solving activity, it provides insights into the ways in which teachers present tasks and interact with children during MR assessment, and exemplifies the ways children respond to the assessment tasks.

Readers should bear in mind that MR assessment aims to determine the most advanced strategy available to the child. This is equally important in the administration of the assessment interview and its analysis. The child's use of this strategy should be spontaneous, that is, unassisted either directly or indirectly by the teacher. As a general rule the child should use the strategy in solving several tasks, rather than only the introductory task for example. Each of the 12 scenarios in this chapter has been selected because in the view of the authors it provides a reasonably clear-cut example of children's problem-solving at a given stage. Readers should aim to identify each strategy used by the child and then determine the most advanced strategy available to the child. The stage identification and a detailed discussion of the reasoning behind the allocation are provided at the end of the chapter.

SCENARIOS OF CHILDREN'S EARLY NUMBER PROBLEM-SOLVING ACTIVITY

Collectively these 12 scenarios exemplify all six stages of SEAL. Each of the stages is exemplified by two scenarios.

Scenario 1: Heather and Tina

Tina was presented with the following three additive tasks: 3 and 2, 5 and 4, and 9 and 6, involving two screened collections. She solved each of these on her first attempt.

H: (Briefly displays and then screens three blue counters and similarly two red counters.) Do you know how many there are altogether?

T: Umm. (Looks at the screen covering three counters for six seconds.) Five!

H: How did you work that out?

T: Umm, I said – umm, umm I read it in my mind and I – and it went three and then I counted the rest and it worked out to five.

H: (Presents the second task of 5 and 4.) Five and four more?

T: (Looks ahead for four seconds then looks to the right for three seconds.) Nine!

H: Hmm. What did you do that time?

T: I just counted them all.

H: Can you tell me what numbers you counted?

T: Hmm, I counted one, two . . . nine.

H: (Presents the third task of 9 and 6.) Nine this time and six more?

T: (Looks in the direction of the screens for nine seconds.) Fifteen!

H: What did you do that time to help you?

T: Well, I did the same, like when it was – there was five there and four there (points at the screens in turn).

H: Hmm, where did you start counting from?

T: Up to nine.

H: You counted up to nine did you?

T: Hmm (nods affirmatively).

H: And then you did what?

T: Well, I said nine and then I counted the rest.

Tina was presented with four Missing Subtrahend tasks, that is, 3 to 2, 8 to 6, 12 to 9 and 6 to 4. She solved the first and last of these only. Heather modified her presentation of the last task in the following way. After partitioning the **minuend** she left the known **difference** unscreened (four counters in this case), whereas on the first three tasks, both the known difference and the missing subtrahend were screened after partitioning. Tina's solution to the last task, that is, 6 to 4, is shown in the following video excerpt:

H: (Arranges six counters into a 3 × 2 array.) Okay there are six there. Can you look away for a moment? (Removes and screens two adjacent counters from one row of three, leaving the remaining four counters unscreened.) Look back. There are only four left. How many did I take away?

T: (Looks at the four counters.) Umm – two!

H: (Unscreens the two counters.) How did you know it was two?

T: (Points to the four counters.) Because I knew there has to be two more there to make six.

Tina was presented with four removed items tasks, that is, 3 r 1, 10 r 2, 15 r 3 and 5 r 2. She solved the first and last of these only. Heather modified her presentation of the last task similarly to the way she modified the last missing subtrahend task, that is, she left the removed items (two in this case) unscreened after partitioning the minuend. For the task of 10 r 2 Tina answered 'five' and for 15 r 3 she answered 'six'. Her strategies for solving these two tasks were not apparent. Tina's solution to the task of 5 r 3 is shown in the following video excerpt:

H: (Briefly displays and then screens five counters.) I'm going to start with five this time. Okay, cover it up. (Removes two counters and leaves them unscreened.) Put my hand under and take two away. How many left?

T: Umm – three!

H: How did you know that?

T: Umm, because I knew there would be two more to make five.

Scenario 2: Tamara and Jack

Jack was presented with the following five additive tasks involving two screened collections: 3 and 2, 5 and 4, 9 and 6, 8 and 5, and 9 and 3. He solved each of these on his first attempt. On the first task (3 and 2) he answered 'five' quickly and when asked how he did it he said 'I just knew it was five'. The following video excerpt begins after Jack had quickly answered 'nine' to the second task (5 and 4).

T: How did you do it?

J: I just knew it was nine and – if you had five and you put up four it would be nine.

T: (Presents the third task.) Okay we've got nine and six. How many altogether?

J: (Looks up for six seconds then raises five fingers on his left hand and one on his right simultaneously). Okay six – (places his left hand on the first screen keeping his fingers raised), wait, nine – (raises his left hand then raises the second finger on his right hand), ten – (lowers the finger just raised) wait, nine – (touches each of his raised fingers in coordination with counting), ten, eleven, twelve, thirteen, fourteen, fifteen.

Jack solved the fourth (8 and 5) task similarly to the way in which he solved the third. His solution involved raising five fingers on his left hand simultaneously and then touching each finger in coordination with counting from nine to thirteen. On the fifth task (9 and 3) Jack quickly answered 'twelve'. On this task it seemed that Jack recalled a known fact. Jack was presented with two missing addend tasks, that is, 4 to 6 and 12 to 15, which he solved. On the first of these he first answered 'eleven' – seeming to misinterpret the task as the additive task of 4 and 6.

Jack was presented with the following four missing subtrahend tasks: 5 to 3, 10 to 6, 12 to 9 and 15 to 11. He solved each of these tasks on his first attempt. On the first task he quickly answered 'two'. Jack's solution to the second task (10 to 6) is shown in the following video excerpt.

T: And now we have six. How many did I take away?

J: How many did you have?

T: Ten.

J: (After seven seconds, raises four fingers.)

T: Okay, how did you do it?

J: Kind of – kind of thinking.

T: Tell me how you were thinking.

J: Well – (mumbles), I think it would be four.

T: (Raises the screen covering four counters.) Well you're right but I want to understand how you did that. (Raises the screen covering six counters.) We started out with ten and now we have six. Tell me how you get four.

J: (After three seconds.) I counted up.

T: Do that for me?

J: (Raises five fingers on his left hand and then points to his thumb.) Ten – I mean ten –. (Lowers his thumb and then raises his right hand above his head with his point finger extended.) Ten! (Touches each finger on his left hand in coordination with counting) nine, eight, seven, six.

T: Okay so you really counted down didn't you?

J: Hmm-mm (affirmatively).

In solving the third task (12 to 9) Jack touched three fingers in coordination with counting sub-vocally. In explaining his solution he said 'I counted down'. In explaining his solution to the fourth task (15 to 11) Jack again said 'I counted down'.

Jack was presented with the following four removed items tasks: 3 r 1, 10 r 2, 15 r 3, 27 r 4. He solved each of these tasks on his first attempt. His strategies typically involved subvocal counting without moving his fingers.

Scenario 3: Wendy and Bill

Bill was presented with three additive tasks involving two screened collections, that is, 5 and 4, 9 and 6, and 8 and 5. On the first task Bill immediately answered 'nine' and explained his answer as follows: 'Because five plus five is ten, and then four plus five must be nine, because it's missing one more from five.' On the second task Bill answered 'fifteen' after 15 seconds. In explaining his answer he said 'well three plus three is six and then there's three more so that makes nine and then there's another three and then there's another three.' The following video excerpt continues after Wendy presented the additive task of 8 and 5 with two screened collections.

W: What would it be if it was eight and five more?

B: (After six seconds.) Thirteen!

W: Yes. How did you do that?

B: Well, it had to be thirteen because there wasn't ten and if there was ten it would be fifteen.

Following this, Bill solved two missing addend tasks, that is, 6 to 10 and 12 to 15. In explaining his solution of 12 to 15 he indicated that he had used 10 and 5 = 15. Then Bill solved the two Missing Subtrahend tasks of 10 to 6 and 12 to 9, and answered 'three' to the task of 15 to 11. In explaining his solution to 12 to 15 he said: 'I can count by threes and I can count back by threes.' The following video excerpt shows Bill's solution to 10 to 6.

W: Look back! There were ten. I've taken some away and now there's only six left. How many did I take away?

B: (Immediately.) Three, I mean four!

W: Why four? How did you know that?

B: Because six plus four is ten and then if I swap it around the other way, it's that way.

Bill solved the removed items tasks of 10 r 2, 15 r 3, 17 r 14 and 27 r 4. On the second of these Bill explained his answer by saying 'because it's only three more from twelve to get to fifteen.' On the task of 17 r 14 Bill answered 'four'. His method of solution was not apparent. Bill's solution to 27 r 4 is shown in the following video excerpt.

W: Twenty-seven and I'm taking out four. What's left?

B: (Looks ahead for 15 seconds.) Twenty-three!

W: Right. How did you know twenty-three?

B: Counted backwards.

Scenario 4: Renae and Carol

R: (Briefly displays and then screens three blue counters.) I'm going to put three blue counters under this screen. (Briefly displays and then screens two red counters.) And I'm going to put two over here. Can you tell me how many I've got altogether?

C: (Places her hands on the screen covering three blue counters.) Three in this one. (Points to the other screen.) Two in that one. Let me see. (Counts subvocally while first placing her hands and head on the first screen and then looking up.) Four?

R: Have a look and see. (Raises the screens.) Were you right?

C: (Touches the blue counters.) Umm yep!

R: Count them for me.

C: (Points to the two red counters.) Two (points to one blue counter), three. (Starts again, pointing to each blue counter in turn.) One, two, three!

R: How many altogether? (Moves the two red counters to a position adjacent to the three blue counters.)

C: (Points to each counter in turn.) One, two, three, four, five!

Renae then posed an addition task involving five red counters that were screened and two blue counters that were unscreened.

C: (Points at the screen in coordination with counting subvocally from 'one' to 'four'. Starts again counting quietly in coordination with pointing at the screen.) One – (attempts to feel the counters), one, two, three, four.

R: There's five under there.

C: (Points at the screen in coordination with counting.) One, two, three, four, five!

R: (Points to the two unscreened counters.) And? (Waves her hand over the screen and the two unscreened counters.) Altogether, five –.

C: (Raises her hands.) That makes ten!

R: (Removes the screen.) What if we take that away. How many now?

C: (Moves the two red counters adjacent to the blue counters and then points to each counter in turn.) One, two . . . seven!

Renae then placed out thirteen blue counters and asked Carol to count them. Carol made three unsuccessful attempts to count these. First, she counted ten of the counters using pointing actions and stopped appearing to lose track. She then started again counting 'one, two . . . twelve, fifteen, fourteen'. Thus making a coordination error, that is, fourteen counts rather than thirteen, and a number word sequence error. Renae then arranged the counters in a line and asked Carol to count them again. On this occasion she again pointed to the counters in turn making three coordination errors, that is, making 16 points instead of 13. She concluded her count with 'fourteen, eighteen, ninety'.

Scenario 5: Terry and Belinda

T: (Briefly displays and then screens three green counters.) Here's three counters. I'm going to cover them up. (Briefly displays and then screens two white counters.) Here's two more counters. How many counters altogether?

B: (Immediately.) Ten.

T: How did you get ten?

B: Because there's three under there (points to first screen) and two under there (points to the second screen.)

Terry restated the task several times, finally removing the screen covering the three counters but Belinda did not attempt to count and did not solve the task. The next task involved five green counters which were unscreened and two white counters which were screened. After two seconds Belinda said 'equals um – ten!' Again Terry restated the task several times, finally removing the second screen so that both collections were unscreened and, as before, Belinda did not attempt to count and answered incorrectly each time. Her answers appeared to be little more than guesses. Terry then directed Belinda's attention to each collection in turn.

T: (Traces around the five green counters.) How many are here?

B: (Looks at the five counters and counts sub vocally.) Five!

T: (Traces around the two green counters.) And how many are there?

B: (Immediately.) Two.

T: (Nods and then pauses.) So how many does that make altogether?

B: (Looks at the two green counters.) Two.

Terry restated the task several times but Belinda did not correctly solve the task. On one occasion she appeared to count subvocally but did not look at the counters when doing so. She answered 'eleven'. Soon after this Terry placed 13 green counters on the desk.

T: How many counters are there altogether? And you can count them. Can you count them to see how many there are?

B: (Pointing at each counter in turn.) One, two . . . thirteen. Thirteen!

T: There's thirteen there. Okay. Alright I'm going to give you some more now. (Adds five green counters making a collection of eighteen.) Now I've given you some more counters Belinda. How many counters are there now?

B: Count 'em?

T: Umm.

B: (Counts quickly, pointing at each counter in turn) One, two . . . seventeen (omits one counter). Seventeen!

After a brief discussion Belinda counted the counters again but more slowly on this occasion and answered 'eighteen!'

Scenario 6: Terry and John

T: (Places out five counters in a row.) How many counters are there?

J: (Looks at the counters.) Three.

T: Count them.

J: (Counts slowly pointing at each counter in turn.) One, two, three, four, five.

T: So how many counters are there?

J: Five.

T: Okay, I'm going to cover up that. (Places a screen on the five counters.) You have to remember there are five. And I'm going to give you two more (places out two counters), how many would we have now altogether?

J: (Looks at the two counters.) Two.

T: (Points to the two counters.) There's two there isn't there? But what if I went (raises the screen and waves her hand over the seven counters), how many are there altogether now?

J: Five. That one and that one and that one (saying 'that one' three times while pointing in turn at the two counters) and that one and that one and that one and that one and that one (points to each of the five counters in turn).

T: Umm, okay (waves her hand over the counters). Altogether there are how many?

J: (Immediately.) Six.

T: Have you got a way of checking that John? How would you check to see if six is how many there are?

J: One, two . . . five (points to each of the five counters in turn). One, two (points to each of the two counters in turn).

Following this Terry moved all the counters together and asked John to count them. In doing so he pointed at the counters in turn but made only six points rather than seven, that is, he incorrectly coordinated his points with the counters. Then John correctly counted eight counters arranged in two rows of four but made coordination errors when attempting to count seven, thirteen and eighteen counters. On these tasks John's counting included several number word sequence errors in the teens, for example, he omitted 'thirteen' and 'seventeen'.

Scenario 7: Tanya and Kelly

Kelly was presented with the following additive tasks involving two screened collections: 3 and 2, 5 and 4, 9 and 6, 8 and 5, and 9 and 3. She solved one task (3 and 2) on her first attempt, three on her second attempt and answered 'sixteen' to the task of 9 and 6. In attempting to solve these tasks Kelly did not count aloud or subvocally – no lip movements were apparent. She typically looked ahead with her hands under the desk. Her solution to one task (8 and 5) is described in the following video excerpt.

T: (Briefly displays and then screens the first collection.) This time there are eight green counters (briefly displays and then screens the second collection) and five yellow counters. How many counters altogether?

K: (Looks ahead with both hands under the desk for ten seconds.) Fifteen!

T: There's eight under there (briefly displays the first collection) and five under there (briefly displays the second collection).

K: (Looks ahead with hands under the desk for 11 seconds.) Thirteen!

Kelly was presented with the following five missing subtrahend tasks: 5 to 3, 6 to 4, 10 to 6, 12 to 9, and 15 to 11. She was typically unsuccessful on these tasks. The following video excerpt shows her attempt at solving the last of these tasks.

T: (Places out 15 counters and asks Kelly to look away. Screens four of the counters.) There's now eleven counters there. How many are hidden under here? (Points to the screen.)

K: (Keeps her hands on the desk for 20 seconds, looking ahead and occasionally glancing at the counters.) Ten.

Kelly correctly solved the following four removed items tasks: 3 r 1, 5 r 2, 10 r 2, and 27 r 4. On the Removed Items task of 15 r 3, she answered 'eleven' instead of 'twelve'. Her solution to 27 r 4 is described in the following video excerpt.

T: (Places a collection of 27 counters in front of Kelly and places a screen over them.) This time there are twenty-seven, right? (Removes four of the counters and places them under a second screen.) I'm taking four of them out. How many are left under there?

K: (Looks ahead for 22 seconds with her hands on the desk.) Twenty-three.

T: Very good! How did you know there's twenty-three under there? That's right. Did you think?

K: Was twenty-seven. And you take twenty-six and twenty-five and twenty-four and twenty-three away.

Scenario 8: Joyce and Jed

Jed correctly solved the following five additive tasks: 3 and 2, 5 and 4, 9 and 6, 8 and 5, and 9 and 3. On the first task Jed's solution strategy was not apparent initially. The following video excerpt continues after Jed had answered 'five'.

Jo: How did you count it up?

Je: You just go – one two, three (in coordination with three points over a screen covering three counters), four, five (in coordination with two points over a screen covering two counters).

Jo: I'm going to take these five disks and put them here (briefly displays and then screens five counters) and I'm going to take four more and put them here (briefly displays and then screens four counters).

Je: (Looks ahead and makes points over the screen covering five counters in coordination with subvocal counts.) One, two, three, four, five (makes three points over the second screen in coordination with counts), six, seven, eight – (makes four points over the second collection in coordination with counts), six, seven, eight, nine!

Following this Jed was presented with the additive task, 9 and 6.

Jo: I'm going to take nine disks and cover them up and I'm going to take six and cover them up (briefly displays and then screens counters as before).

Je: (Slaps his hand on the first screen.) Nine, nine under – nine – nine (makes points over the second screen in coordination with counting slowly), ten, ee – leven I think, eleven, twelve, thirteen, fourteen. (Starts counting again from eleven in coordination with points over the screen) eleven – eleven, twelve, thirteen, fourteen, fifteen. Fifteen!

Jo: (Points to the first screen.) You thought there were nine under here. (Points to the second screen.) And then you started counting ten, eleven. How did you remember how many were under here (indicates the second screen)?

Je: (Makes two points over the second screen.) Because, I knew there were three right here and three right here, makes six.

The following video excerpt begins after Joyce presented Jed with the next additive task, that is, 8 and 5.

Je: (Points to the screen covering eight counters.) Eight (places his hand above the screen covering five counters and counts aloud in coordination with points), nine, (after three seconds) ten, (after eight seconds) eleven, twelve, thirteen, thirteen!

Jo: (Presents the next task, that is, 9 and 3.) I'm going to put nine here and three here.

Je: (Places his hand on the first screen.) Nine – (looks at the second screen and makes three points over the screen in coordination with counting), ten, eleven, twelve, twelve!

Jed was presented with two missing addend tasks – 4 to 6 and 12 to 15 – and three missing subtrahend tasks – 6 to 4, 10 to 6 and 12 to 9. Jed correctly answered only one of these tasks, that is, 6 to 4 and did not appear to have a strategy for either kind of task. For the missing addend task of 12 to 15 he answered 'ten'. For the missing subtrahend task of 10 to 6 he answered 'one' and then 'two' and for the final missing subtrahend task of 12 to 9 he answered 'seven'.

Jed solved three removed items tasks, that is, 3 r 1, 5 r 2, 10 r 2, but did not solve the task of 15 r 3, answering 'seventeen'. Jed's solution to the task of 10 r 2 is shown in the following video excerpt.

Jo: (Briefly displays and, then screens ten counters.) There are ten there now Jed.

Je: (Raises ten fingers and then puts his hands under the desk.)

Jo: (Removes and screens two counters.) I'm going to take two away. How many did I leave under here?

Je: (Looks at his hands under the desk.)

Jo: (Indicates the top of the desk.) Would you put your hands up here Jed so I can see you work with your hands.

Je: (Places his hands above the desk with five fingers raised on his left hand and three raised on his right hand. Points to each finger on his left hand in coordination with counting.) One, two, three, four, five (points to the three raised fingers on his left hand in coordination with counting), six, seven, eight, eight!

Scenario 9: Kathryn and James

James was presented with three additive tasks involving two screened collections: 3 and 2, 5 and 4 and, 9 and 6. He solved each of these on his first attempt. In solving 3 and 2 he quickly counted subvocally from three to five. In solving 5 and 4 he quickly answered 'nine' and did not appear to count. His solution to 9 and 6 is shown in the following video excerpt.

K: (Poses the task.) Nine and six more?

J: (Looks ahead for ten seconds with hands under the desk.) Fifteen!

K: How did you do that?

J: 'Cos you add 'em up – 'cos umm –, like it – you start from nine and then you count on how much more.

James was presented with four missing subtrahend tasks: 3 to 2, 8 to 6, 12 to 9 and 15 to 11. He solved each on his first attempt. His solution to the second, third and fourth tasks are described in the following video excerpt:

K: (Poses the task of 8 to 6.) . . . And I've got six left. How many did I take away?

J: (Looks ahead with his hands under the desk. Answers after three seconds.) Two.

K: How did you know that?

J: 'Cos when that's up to eight, and you say – you take away two – you count backwards to two and you got the right answer.

K: (Poses the task of 12 to 9.) . . . Had twelve. Took some away and I've got nine.

J: (As before, looks ahead with his hands under the desk. Answers after six seconds.) Three.

K: That's clever. How did you do that?

J: Well, you start from twelve and you had to count back from twelve to see what number it was.

K: (Poses the task of 15 to 11.) . . . And there's eleven left. How many did I take away?

J: (As before, answers after eight seconds.) Four.

K: Tell me the numbers you said in your head that time.

J: Fifteen, fourteen, thirteen, then twelve.

Following this James solved the following three removed items tasks on his first attempt: 3 r 1, 10 r 2, 15 r 3. When solving the first two tasks he responded quickly and on the third he counted subvocally with his hands under the desk and, after ten seconds in all, answered 'twelve'. In explaining his answer he said, '. . . you've got to take away fifteen and fourteen, and then take away thirteen'. James was finally presented with the following three missing addend tasks and solved each on his first attempt: 4 to 6, 5 to 9 and 18 to 23. In solving the first task he responded quickly. His methods for solving the second and third were similar to each other in that he looked ahead with his hands under the desk and responded after about six seconds.

Scenario 10: Meg and Matthew

Me: Three counters here (momentarily unscreens a collection of three red counters). Two there (momentarily unscreens a collection of two green counters). How many altogether?

Ma: (Quickly raises three fingers on his left hand and then two simultaneously on his right hand. Counts subvocally using his right index finger to point at each raised finger on his left hand and then his left index finger to point at each raised finger on his right hand.) Five!

The next task was similar to the one above and involved five red counters and four green counters. Matthew used an exactly similar strategy and quickly answered 'Nine!' Meg similarly presented the next task involving nine red counters and six green counters.

Me: I have nine counters here and six counters here. How many altogether?

Ma: (Immediately). I don't know. I don't know six and nine because –.

Me: You might be able to work it out a different way.

Despite prompts from Meg, Matthew did not attempt a counting strategy. Meg removed the screens and asked Matthew to count the counters. He quickly counted from one to fifteen pointing at each counter in turn. The next three tasks were presented similarly to those above except that only the first collection was screened. The first task involved five red and two green, the second four and four and the third seven and five. Matthew easily solved the first and second tasks using his fingers as before but was quite unable to solve the third task. Following this Meg asked him to count out thirteen and then eighteen counters from a pile. He solved both tasks by counting quickly from 'one'.

Scenario 11: Ivan and Rhett

I: I'm going to give you some counters now. (Briefly displays and then screens three red counters.) Three red ones. I'm going to hide them under there. (Briefly displays and then screens two green counters.) And two green ones. Hide them under there. (Waves his hand over both screens.) How many counters have you got altogether?

R: (Counts subvocally while looking straight ahead. Continues in this vein for 30 seconds.) Four.

I: Let's have a look. (Unscreens both collections.)

R: (Beginning with the three red counters, counts subvocally while pointing at each counter in turn. Then looks at Ivan and smiles.) Five.

I: Okay. Let's try this one. This time I'll give you five red ones. (Briefly displays and then screens five red counters.) Now hide those under there. (Places out two green counters which remain unscreened.) And two green ones.

R: (Looks at the two green counters for three seconds and then looks straight ahead for three seconds.) I don't know.

I: (After two seconds.) Can you work it out? Think hard.

R: (Shakes his head indicating 'no'.) (Looks ahead for 23 seconds.) Can't think of it.

I: (Removes the screen.) What about this one as well. What if I give you . . . (pauses).

R: (Beginning with the five red counters, counts subvocally while pointing at each counter in turn.) Seven.

I: Seven right. What if I give you . . . (removes one of the five red counters and screens the remaining four) four red ones . . . (places out two more green counters leaving all four unscreened) and four green ones?

R: (Looks ahead for two seconds and then looks at the four green counters. Counts subvocally while pointing at each counter in turn. Looks up and continues counting subvocally.) Eight?

I: (Removes the screen.)

R: (Beginning with the four red counters, counts subvocally while pointing at each counter in turn. Looks at Ivan and smiles.) Eight.

I: You were right. What about if I give you . . . (places out three more red counters and screens all seven) seven red ones . . . (places out one more green counter and leaves all five unscreened) and five green ones.

R: (Looks ahead for one second and then looks at the five green counters. Counts subvocally while pointing at each counter in turn. Looks up and continues counting subvocally.) Twelve?

I: How did you work that one out?

R: (Looks ahead but does not answer.)

I: (After five seconds.) I saw you doing some things. Can you tell me what you where doing?

R: (Immediately, while smiling.) Counting.

I: What numbers were you counting? (After six seconds.) What did you count?

R: (Looks ahead for five seconds and then points to the unscreened collection of five green counters.) Those, I counted.

I: Yes. (After five seconds, points at the unscreened counters.) There is not twelve there though is there? So how did you know there was twelve?

R: (Shrugs his shoulders.) I don't know.

I: (Unscreens the seven red counters.)

After this Ivan presented Rhett with three missing subtrahend tasks (3 to 2; 8 to 6; 6 to 4) and three Removed Items tasks (3 r 1, 10 r 2, 5 r 2). Rhett solved the introductory tasks only (3 to 2 and 3 r 1) and was generally unsuccessful on the other tasks. On these tasks he did not seem to use a strategy involving counting back, and in most cases his answers seemed to be little more than guesses.

Scenario 12: Sandra and Ben

Ben was presented with five additive tasks involving two collections, that is, 3 and 2, 5 and 4, 9 and 6, 8 and 5, and 9 and 3. On the first task (3 and 2) Ben answered 'five' after eight seconds but his solution strategy was not apparent. His solution to 5 and 4 is shown in the following video excerpt.

S: (Poses the task.) Five and four?

B: (Rubs his face with his right hand.) I know. That . . . that is, ten.

S: (Places a hand on each screen.)

B: (Quickly.) Nine!

S: Pardon?

B: Is it nine?

S: Well you tell me. Five and four?

B: Five and four? Is nine.

S: (Unscreens both collections.) Have a look. See if you were right.

S: (Poses the next task.) Nine and six?

B: (Looks to his right.) Nine and six is sixteen. Actually . . . it is fifteen.

S: How do you know that?

B: (Immediately.) 'Cause, if it was ten it would be sixteen and if it was nine it would be fifteen.

S: (Poses the next task.) What about eight and five? Eight and five?

B: Is ten.

S: (Unscreens both collections.)

Ben counted from one to thirteen in coordination with pointing at each counter in turn. After a brief discussion Sandra presented the next task.

S: Nine and three?

B: (Immediately.) Nine and three is . . . twelve.

S: How did you get that?

B: (Immediately.) 'Cause, if it was ten and three it would be thirteen and you just cut . . . cut off one.

Sandra then presented Ben with three missing addend tasks, that is, 4 to 6, 12 to 15, and 8 to 10. Ben answered 'three' on the first task, and answered the second and third tasks correctly. His strategies for solving these three tasks were not apparent. Following this Ben solved three missing subtrahend tasks, that is, 5 to 3, 10 to 6 and 12 to 9. He used a finger pattern for ten to solve the second of these but his strategies for solving the first and third were not apparent. The following video excerpt begins after Ben answered 'three' on the last of these tasks.

S: How did you know that one?

B: 'Cause (raises his thumb), twelve . . . and (raises his point finger) ten . . . (lowers his point finger) twelve, (raises his point finger) and eleven (raises his middle finger), and ten are 'tooken' away and that makes nine.

Following this Ben also solved three Removed Items tasks, that is, 10 r 2, 15 r 3 and 27 r 4. On the last of these he first answered 'twenty-four'. Sandra then indicated that he was incorrect and he answered 'twenty-three'. Ben used his fingers to solve this task, and in doing so, he concealed his fingers. This was the second occasion that he did this, having also concealed his fingers on the missing subtrahend task of 10 to 6. In the case of solving 27 r 4 it was likely that Ben used his fingers to keep track of counting back from 27.

SOLUTIONS

Scenario 1: Heather and Tina – Solution

Tina solved the three additive tasks presented to her and the evidence suggests that she counted from one when doing so. Each of the three additive tasks involved two screened collections and it is clear that Tina did not count perceptual items (that is visible items) on her solutions. This suggests that Tina was at Stage 2: Figurative Counting. In the case of the missing subtrahend tasks, Tina did not display a general strategy for solving these tasks. Solving the introductory task of '3 to 2' was not a sufficient indicator of a more advanced strategy. Similarly, in solving the task of '6 to 4' her solution seemed to depend on the four counters being unscreened. There is no indication that she used the counting-down-to strategy. In similar vein, Tina did not use counting-down-from to solve the removed items tasks. She was able to solve the introductory task and her solution to the last task seemed to depend on the three counters being unscreened. Thus Tina is judged to be at Stage 2: Figurative Counting.

Scenario 2: Tamara and Jack – Solution

Jack used a range of advanced strategies involving counting-by-ones to solve additive and subtractive tasks. He used counting-up-from to solve all but one of the additive tasks. He solved two missing addend tasks although he may have initially misinterpreted the first. Finally, Jack used counting-down-to to solve missing subtrahend tasks. Thus Jack was at least at Stage 4. On three of the additive tasks, that is, 3 and 2, 5 and 4, and 9 and 3, Jack answered quickly. In doing so Jack provided some indication that his strategies on these tasks did not involve counting-by-ones. His explanation of his solution to the second of these (5 and 4) suggests an awareness of the finger pattern for nine consisting of five fingers on one hand and four on the other. Overall, his solutions do not constitute sufficient evidence that he is at Stage 5. His solutions could be attributed to addition facts that he knows, for example $3 + 2 = 5$, or can work out quickly, for example $5 + 4 = 9$. Beyond this there is little indication that Jack can use a range of non-count-by-ones strategies. Thus Jack is judged to be at Stage 4: Intermediate Number Sequence.

Scenario 3: Wendy and Bill – Solution

Bill used a range of non-count-by-ones strategies to solve additive and subtractive tasks. He used the known fact of 5 + 5 to solve 5 and 4 and similarly 10 + 5 to solve 8 and 5. In solving 9 and 6 he seemed to be able to regard nine as three threes and six as two threes. He used the known addition fact of 6 + 4 = 10 to work out the missing subtrahend task of '10 to 6'. In the final example Bill used counting-down-from to solve a removed items task. Thus in some cases Bill might use a counting strategy. Nevertheless he has a range of robust non-count-by-ones strategies and was clearly at Stage 5: Facile Number Sequence.

Scenario 4: Renae and Carol – Solution

Carol made two types of errors when attempting to count the collection of 13 counters. First, she makes a coordination error on each of her two attempts. On her first attempt she made 14 counts rather than 13 and on her second attempt she made 16 counts. Secondly, Carol made a number word sequence error on each of her two attempts. For these reasons Carol is judged to be at Stage 0: Emergent Counting.

Scenario 5: Terry and Belinda – Solution

Belinda correctly counted a collection of 13 counters. On her first attempt to count a collection of 18 counters Belinda answered 17 and on her second attempt correctly answered 18. This indicates that Belinda was at least at Stage 1. Belinda was unable to solve tasks involving two screened collections, for example, she did not attempt to count from one or count-on to solve these tasks. This indicates that Belinda was not at Stage 2. Thus Belinda was at Stage 1: Perceptual Counting. On each of the two tasks involving two screened collections, when Belinda did not solve the task, Terry removed the screens and asked Belinda how many counters in all. Of interest is that in these cases Belinda also did not use counting. She did not seem to conceive of the two collections as being reorganized into one collection that could be counted. This is typical of some children at Stage 1, and also some children at Stage 0.

Scenario 6: Terry and John – Solution

On two occasions John made a coordination error when attempting to count seven counters. He also made coordination errors when attempting to count 13 and 18 counters. John also made number word sequence errors in the teens when attempting to count collections of counters. This indicates that John was at Stage 0: Emergent Stage. When asked to count the counters which were arranged in a collection of five and a collection of two, John counted each collection separately. As in the case of Belinda in Scenario 5, John did not seem to be able to regard the counters as being reorganized into one collection which could be counted.

Scenario 7: Tanya and Kelly – Solution

Kelly was able to solve additive tasks and Removed Items tasks but was not able to solve missing subtrahend tasks. Although Kelly did not count aloud or move her lips, the times taken to solve the tasks are consistent with her using a strategy involving counting-by-ones. Kelly may have been using her fingers under the desk to keep track of her counts. That she could not solve Missing Subtrahend tasks indicates that Kelly was less advanced than Stage 4. Whether Kelly counted-on or counted-from-one when solving the additive tasks is not apparent. Nevertheless her solution of four removed items tasks, and her explanation of her solution of '27 r 4' in terms of counting back provides sufficient evidence of advanced counting-by-ones strategies. Therefore Kelly is judged to be at Stage 3: Initial Number Sequence.

Scenario 8: Joyce and Jed – Solution

On the basis of his performance on the various subtraction tasks Jed is no more than Stage 3. Although he did solve one missing subtrahend task he did not appear to have a general strategy for these tasks, for example, counting-down-to. In similar vein, Jed did not solve the two missing addend tasks and apparently did not use counting-up-to to attempt to solve these tasks. Jed also does not appear to have used counting-down-from to solve the removed items tasks. What is clear in the descriptions of Jed's solutions is that he used counting-on to solve the three additive tasks of 9 and 6, 8 and 5, and 9 and 3, and counted from one to solve 5 and 4. Why Jed counted-on on the last three tasks is not apparent. His use of counting-on was apparently spontaneous, in that Joyce did not appear to assist him. On the basis of his solutions of the last three additive tasks Jed is judged to be at Stage 3: Initial Number Sequence. That Jed solved three Removed Items tasks serves to strengthen the case for classifying him at Stage 3.

Scenario 9: Kathryn and James – Solution

James was able to solve all three types of subtractive tasks as well as additive tasks, and correctly answered all of the tasks presented to him. James's solutions typically involved an advanced counting-by-ones strategy. James used counting-up-from to solve additive tasks, counting-up-to to solve missing addend tasks, counting-down-from to solve removed items tasks and counting-down-to to solve missing subtrahend tasks. Solving missing subtrahend tasks in this way is a strong indication that James was at Stage 4 rather than Stage 3. In solving the additive task of 5 and 4 the indication is that James did not use counting-by-ones because he answered quickly. Also, James may not have used counting-by-ones on the subtractive tasks of 3 r 1, 10 r 2 and 4 to 6, although it is difficult to discern counting-by-ones on tasks such as these where only one or two counts are required. In overall terms, there is little or no evidence to indicate that James is at Stage 5, that is, using a range of non-count-by-ones strategies. Therefore, on the basis of his facile use of advanced counting-by-ones strategies and, in particular, his use of counting-down-to to solve Missing Subtrahend tasks, James is judged to be at Stage 4: Intermediate Number Sequence.

Scenario 10: Meg and Matthew – Solution

Matthew was clearly at least at Stage 1 because he successfully counted collections of 13, 15 and 18 counters. Matthew solved tasks involving two collections in cases where both collections were screened as well as in cases where only one collection was screened. In solving these tasks Matthew always counted from 'one' and thus he was not at Stage 3. Thus we can conclude that Matthew was at Stage 1 or 2. Matthew solved the following four additive tasks, 3 and 2, 5 and 4, 5 and 2, and 4 and 4 using the same strategy for each. This strategy involves raising fingers on his left hand to signify the counters in the first collection, then raising fingers on his right hand to signify the counters in the second collection and, finally, counting all of the raised fingers from one. Clearly, this strategy is viable in additive tasks where each addend is not greater than five. On each of the two tasks where one or both addends were greater than five, that is, 9 and 6 and 7 and 5, Matthew did not solve the task and did not appear to have any strategy available to him. Although Matthew may appear to have satisfied the criteria for Stage 2 because he solved four additive tasks in which one or both collections were screened, he is judged to be at Stage 1 rather than Stage 2. His strategy is referred to as 'building perceptual replacements', that is, his raised fingers are the perceptual items that have replaced the screened counters.

Matthew's strategy is a particular case of a strategy commonly used by young children to solve additive and subtractive tasks. In MR we have called this strategy 'counting forward from one three times'. Children typically use this strategy when they have materials which they can form into collections that signify addends, sums, minuends, and so on. Thus a child may use counters to solve 9 and 6 by counting out nine counters, then six counters and then counting all of the counters from one to 15. Similarly, a child may use counters to solve 12 – 9 by counting out 12 counters, then counting out and separating nine of the 12 counters, and then counting the remaining three. When counters are not available a child may use the fingers as in the case of Matthew but, typically, the strategy is viable for addition only when the two addends are no greater than 5, and viable for subtraction only when the minuend is no greater than 10. Children can become quite facile in their use of finger patterns as part of this strategy, for example children will raise fingers simultaneously to signify a number. In solving 5 and 3, for example, a child might raise five fingers on one hand simultaneously, then raise three fingers on the other hand simultaneously and then answer 'eight' without counting from one.

A comment on teaching can be made at this point. Consider a situation in which children are given the task of working out written additions or subtractions, for example, 5 and 2, 3 and 8, 14 – 7, 12 – 10, and so on, and are encouraged to use materials to work out their answers. In this situation children typically use the strategy of counting forward from one three times, that is, they count out a number of counters to signify the first number, and so on. Doing tasks of this kind is likely to encourage or reinforce the use of strategies involving perceptual counting and thus discourage advancement in terms of SEAL.

The strategy used by Matthew and the corresponding one for subtraction (as above) should not be confused with advanced counting-by-ones strategies in the particular case where the child uses fingers to keep track of the number of counts. Thus a child who solves an additive task such as 8 and 5 by raising five fingers in sequence to keep track of counting from 'nine' to 'thirteen' is using a Stage 3 strategy and this strategy should not be confused with the strategy of building perceptual replacements. In the case where the child raises five fingers prior to commencing their count this is also classified as a Stage 3 strategy. Similarly, children at Stage 3 or Stage 4 will use finger patterns to keep track of counting when solving various types of subtractive tasks. As an example, a child at Stage 4 might solve the missing subtrahend task of 16 to 12 by raising four fingers in turn while counting from 'fifteen' to 'twelve'. It is conceivable that a child might solve the task of 8 and 5 involving two screened collections by counting from 'one' to 'eight' and then sequentially raising five fingers on one hand to keep track of counting from 'nine' to 'thirteen'. This strategy is not very common, probably because children who can use their fingers in this way usually count-on rather than count from one, that is, they are at Stage 3 at least. Nevertheless, the strategy just described would exemplify Stage 2: Figurative Counting.

Scenario 11: Ivan and Rhett – Solution

In this scenario Rhett is presented with four additive tasks involving two collections, that is, 3 and 2, 5 and 2, 4 and 4, and 7 and 5. On the first task both collections were screened, whereas on the other three tasks the first mentioned collection only is screened. On the first task Rhett took a relatively long time to answer, that is, 30 seconds, and then answered 'four' rather than 'five'. It is reasonable to assume that because of Rhett's apparent difficulty with this task, Ivan decided that, on subsequent additive tasks, he would unscreen one of the two collections. Although Rhett did not provide any answer on the second task he correctly answered both the third and fourth tasks. It is clear that Rhett counted from one when solving the third and fourth tasks. This and his apparent lack of a strategy to solve subtractive tasks indicates that he was no more than Stage 2.

Rhett's solutions to the third and fourth additive tasks are unusual to some extent. Both tasks involved a screened and an unscreened collection rather than two screened collections, and in both tasks Rhett first counted the unscreened collection rather than the screened collection. In continuing his count, to count the second screened collection, Rhett was able to keep track of four counts in the case of the third task, and seven counts in the case of the fourth task. For this reason Rhett is judged to be at Stage 2: Figurative Counting, rather than Stage 1.

Scenario 12: Sandra and Ben – Solution

Ben solved a wide range of additive and subtractive tasks and, although his strategies were often not apparent, it was very clear that he was not counting from one. Thus Ben is at least Stage 3. In explaining the strategy he used to solve the missing subtrahend task of 12 to 9, Ben counted-down-to and used his fingers to keep track of three counts. This was indicative of a Stage 4 strategy. In the case of three of the additive tasks Ben indicated that he could use non-count-by-ones strategies. On the first task (5 and 4) he answered 'ten' and then quickly said 'nine'. He did not appear to use a counting strategy on this task and thus it is likely that he used the fact that five and five make ten to work out five and four. In explaining his solution to 9 and 6 he was aware that ten and six make sixteen, and in explaining his solution to 9 and 3 he was aware that ten and three make thirteen. In general terms Ben's solution strategies were not easily discernible. His advanced thinking was more apparent in his explanations than his solutions. Nevertheless he provided three indications of non-count-by-ones strategies and therefore is judged to be at Stage 5: Facile Number Sequence.

In the next chapter we continue to expand on SEAL and in particular on the Stage 5 child. We also present the second aspect of Part A of the LFIN by introducing the model for Tens and Ones.

6

Assessment Interview Schedule 1.2

Summary

In this chapter we set out the task groups in the Assessment Interview Schedule 1.2. This interview assesses children's numerical knowledge and strategies that are beyond Stage 3: Initial Number Sequence. Two of the task groups are concerned with the model for the allocation of levels for the child's knowledge of tens and ones, base-ten strategies. The third task group involves non-count-by-ones which will enable more information to be gathered as to whether a child is Stage 5 on the Learning Framework. Non-count-by-ones refers to a class of strategies which involves aspects other than counting-by-ones. Non-count-by-ones strategies are used to solve addition and subtraction tasks.

The Diagnostic Assessment Interview 1.2 (Assessment 1.2) contains the assessment tasks for the second part of Part A of the LFIN. Assessment 1.2 is administered at a later session than 1.1 and only if the child has attained at least Stage 3 in terms of SEAL. Table 6.1 sets out the groups of tasks from Assessment 1.2 and indicates for which of the models each group of tasks is relevant.

Table 6.1 Task Groups and associated models for Assessment 1.2

Group of tasks	Model
1. Tens and ones tasks – strips	Base-Ten
2. Tens and ones tasks – uncovering	Base-Ten
3. Horizontal sentences	Base-Ten
4. Tasks to elicit non-count-by-one strategies	SEAL: Stage 5

BASE-TEN ARITHMETICAL STRATEGIES

Around the time they attain Stage 3, 4 or 5 of the SEAL, children typically begin to develop knowledge of the tens and ones structure of the numeration system. Of course children can, and should, solve addition and subtraction tasks involving two-digit numbers (that is from 10 onward) long before they develop knowledge of the tens and ones structure. For children who have attained Stage 5, development of knowledge of the tens and ones structure becomes increasingly important. There is a progression of three levels in children's development of base-ten arithmetical strategies. The model for the development of base-ten arithmetical strategies is adapted from research by Cobb and Wheatley (1988) and is shown in Table 6.2.

Table 6.2 Model for Development of Base-Ten Arithmetical Strategies

---

Level 1: Initial Concept of Ten. The child does not see ten as a unit of any kind. The child focuses on the individual items that make up the ten. One ten and ten ones do not exist for the child at the same time. In addition or subtraction tasks involving tens, children at this level count forward or backward by ones.

Level 2: Intermediate Concept of Ten. Ten is seen as a unit composed of ten ones. The child is dependent on re-presentations (like a mental replay or recollection) of units of ten such as hidden ten strips or open hands of ten fingers. The child can perform addition and subtraction tasks involving tens where these are presented with materials such as covered strips of tens and ones. The child cannot solve addition and subtraction tasks involving tens and ones when presented as written number sentences.

Level 3: Facile Concept of Ten. The child can solve addition and subtraction tasks involving tens and ones without using materials or re-presentations of materials. The child can solve written number sentences involving tens and ones by adding or subtracting units of ten and ones.

Note: A necessary condition for attaining Level 1 is attainment of at least Stage 3 in the Stages of Early Arithmetical Learning.

The tasks which follow indicate how the child might use strategies that incorporate knowledge of the tens and ones structure of two-digit numbers and the types of strategies they might use. These tasks enable the determination of the child's level in terms of the model for the Development of Base Ten Arithmetical Strategies.

TASK GROUP 1: Tens and Ones Tasks

The Tens and Ones tasks are divided into four subsections:

(a) Counting by Tens with equipment
(b) Incrementing by Tens off the decade
(c) Uncovering tasks with Tens and Ones separate
(d) Uncovering tasks with Tens and Ones combined

(a) Counting by Tens with Equipment

Task Group 1(a) involves the use of ten strips. A ten strip is a strip of cardboard containing a row of ten dots. The purpose of these tasks is to determine whether the child can increment by tens in situations where the ten strips are displayed rather than screened and each increment is by one ten only. This is the forerunner to the development of place value knowledge. The interviewer places the strips on the table one at a time, and the child's task is to say how many dots there are after each new strip is placed on the table. The number of dots is 10, 20, 30, and so on. On completion the strips are gathered and the child is asked to recall how many dots there were and how many strips this constituted. The assessor should note whether the child is able to regard a ten strip simultaneously as one ten and ten ones, that is both as a unit and as a composite.

(a)   Counting by tens with 'strips' – informal familiarization with material

(i) Put down a ten strip. *How many do we have?* If the child says 'one', ask, *How many dots are there?*

(ii) *How many altogether?* Put down one ten strip at a time to 8 strips.

10 20 30 40 50 60 70 80

(iii) Pick up all the strips.

How many dots do we have?

How many strips are there?

(b) Incrementing by Tens off the Decade

The second task, 1(b), Incrementing by ten off the decade, commences with putting out a four strip (that is, a strip containing four dots only), and then a series of ten strips. Thus the incremented number of dots is 4, 14, 24, 34, 44, and so on. If further information is required on the child's ability to increment by ten off the decade the whole task can be repeated with either the 3 strip and/or the 7 strip. Incrementing off the decade is usually more difficult than incrementing on the decade.

(b)   Incrementing by ten

(i) Place out the 'four dot' strip. *How many dots are there?*

(ii) Place out a ten strip to the right of the four strip. *How many dots are there altogether?*

(iii) Continue placing ten strips to the right of the four strip. *How many dots are there altogether?*

24   34   44   54   64   74

(iv) If necessary, repeat the whole task with either the 3 strip or the 7 strip.

(c) Uncovering Tasks with Tens and Ones separate

The third and fourth tasks, 1(c) and 1(d), uncovering tasks with tens and ones, shown below, involve the use of two large boards containing columns of ten dots and columns containing fewer than ten dots. These are referred to as the uncovering tasks and involve increasingly complex ways of incrementing by tens and/or ones. Two screens are used to cover the boards. The task begins by revealing one section as indicated by the arrows. The screen is then moved to reveal the next section and the previous section is re-screened. The sheets are progressively uncovered and the child's task is to determine the number of uncovered dots in all. The uncovering continues with the child incrementing from the screened total. Hence the count for Board One goes 10, 13, 33, 37, 40, 50, 52, 72 and for Board Two 4, 14, 34, 46, 71. It is important to provide sufficient time for the child to think about the tasks and to reflect on the results of their thinking. The assessor needs to observe closely to determine the child's strategy. For example, does the child revert to counting by ones? If so, at which point? Also does the child count the ones then the tens?

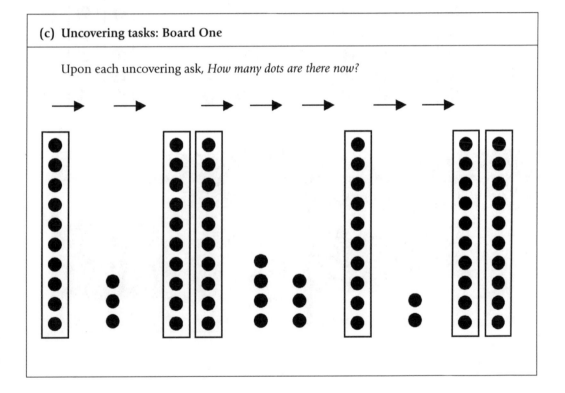

(c) **Uncovering tasks: Board One**

Upon each uncovering ask, *How many dots are there now?*

(d) Uncovering tasks: Board Two

Upon each uncovering ask, *How many are there now?*

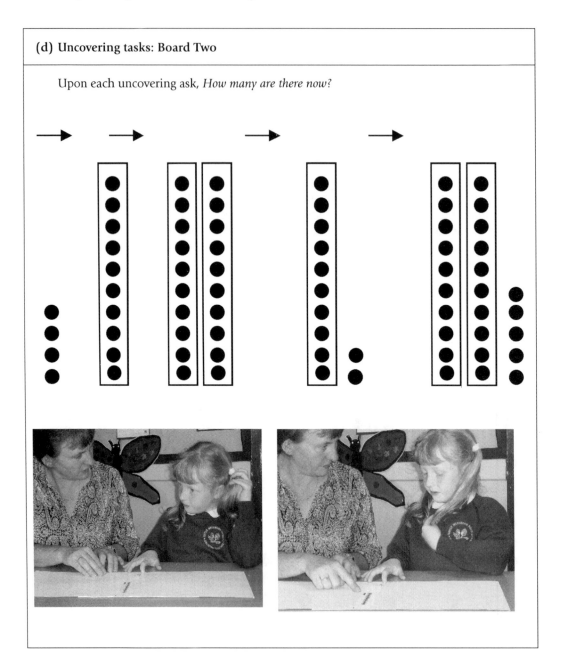

TASK GROUP 2: Horizontal Sentences

2.	**Horizontal Sentences**

(a) *Do you have a way to figure out what is?*
16 + 10 =
'So what is 16 + 9?'

(b) *Do you have a way to figure out what is?*
42 + 23
If correct ask, 'Do you have another way to work it out or check?'

(c) *Do you have a way to figure out what is?*
38 + 24
If correct ask, *Do you have another way to work it out or check?*

(d) Repeat the above questions for
39 + 53

(e) 56 – 23

(f) 43 – 15

(g) 73 – 48

The task items in the horizontal sentences group present the child with written problems involving two-digit addition and subtraction. Following the presentation of a decrementing task without equipment, 2(a), the methodology for presenting questions 2(b)–2(g) follows an identical pattern. The tasks are printed on individual cards and the child is asked to read the card. This is followed by the question, 'Do you have a way to figure out what is ...?' It is advisable to probe the child's thinking if the strategy is not evident. The assessor can also ask if the child has another way to solve the problem or to check their answer.

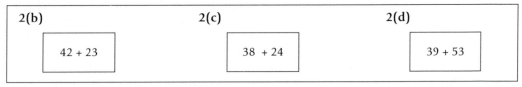

2(b)	2(c)	2(d)
42 + 23	38 + 24	39 + 53

At this point it may be useful to discuss some of the strategies children employ. We have found that the most common strategy on the above additive tasks is to work separately with the tens and ones, and then combine them at the end. For example, in 42 + 23 the 40 and 20 are added first to make 60, then the 2 and the 3 are totalled to 5. Finally the 60 and 5 are combined to arrive at 65. Some children may combine the ones first and others will combine the tens first. Wherever they start, this method is referred to as the 'split' strategy. The same strategy can be used for 38 + 24 and 39 + 53 but additional steps are required because the total of the ones constitute an additional ten.

Some children may use a 'jump' strategy. This involves the children jumping from the first number. For example, 42 + 23 becomes 42, 52, 62 (by incrementing by two jumps-of-ten) before finally adding 3 to reach 65. The problem, 38 + 24, perhaps would read 38, ... 58, a jump of twenty, and then the adding of the four which could be by ones, for example, 58 ... 59, 60, 61, 62, or by 2 to 60 and then 2 to 62 (bridging through ten). A third procedure might be observed whereby the child bridges to 40 by adding two, then adds two tens and 'finally' adds on the remaining two, thus showing decompositition of four into 2 + 2 and bridging to the decades. The item 39 + 53 affords the opportunity to see if the child has the strategy jump-via-ten. This would appear as 39 and 1 = 40, and five jumps-of-ten would be 40... 50, 60, 70, 80, 90, then add the 2 = 92. A similar, but not identical, method may be used which we refer to as 'transforming'. This is where the child would change the problem 39 + 53 to read 40 + 52 by adding one to one side and reducing the other side of the sum. This may seem similar to a jump-via-ten but it is different because it involves a non-count-by-ones strategy termed 'compensating'.

Whatever the strategy or strategies used by the child it is interesting to see if they can be applied to subtractive tasks.

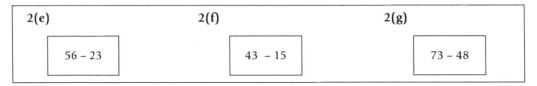

2(e)	2(f)	2(g)
56 – 23	43 – 15	73 – 48

The child who uses the 'split' strategy may continue to use the same for the solution of the above. 56 – 23 should not pose a problem, but 43 – 15 and 73 – 48 might well present difficulty. Here a mixture of split and jump (split/jump) strategies may be observed. For example, with   43 – 15 the tens are worked with first and then the units sequentially 40 – 10 = 30; 30 + 3 = 33; 33 – 5 = 28. Another mixed split strategy uses the notion of 'how many units short'. This would appear in the sum 73 – 48 as 70 – 40 = 30; 3 – 8 = –5 (5 short); leading to 30 – 5 = 25. Children who possess the jump strategy will not encounter the same complexity but be able to use decrementing by tens and ones. 43 – 15 could be solved as 43 – 10 = 33; 33 – 3, – 2 (33 to 30 to 28). Transforming could appear in 73 – 48 as 75 – 50 by adding two to each side.

Determining the Child's Level of Tens and Ones

Children are judged to be at Level 1 if they are unable to increment by tens in the tasks involving base-ten materials, that is, Task Groups 1(a), 1(b), 1(c), and 1(d). To be judged at Level 2 the child would be expected to increment by tens on the above tasks and demonstrate incrementing in the Uncovering Tasks. However, it is not necessary for the child to correctly answer each increment on both boards. For example, if they completed up to 34 on Board Two but could not answer the remaining strips correctly they could still be considered Level 2. The final section of Board Two involves incrementing by both tens and ones and often this is a step too far for some children. Children at Level 2 are unable to solve the written problems involving two-digit addition or subtraction presented in written format illustrated in the horizontal sentences questions, Task Group 2. Finally, children are judged to be at Level 3 if they are able to increment by tens when solving the bare number tasks that do not involve base-ten materials, that is, the horizontal sentences questions. It is not necessary for children to correctly answer all of these tasks. However, it is important to note whether they can solve addition but not subtraction or solve both operations. Also it is beneficial to identify the strategies they use to solve tasks and whether they have multiple strategies or are dependent upon a particular one.

TASK GROUP 3: Tasks to Elicit Non-Count-By-Ones Strategies

Task Group 3 is concerned with assessing the child's ability to use strategies which are characteristic of Stage 5 on SEAL. There are six subtasks, a–f, and these include two addition, two subtraction and two addition and subtraction questions.

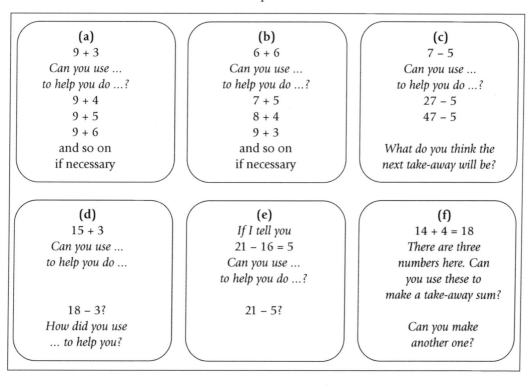

(a)
9 + 3
Can you use …
to help you do …?
9 + 4
9 + 5
9 + 6
and so on
if necessary

(b)
6 + 6
Can you use …
to help you do …?
7 + 5
8 + 4
9 + 3
and so on
if necessary

(c)
7 – 5
Can you use …
to help you do …?
27 – 5
47 – 5

What do you think the
next take-away will be?

(d)
15 + 3
Can you use …
to help you do …

18 – 3?
How did you use
… to help you?

(e)
If I tell you
21 – 16 = 5
Can you use …
to help you do …?

21 – 5?

(f)
14 + 4 = 18
There are three
numbers here. Can
you use these to
make a take-away sum?

Can you make
another one?

In the first four tasks, (a–d), the child is first asked to solve a written task involving addition or subtraction. Since these tasks should only be administered to children who are beyond Stage 3 they are expected to be able to solve the first task. Following the correct response, further written number statements are placed under the original and the child is asked if they are able to use their solution to solve related tasks. Of interest is the extent to which the child uses a given number sentence to solve a related number sentence.

The instructions for the tasks are as follows.

Task (a)

The '9 + 3' card is placed on top of a blank sheet of paper. The assessor asks the child whether they can work out the sum and then writes down the correct response '= 12' to the right of '9 + 3'. If an incorrect response is given the assessor re-poses the question. Assuming a correct response is received the '9 + 4' card is placed below the '9 + 3' card. The cards are indicated in turn and the child is asked, 'Can you use this (pointing to 9 + 3 = 12) to help you do 9 + 4?' 'What is the answer?' The key question is then asked, 'How did you use this to work out this?' Similarly, the

9 + 5 and 9 + 6 are presented. To confirm the non-count-by-ones strategy being used (incrementing by one from a constant number) the assessor could ask the child to predict the next card and explain why they have decided on that. If the child continues to calculate each sum they are not showing a non-count-by-ones strategy.

Tasks elicit to Non-Count-By-Ones strategies

6 + 6   = 12

Posing the task

6 + 6   = 12

7 + 5

Can you use this information to help you work out 7 + 5?

6 + 6   = 12

7 + 5   = 12

8 + 4

Can you use this information to help you work out 8 + 4?

6 + 6   = 12

7 + 5   = 12

8 + 4   = 12

9 + 3

Can you use this information to help you work out 9 + 3?

Task (b)

A new sheet of paper is required but the task is presented as described above. The child is asked to work out 6 + 6, and the assessor writes the answer to the right. The '7 + 5' card is placed below the '6 + 6' card. The cards are indicated in turn and the child asked, 'Can you use this to help you work out this?' 'What is the answer?' 'How did you use this to work out this?' Continue in a similar way with the next card, 8 + 4. We anticipate that some children will carry forward the strategy of incrementing by ones from the previous task item, so it may be necessary to ask them to read the second card carefully. The strategy required is termed 'compensation for addition' and this may be confirmed by asking the child to predict the next sum and to give their reasoning.

Task (c)

This is the first of the subtractive tasks. The task will examine incrementing by two groups of ten and the knowledge of a known fact, 7 – 5. The child is asked to work out 7 – 5, and the answer is written to the right. The '27 – 5' card is placed below the '7 – 5' card. The questioning is posed as before. The card, '47 – 5' is similarly posed. If necessary the child can be asked to predict the next question.

Task (d)

In this task the non-count-by-ones strategy to look for is the use of addition to solve subtraction. Only two cards are used. Following the child's correct response to the presentation of the card 15 + 3, and the writing of the total alongside, the child is presented with the '18 – 3' card below the '15 + 3' card. The cards are indicated in turn and the same questions are posed. *'Can you use this to help you work out this? What is the answer?'* and *'How did you use this to work out this?'* The child is asked to explain the reasoning behind their statements.

Task (e)

The '21 – 16 = 5' card is placed out and the '21 – 5' card is placed below it. The child is told that 21 take away 16 is 5, and asked whether they can use the information to work out 21 – 5? The non-count-by-ones strategy is using a known subtraction fact to work out an associated subtraction problem.

Task (f)

This task differs from the above. The child is shown a card on which is written '14 + 4 = 18' and asked to read it aloud. Then five cards bearing the numbers and symbols, '14', '4', '18', '=', and '–' are put on the table. Care is taken to place the '18' card to the right of the other numbers. The child is then required to use the three numbers and the two symbol cards to make a take-away sum. If they are successful they are asked if they have another way of making a subtraction sentence. The non-count-by-ones strategy concerns deriving a subtraction fact from an addition fact.

In addition to the above a child might use the following strategies.

▶ *Compensation for addition.* Six and four is the same as five and five.
▶ *Compensation for subtraction.* Nine take away four is five because eight take away four is four.

▶ *Commuting for addition.* Two and nine is the same as nine and two.
▶ *Using addition for subtraction.* Four and four is eight so eight take away four is four.
▶ *Using doubles and near doubles.* Five and five is ten so five and four is nine.
▶ *Using a known fact.* Seven and three is ten so seven and four is eleven.
▶ *Addition by partitioning using five as a base.* Four and three is the same as four and one and two.
▶ *Subtraction by partitioning using five as a base.* Seven take away four is seven take two – five, and five take two – three.
▶ *Addition using ten as a base.* Seven and six is the same as seven and three – ten, and three more – thirteen.
▶ *Subtraction using ten as a base.* Fifteen take away four is eleven because fifteen take away five is ten and four is one less than five.

When is the Child at Stage 5?

Stage 5 is characterized by the use of non-count-by-ones strategies, that is, strategies which include procedures which do not involve counting by ones. There are many instances where a child uses several Stage 5 strategies in the course of solving tasks in Assessment 1.1, Task Groups 8 and 9. As a general rule, at least three instances of Stage 5 strategies on Assessment 1.1 are necessary for the child to be judged to be at Stage 5. In the case of children who show one or two instances only, solutions in Task Group 3 of 1.2, Non-Count-by-Ones Strategies, should also be considered. Experience has shown that in 1.2: Task Group 3, for many children, their response is indicative of Stage 5 on some but not all of the six items. The criterion stated above is applied once again. If they show at least three instances of Stage 5 strategies across Tasks Groups 1.1:8, 9 and 1.2:3 then the child is judged to be at Stage 5. In this way the criterion can be applied to Assessment 1.1 only, Assessment 1.2 only or collectively across both assessments 1.1 and 1.2.

To summarize, the interviewer should keep an open mind with regard to the kinds of strategies children might use on these tasks. For example, a child might use an expected strategy to solve some of these tasks and use unexpected and idiosyncratic strategies to solve others. In determining whether the child is at Stage 5, the interviewer should take account of the child's use of Stage 5 strategies in these six tasks and add this to knowledge gained in the additive and subtractive tasks in Assessment 1.1 (that is, Task Groups 8 and 9).

In the next chapter we look at the assessment schedules for Part C of the LFIN.

7

Part C of the LFIN: Assessment Interview Schedules 2.1 and 2.2

Summary

Assessments 1.1 and 1.2 are intended to assess knowledge of number words and numerals and counting strategies. In this chapter we have presented Assessments 2.1 and 2.2 which are intended to assess the topics of structuring numbers to 10 and to 20. Schedules 1.1 and 1.2 can be used separately or in conjunction with Schedules 2.1 and 2.2. Schedules 2.1 and 2.2 can also be used separately. In the case of children regarded as very early number learners, Assessment 1.1 would be an appropriate beginning. In the case of children regarded as more advanced, Assessment 1.1 or 2.1 could be a starting point.

In this chapter we return to Part C of the LFIN, which is concerned with Structuring Number. Part C contains five aspects which are considered important in children's early number learning. The five aspects are Combining and Partitioning; Spatial Patterns and Subitizing; Temporal Sequences; Finger Patterns and Base-five (**Quinary**-based) Strategies. Not only are these aspects closely integrated with the Counting and Number Words and Numerals (Parts A and B) but also the aspects themselves share close interrelationships. For a full discussion of the five aspects assessed in 2.1 and 2.2 see Chapter 2. All these aspects, with the exception of Temporal Patterns, are assessed in Assessment Interview Schedules 2.1 and 2.2, hereafter referred to as Assessment 2.1 and Assessment 2.2.

Assessment 2.1 is concerned with Early Grouping: Structuring Numbers One to Ten. Being able to solve problems in the range 1 to 10 involves learning to combine and partition numbers. First, we examine a child's ability to ascribe number to flashed spatial patterns. Then we assess their facility with finger patterns before moving to spatial configurations in frames. These tasks will see whether they can combine and partition numbers using doubles, and five and ten as reference, or anchor points.

In Assessment 2.2, Advanced Grouping, we extend the range of numbers to twenty. Where previously in Assessment 2.1 we were looking at the building blocks for calculations in Assessment 2.2 we are looking at the child's ability to 'automatize' addition and subtraction in the range 1 to 20. Thus we assess strategies involving doubles, near doubles, and using 5 and 10 with numbers in the range 1 to 20.

The structure of the chapter is as follows. We begin by describing the task groups in 2.1 and how they are administered. Since task groups in both Assessment Interviews 2.1 and 2.2 do not have models to provide a level of performance, we provide a range of responses which children tend to make. Close observation of these behaviors will enable the assessor to have a defined focus and basis for building the child's profile report. The full assessment interview schedules and associated record keeping are presented in the Appendices 3 and 4.

ASSESSMENT INTERVIEW SCHEDULE 2.1: EARLY GROUPING – STRUCTURING NUMBERS 1 TO 10

The task groups in Assessment 2.1 are:

1. Subitzing and Spatial Patterns
2. Finger Patterns 1 to 5
3. Finger Patterns 6 to 10
4. Five Frame Patterns
5. Five-wise Patterns on a Ten Frame
6. Pair-wise Patterns on a Ten Frame
7. Combining to Make Five
8. Combining to Make Ten.

TASK GROUP 1: Subitizing and Spatial Patterns

Subitizing, as explained in Chapter 2, means 'to apprehend directly the number of dots in an unstructured stimulus display without counting them'. The term 'spatial patterns', in the context of early arithmetic, is more general or more inclusive. This task group relates to strategies that arise in situations involving spatial configurations of various kinds. In early number there is a range of instructional settings for which spatial pattern or spatial arrangement seems to be a dominant feature. These include the various dots cards with regular patterns, dot cards with random or irregular arrays, rows of counters arranged by twos or fives and with colour differentiating each group of five or ten and the ten frame. Activities involving spatial patterns and subitizing have an important role in young children's numerical development.

The subitizing and spatial patterns task group has three subsections of increasing complexity, ranging through regular patterns, irregular configurations and configurations involving two domino patterns. Before commencing each task item, the assessor should ensure that the cards are correctly sorted in each pile, that is, as in the schedule shown below. The verbal instructions are, '*I am going to show you some cards that have dots on them and I would like you to tell me how many dots you see.*' When flashing each card, ensure that it is held vertically and stationary for the required time, that is, for half a second. The child should not have time to count the dots. If one, or two, wrong responses are given in each subsection the particular item, or items, should be revisited. However, if more incorrect responses are given the section should be curtailed.

Spatial Patterns

---

1. Subitizing and Spatial Patterns

Show each card briefly, for about half a second, saying, *I'm going to show you some cards very quickly. Tell me how many spots are on each one.*

(a) Flashed Regular	4	3	2	5	6
(b) Flashed Irregular	6	7	4	5	8

When a card is flashed, the child might immediately recognize the pattern in the sense of recalling the number name that corresponds to the pattern. Alternatively, the child might take a few seconds to answer, in which case they might be visualizing the pattern and attempting to count the dots in their visualized image. The delay may be accompanied by head nods or hand movements and/or verbal or non-verbal utterances.

The final part of the subitizing and spatial patterns task uses domino cards. These are flashed for half a second. Initially the questioning is very open, '*What did you see?*' This invites the child to tell as much as they can so that we may gain an insight into their emerging strategies for combining and partitioning. If the child is unable to respond, then the supporting questions may be used. An important goal in early numeracy is for children to develop strong conceptually based spatial patterns. The term 'conceptually based' is used to indicate that the child can visualize a pattern for 'four' for example, in the absence of any visibly available pattern (that is, a pattern for four is neither displayed nor flashed). These conceptually based patterns can form a basis for children's emerging strategies for combining and partitioning small numbers (for example, numbers in the range 1 to 10).

---

1. **Subitizing and Spatial Patterns**

    (c) Domino Cards
    Show each card briefly, for about half a second, saying, *I'm going to show you some cards very quickly.*
    (i)   *What did you see?*

    (ii)   *Tell me how many spots are on one side.*

    (iii)   *Tell me how many spots are on the other side.*

    (iv)   *How many are there altogether?*

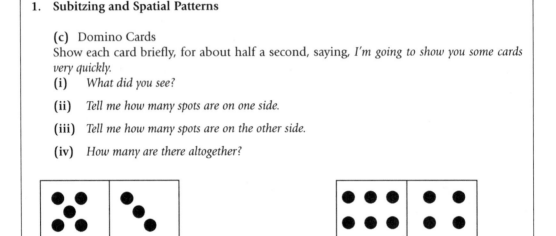

There are no models for subitizing and spatial patterns.

TASK GROUP 2: Finger Patterns 1 to 5

There are variations in the extent to which children spontaneously use their fingers in numerical situations. In this task group we ask children to make numbers first on one hand and then by using two hands. The assessor is advised to observe closely to see if the child needs to look at their fingers in order to make the finger patterns for the numbers 1 to 5. If they do, they may have to count their fingers slowly from one in order to make a pattern corresponding to the required number. Some may need to count their fingers to confirm the numerosity of the finger pattern they have made. The assessor should also note whether the child raises some fingers simultaneously and then raises other fingers in turn.

2. **Finger Patterns 1 to 5**

    (a) *Show me three on your fingers*

    3   2   5   1   4

    (b) *Using two hands show me*

    3   2   5   4

TASK GROUP 3: Finger Patterns 6 to 10

Task Group 3: Finger Patterns 6 to 10, is posed to see if the child has developed more sophisticated ways of reasoning about finger patterns. The initial question is posed, *'Show me "x" on your fingers'* and if successful they are asked if they have another way of making that number. There are many different responses for the assessor to look for and take note of. For example, the assessor should observe whether the child makes the finger pattern for five by raising the fingers sequentially or whether they raise them simultaneously. The former may continue to raise individual fingers to the required amount, while the latter, having simultaneously raised five as a hand, may now count-on from five. Some children may produce five and the remainder simultaneously. When the second question is posed, *'Show me ... a different way'*, observe whether the child uses a systematic approach to producing the new solution or whether the question is seen as a new, unrelated task. Some children may not solve this in a cumulative or additive sense as shown above but raise ten fingers and then proceed to reduce the amount to the required total.

Finger Patterns

3. **Finger Patterns 6 to 10**

    (a) *Show me 6 on your fingers*

    (b) *Show me 6 a different way*

    (c) *Show me 9 on your fingers*
    (d) *Show me 10 on your fingers*
    (e) *Show me 8 on your fingers*
    (f) *Show me 8 a different way*

TASK GROUP 4: Five Frame Patterns

The five frame is simply that, a horizontal or vertical frame of five squares upon which a number of spots have been placed. The card is flashed for half a second as in the subitizing and spatial patterns tasks. The objective of the task is to assess the child's facility with partitions of five. For example, do they know the patterns on the five frame? Related to this is whether they can say the number of spots seen and the number of empty squares without counting them? The first question is open ended to allow the child the opportunity to tell you as much as possible. The assessor could probe to see if they have more to tell. If not, then the second question can be posed.

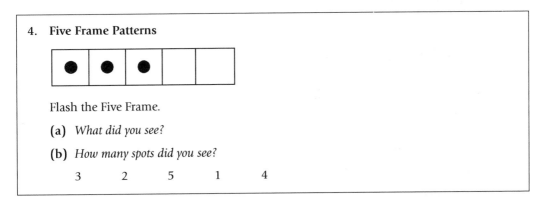

4. **Five Frame Patterns**

Flash the Five Frame.

(a) *What did you see?*

(b) *How many spots did you see?*

3   2   5   1   4

TASK GROUP 5: Five-wise Patterns on a Ten Frame

The ten frame is two five frames designed to assess the child's knowledge of the number five as a base. It follows on from the use of finger patterns and the five frame tasks. In the Mathematics Recovery Teaching programme using five as a base is given special emphasis in order for them to incorporate it in their additive and subtractive strategies. Examples of five-wise patterns are:

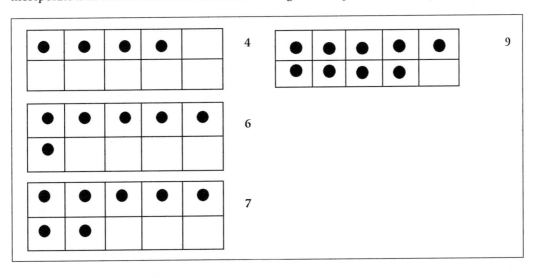

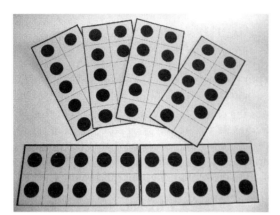

It may be argued that ten is the base in the setting posed in this task. We do not see five as replacing ten as a base but rather that five is a useful additional base. Some texts refer to five as an anchor or reference point. We would argue that there is considerable advantage associated with five being used as an additional base along with ten as it has the potential to reduce reliance on counting-by-ones. The card is flashed for half a second and the questions posed as above.

Five-wise patterns on a Ten Frame

5. **Five-wise Patterns on a Ten Frame**

Flash five-wise cards 1–10

(a) *What did you see?*

(b) *How many spots did you see?*

7   10   8   6   9

TASK GROUP 6: Pair-wise Patterns on a Ten Frame

Pair-wise patterns use two as a base unit and relate to odd and even numbers and doubles and near doubles. Some patterns are shown below:

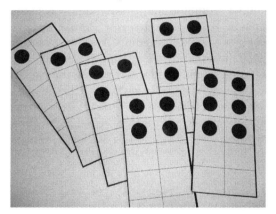

Pair-wise patterns on a Ten Frame   'What do you see?'

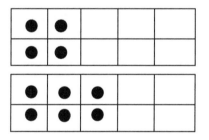

4

7

6

9

The pattern is superimposed on a ten frame and presented as for the previous group.

---

6. **Pair-wise Patterns on a Ten Frame**

Flash pair-wise cards 1–10

(a) *What did you see?*

(b) *How many dots did you see?*

4	2	5	1	3
7	10	8	6	9

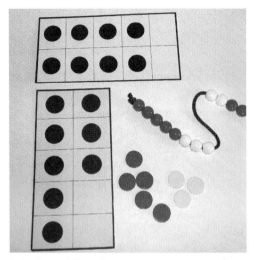

Pair-wise and Five-wise patterns

This task will expose to what extent the child has developed conceptually based images for the numbers one to ten in a different context to the five-wise pattern. Again the initial open-ended question is posed to offer the child the opportunity to use the flashed image to show their ability to combine and partition numbers in the range 1 to 10. The assessor should observe whether the child attempts to count the dots while the pattern is being flashed. Alternatively the child might attempt to visualize the pattern and attempt to count using the visualized image. This may be detected by a series of head or eye movements accompanied by verbal or subvocal counting.

TASK GROUP 7: Combining to Make Five

This task group follows on from Task Group 4, Five-Frame Patterns, but now the child does not have the support of the equipment to give the corresponding number. It has become a verbally posed task that does not include using frames to assess the child's knowledge of the combinations to make five. The instructions are, 'I will say a number and you say the number that goes with it to make five'.

---

7. **Combining to make five**

    I will say a number and you say the number that goes with it to make five.

    4   2   1   3   5

TASK GROUP 8: Combining to Make Ten

This task group extends the previous task by assessing the child's ability to make various combinations of ten presented as verbal questions. There are six questions in the group. The first three look for the child to generate combinations to make ten. The second group are termed missing addend problems such as, 'I have 8 apples, how many more do I need to make 10?' This is equivalent to saying 8 + [ ] = 10. This is a similar task to the Missing Addends in Assessment Interview 1.1:8(e) but is presented without equipment.

8. **Combining to make ten**

    (a) *Tell me two numbers that add up to 10.*

    (b) *Tell me 2 other numbers that add up to 10.*

    (c) *Can you tell me another two?*

    (d) *I have 8 apples, how many more do I need to make 10?*

    (e) *I have 4, how many more to make 10?*

    (f) *I have 7, how many more to make 10?*

ASSESSMENT INTERVIEW SCHEDULE 2.2: ADVANCED GROUPING – STRUCTURING NUMBERS 1 TO 20

We now turn to the presentation of Assessment Interview Schedule 2.2. This extends Assessment 2.1 by including numbers in the range 1 to 20. In particular we will be looking to see how facile the child is with addition and subtraction in the range 1 to 20 using doubles, and using 5 and 10 as reference points. Equipment in the form of flashed cards is used in the first task group. This is followed by the presentation of additive and subtractive written number sentence problems. Finally, we look at the child's ability to use relational thinking, that is, using the solution to one number problem to deduce the answer to a related problem. The items are arranged in order of difficulty.

The task groups in Assessment 2.2 are:

1. Doubles
2. Near Doubles
3. Addition Using Five, Ten or Doubles, and so on.
4. Subtraction Using Five, Ten or Doubles, and so on.
5. Addition and Subtraction with One Addend/Subtrahend Greater than Ten
6. Relational Thinking

TASK GROUP 1: Doubles

In the Mathematics Recovery Programme initial tasks typically involve materials. In this task item we use a setting similar to the arithmetic rack, which is an abacus-like device containing two rows of beads. In each row there are ten beads. The ten beads appear as a group of five of one colour and a group of five of another colour.

The Arithmetic Rack and cards

First, three tasks, each involving a double is shown on spot cards for approximately two seconds. Then the child is asked to describe what they saw. If the answer is comprehensive then there is no need to probe further. However, if the child is hesitant then the subordinate questions, (ii) to (iv), can be posed. These tasks are followed by doubles 6 to 9 not in numerical order.

The cards were flashed for a longer time than in the subitizing and spatial pattern tasks in Assessment 2.1 but it is still necessary to allow sufficient time for the child to think and reflect upon their thinking.

---

1.   **Doubles**

Show spot cards (two seconds)

	(a) 5 + 5	(b) 4 + 4	(c) 2 + 2

(i)   *What do you see?*

(ii)   *How many on the top row?*

(iii)   *How many on the bottom row?*

(iv)   *How many altogether?*

	(d) 7 + 7	(e) 9 + 9	(f) 6 + 6	(g) 8 + 8

(v)   *What do you see?*

(vi)   *How many on the top row?*

(vii)   *How many on the bottom row?*

(viii)   *How many altogether?*

TASK GROUP 2: Near Doubles

The presentation of near doubles differs from doubles because the cards are not used. The child works from the written number sentence. The child might use visualized images of the dot pattern. If the child gives a correct response ask if they have another way of solving the problem.

---

2. **Near Doubles**

    Show the number task.

    Can you work this problem out?

    How did you do that?

    Do you have another way to work it out?

    (a) 5 + 6   **(b)** 4 + 3   **(c)** 7 + 6

    (d) 9 + 8   **(e)** 8 + 7   **(f)** 3 + 2

TASK GROUP 3: Addition Using Five, Ten or Doubles, and so on.

Task Groups 3, 4 and 5 assess the child's facility to use number relationships and the properties of operations. Task Group 3 involves addition tasks and Task Group 4 involves subtraction tasks. Task Group 5 has a mixture of addition and subtraction. We are looking to see if the child has ways of reorganizing the task by using five or ten as a reference point or using their knowledge of doubles. Each problem is presented on a card.

---

3. **Addition Using Five, Ten or Doubles, and so on**

    Show the number task. *Do you have a way to work out this problem?*

    How did you do that?

    (a) 9 + 3   **(b)** 8 + 5   **(c)** 9 + 6

    (d) 8 + 6   **(e)** 5 + 7   **(f)** 4 + 9

TASK GROUP 4: Subtraction Using Five, Ten or Doubles, and so on

4. **Subtraction using Five, Ten or Doubles, and so on**

    Show the number task. *Do you have a way to work out this problem?*
    How did you do that?

    (a) 17 – 7   (b) 11 – 4   (c) 12 – 9

    (d) 17 – 8   (e) 13 – 5   (f) 14 – 8

TASK GROUP 5: Addition and Subtraction with One Addend/Subtrahend Greater than Ten.

5. **Addition and Subtraction with One Addend/Subtrahend Greater than Ten**

    Show the number task. *Do you have a way to work out this problem?*
    How did you do that?

    (a) 13 + 5   (b) 11 + 8

    (c) 19 – 7   (d) 17 – 15

TASK GROUP 6: Relational Thinking

In this task group we assess the child's understanding of number relationships. In each task the first card is placed on the table. The child is asked to read it and asked whether they have a way to work it out. If correct, the second card is placed below the first and they are asked to use their first solution to calculate the answer to the second. We are not looking for the child to calculate the answer to the second problem but, rather, whether the child sees relationships between the numbers. The assessor is encouraged to probe the responses for clarification.

Task item 6(a) concerns the commutative law. By this we mean that it does not matter in what order the numbers are added. Both addition and multiplication are commutative. Here we present addition. Later, in Assessment Interviews Schedules 3.1 and 3.2, we will assess commutativity in multiplication tasks.

6. **Relational Thinking**

    (a) Present the card
        What does this say?
        Can you work it out?

        14 + 2

        Can you use this number sentence
        to help you work out … ?

        2 + 14

Task 6(b) is similar in presentation and questioning to Assessment 1.2:3(b) – Non-Count-by-Ones Strategies. Each card is presented in turn and the child is asked to state how they used the information from the solution of the first problem to answer the subsequent problems. It is intended to expose the compensation strategy and we look for the child to explain how one number increases as the second decreases. To confirm the strategy it is helpful to ask the child if they can predict the next question.

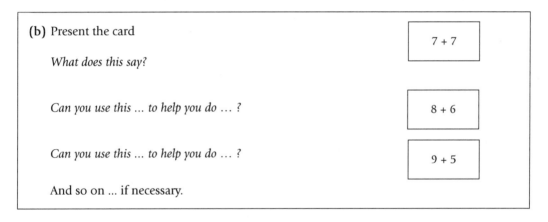

(b) Present the card

7 + 7

What does this say?

Can you use this … to help you do … ?

8 + 6

Can you use this … to help you do … ?

9 + 5

And so on … if necessary.

Only two cards are presented in task 6(c) 13 + 4 and 17 – 4. The questions are posed as before. The strategy involves using addition to solve subtraction.

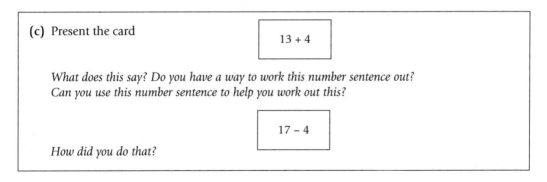

(c) Present the card

13 + 4

What does this say? Do you have a way to work this number sentence out?
Can you use this number sentence to help you work out this?

17 – 4

How did you do that?

The final question is very open ended in that no calculation is required. The number sentence 6 + 8 = 14 is shown and the child is asked to use the information to respond to an addition problem and a related subtraction problem. If correct responses are given, the final question is posed which will see if the child can derive additional information from their solutions.

(d) Present the card

$$6 + 8 = 14$$

Can you use this number sentence to help you work out this?

(i)

$$8 + 6$$

(ii)

$$14 - 6$$

(iii) *What other number facts would you know from this?*

8
Assessment Interview Schedules 3.1 and 3.2

Summary

We now turn to Part D of Learning Framework in Number. In this chapter we set out an overview of the development of children's early multiplication and division knowledge and strategies together with an associated model consisting of five levels. For each level, an explanation and an illustration in the form of a protocol of a child's solutions of multiplicative or divisional tasks is provided. The Assessment Interview Schedules 3.1 and 3.2 for multiplication and division knowledge and strategies are set out together with guidance for their administration. We conclude the chapter with five scenarios taken from classroom situations and challenge the reader to identify the child's level, solutions and explanations. We also provide guidelines for determining levels of early multiplication and division knowledge. The complete assessment interview schedules are provided in the Appendices 5 and 6 together with the associated record keeping and reference guides.

DEVELOPMENT OF EARLY MULTIPLICATION AND DIVISION KNOWLEDGE AND STRATEGIES

This chapter draws on an extensive range of research in the area of multiplication and division (see Mulligan, 1998). Children's early multiplication and division knowledge and strategies result from cognitive reorganizations of their counting, addition and subtraction strategies.

However, it has long been recognized that multiplication is not simply a process of repeated addition, and that division is not simply a process of sharing. Multiplication and division knowledge differs from addition and subtraction mainly because the former incorporates the ability to use equal groups as 'abstract composite units' (Steffe, 1992b): 'An abstract composite unit [is] the result of applying the integration operation to a numerical composite or to a symbolized numerical composite. The child focuses on the unit structure of a numerical composite e.g. one ten, rather than on the unit items e.g. ten ones' (Steffe and Cobb, 1988, p. 334). In the case of multiplication or division an abstract composite unit is a collection of items that is viewed as one thing. For example, a child for whom three is an abstract composite unit can regard three items as 'one three'. The child can also regard three items as 'three ones'. This follows from the description of an abstract composite unit given above because an abstract composite unit is a cognitive advancement on a numerical composite.

The child who has advanced multiplication and division knowledge can conceptualize a group of equal groups as a composite of composite units. In the case of three sixes, for example, the child is aware of three as a composite unit and, at the same time, aware of each of the groups of six as a composite unit. 'For a situation to be established as multiplicative, it is necessary at least to co-ordinate two composite units in such a way that one of the composite units is distributed over elements of the other composite unit' (Steffe, 1994, p. 19). Thus a framework of the development of multiplication and division knowledge should account for the acquisition of a cognitive structure based on equal grouping which is at the heart of multiplicative reasoning (Anghileri, 1989; Confrey, 1994; Kouba, 1989; Steffe, 1992b).

Research shows that children as young as 4 or 5 years old can solve simple multiplicative and divisional tasks by using materials and counting. Studies show that young children can develop multiplication and division concepts in the first years of schooling and highlight that teaching practices may not necessarily focus on children's potential mathematical development (Carpenter et al., 1993; Clark and Kamii, 1996; Hunting et al., 1996; Kouba, 1989; Mulligan and Mitchelmore, 1997). On the other hand, there is growing evidence that once children reach the primary (elementary) grades (that is, the fourth year of school and around 8 years of age) many are unable to solve problems involving multiplication and division or apply multiplicative number facts with meaning. Children need to be presented with specific problem-based situations designed to encourage the construction of abstract composite units. This will promote a range of increasingly sophisticated strategies based on counting in multiples, and addition and subtraction. This is a necessary phase for children before they acquire facile strategies for multiplying and dividing and, related to this, 'automatized' knowledge of multiplication and division facts.

Children may use identical or very similar strategies for solving both multiplicative and divisional tasks, except that, in the case of division, the child will form and count composite units based on a given divisor. Interestingly, it has been found that division is not necessarily more difficult than multiplication and, in many cases, a divisional task may be easier than a corresponding multiplicative task. For example, it may be easier for a child to share counters into equal groups and count the number of groups rather than keep track of a larger number of composite groups as is necessary in the case of multiplication. Research indicates that teaching children to share and group small numbers into equal parts can facilitate the development of relatively sophisticated multiplication and division strategies, that is, strategies more advanced than counting by ones.

In this chapter a model of early multiplication and division knowledge consisting of five levels is presented. Links between this model and the Stages of Early Arithmetical Learning model (Chapter 4) can easily be drawn. For example, Stage 3 and Stage 5 are characterized by the construction of numerical composites and abstract composite units respectively. Thus one would expect children at Level 1 in terms of early multiplication and division to have attained Stage 3 in terms of SEAL.

MODEL OF THE DEVELOPMENT OF EARLY MULTIPLICATION AND DIVISION KNOWLEDGE

The five levels in children's development of early multiplication and division knowledge are now presented. The model is adapted from that developed by Mulligan (1998). The level is defined and is then further exemplified by a discussion and a classroom scenario.

LEVEL 1: INITIAL GROUPING

Level 1: Initial Grouping. Uses perceptual counting (that is, by ones) to establish the numerosity of a collection of equal groups, to share items into groups of a given size (quotitive sharing), and to share items into a given number of groups (partitive sharing).

The child at Level 1 can establish the numerosity of a collection of equal groups when the items are visible and counts by ones when doing so, that is, the child uses perceptual counting (see Stage 1 of SEAL). The child can make groups of a specified size from a collection of items. For example, given 12 counters the child can arrange the counters into groups of three thereby obtaining four groups. This is referred to as quotitive sharing, and is also known as the grouping aspect of division. The child can also share a collection of items into a specified number of groups, for example, given 20 counters the child can share the counters into five equal groups. This is referred to as partitive sharing and is also known as the sharing aspect of division. The child does not count in multiples.

Scenario 1: Kim and Beau

At the beginning of his interview Beau arranged 18 counters into groups of three obtaining six groups. He also shared 20 counters into five equal groups. In each of these tasks Beau was asked to count the total number of counters, and he counted by ones to do so. The interview continued as follows:

K: Can you count by twos for me and I'll tell you when to stop.
B: (Extends two fingers on his right hand. Points over the desk with his two extended fingers in coordination with each number word.) Two, four, six, eight, ten, (looks towards Kim) twelve.
K: Can you go any further?
B: (Shakes his head.) Umm, no.
K: Can you count by fives for me?
B: Yep. (Extends five fingers on his right hand.) Umm – (touches the desk with his right hand in coordination with each number word) ten, twenty (softly) I think, umm –.
K: Try counting by fives this time. Five –.
B: (Counts slowly and touches the desk in coordination with each count.) Five, ten, umm (looks at Kim) seven?
K: Stop there. Try counting by threes for me and I'll tell you when to stop.
B: (Extends three fingers on his right hand. Counts slowly and touches the desk in coordination with each count.) Ten, twenty, thirty –, umm ten – .
K: Okay, stop there. (Places out five rows of three counters arranged in a 5 × 3 array.) Can you count by threes this time and tell me how many counters are there?
B: (Places a finger on each counter in the first row and then the second row in coordination with counting.) Ten, twenty –.
K: Can you count by threes?
B: (As before, places fingers on counters in the first row and then the second row.) Three, ten – (looks at Kim).
K: Okay, stop there.

Discussion of Scenario 1

Beau could produce the number word sequence of multiples of two, up to twelve. But he could not produce multiples of five or three. When asked to count a 5 × 3 array of counters by threes, he was unable to do so. Beau was able to share collections of counters into groups of a specified size and into a given number of equal groups, and when doing so counted the total number of counters by ones. Beau's strategies are indicative of Level I: Initial Grouping.

LEVEL 2: PERCEPTUAL COUNTING IN MULTIPLES

> **Level 2: Perceptual Counting in Multiples.** Uses a multiplicative counting strategy to count visible items arranged in equal groups.

The child at Level 2 has developed counting strategies that are more advanced than those used in Level 1. These counting strategies fall into three categories.

▶ *Perceptual rhythmic counting.* Rhythmic counting involves counting all the items contained in several equal groups by ones and emphasizing the number word reached after each group is counted, for example, when counting three groups of four the child emphasizes 'four', 'eight' and 'twelve', that is, 'one, two, three, *four*', and so on.
▶ *Perceptual double counting.* Double counting involves counting all the items contained in several equal groups by ones in coordination with counting the number of groups by ones, for example, 'one, two, three, four – *one*; five, six, seven, eight – *two*', and so on.
▶ *Perceptual skip counting.* Skip counting involves counting by threes, fours, and so on when counting all the items contained in several equal groups.

Each of the above strategies is given the label 'perceptual' (for example, perceptual rhythmic counting) because of the child's reliance on visible items. These multiplicative counting strategies involve implicitly or explicitly counting in multiples. After sharing a collection into equal groups the child uses one of these strategies to count all the items contained in the groups, which are necessarily visible. The child is not able to count the items in situations where the groups are screened.

Scenario 2: Sarah and Delise

At the beginning of her interview Delise arranged 16 counters into groups of two obtaining eight groups. She also shared 30 counters into six equal groups. When asked to count the total number of counters Delise counted by twos to sixteen on the first task and by fives to thirty on the second task. The interview continued as follows:

S: Count by fives and I'll tell you when to stop.
D: Five, ten, fifteen, (pauses briefly) twenty, twenty-five, (pauses briefly) thirty, thirty-five, forty.
S: Stop there please. This time count by threes and I'll tell you when to stop.
D: Three, six, nine, (after two seconds) twelve, (after three seconds) fifteen.
S: Okay stop there please. (Places out six rows of three counters arranged in a 6 × 3 array.) Can you count by threes and tell me how many counters are there?
D: (Points to each row in turn.) Three, six, nine, (pauses briefly) twelve, fifteen, (after two seconds) eighteen!

Discussion of Scenario 2

Delise could produce the number word sequence of multiples of five, up to forty, and the number word sequence of multiples of three up to fifteen. She also counted by threes to establish the numerosity of a 6 × 3 array of counters and, in similar vein, counted by twos to sixteen and by fives to thirty on tasks involving collections of counters that she had arranged into equal groups. Delise's strategies are indicative of Level 2: Perceptual Counting in Multiples.

LEVEL 3: FIGURATIVE COMPOSITE GROUPING

> **Level 3: Figurative Composite Grouping.** Uses a multiplicative counting strategy to count items arranged in equal groups in cases where the individual items are not visible.

The child at Level 3 has developed counting strategies which do not rely on items being visible and which do not involve counting by ones. For example, if the child is presented with four groups of three counters, where each group is separately screened, the child may use skip counting by threes to determine the number of counters in all, that is 'three, six, nine, twelve'. From the child's perspective each of the four screens symbolizes a collection of three items but the individual items are not visible.

Scenario 3: Anna and Jenna

A: (Places out six containers.) Jenna I have six containers here. (Takes one container and empties out three counters.) And in each container there are three counters. (Replaces the three counters.) How many counters would there be altogether?

J: (Looks ahead for seven seconds.) Eighteen!

A: Tell me how you worked that out.

J: (Points to each of the six containers in turn.) I said three, six, nine, twelve, fifteen, and then I just counted on – three.

A: Tell me the numbers that you used to count on. You got to fifteen, and then you said?

J: (After three seconds, while looking at Anna makes three pointing actions in coordination with counting.) Sixteen, seventeen, eighteen.

Discussion of Scenario 3

Jenna used skip counting by threes up to fifteen to count five groups of three counters and then counted-on by ones to count the sixth group of three counters. Jenna's strategy is indicative of Level 3: Figurative Composite Grouping, because she counted in multiples of three to fifteen in order to count six groups of three, in the case where the individual items in each group are screened.

LEVEL 4: REPEATED ABSTRACT COMPOSITE GROUPING

> **Level 4: Repeated Abstract Composite Grouping.** Counts composite units in repeated addition or subtraction, that is, uses the composite units a specified number of times.

The child at Level 4 has constructed a conceptual structure labeled an 'abstract composite unit' in which the child is simultaneously aware of both the composite and unitary aspects of three, for example. The child can use repeated addition to solve multiplication tasks and repeated subtraction to solve division tasks, and can do so in the absence of visible or screened items. On a multiplicative task involving six groups of three items, in which each group is separately screened, the child is aware of each group as an abstract composite unit.

Scenario 4: Emily and Jamal

E: If twelve cakes were shared among the children and they got four cakes each, how many children would there be?

J: (After two seconds.) Three!

E: How did you work that out?

J: Umm, I was trying to figure it out by fours.

E: Okay. So how did you figure it out by fours? What did you do?

J: One, two, three, four (slight pause), five, six, seven, eight (slight pause), nine, ten, eleven, twelve. (Looks at Emily.)

E: Hmm, hmm. (Looks at Jamal.)

J: (After two seconds.) By counting one, two, three, fours.

E: Hmm, hmm. And then what did you do after you went one, two, three, four?

J: I –, I tried to figure out what three fours equalled and it equalled twelve.

E: (Places out seven piggy banks and a large collection of counters.) I want you to use exactly twenty counters to make piggy banks that have five counters in them. And tell me how many piggy banks you need?

J: (Immediately, while shrugging his shoulders, looking at Emily and smiling.) Four!

E: How did you do that?

J: I counted. (Points to four piggy banks in turn.) Like, that was one five, ten, fifteen, twenty.

Discussion of Scenario 4

Jamal's solution to the first task was relatively sophisticated because when he counted by ones from one to twelve, he was double counting. His count from one to twelve was an object on which he could focus in order to determine how many times he made four counts. Presumably Jamal anticipated he could do this prior to commencing his count. Jamal's explanation 'By counting one, two, three, fours' is ambiguous because the number of groups (that is, three) is one less than the number in each group (that is, four). Thus Emily interpreted this explanation as a count from 'one' to 'four' whereas, for Jamal, 'fours' in his explanation referred to groups of four. His explanation referred to counting the groups of four rather than the items in one of the groups (for example, the first group). Jamal solved the second task by counting by fives to twenty and keeping track of the number of counts. Emily provided seven piggy banks and a large collection of counters but Jamal did not use the counters in his solution. Inherent in each of Jamal's solutions is the construction of an abstract composite unit. On the first task Jamal simultaneously regards 'four' as four ones (that is, in his count by ones from one to twelve) and one four (that is, in his keeping track of the number of times he makes four counts). Similarly on the second task, the multiples of five ('five', 'ten', and so on) signify for Jamal both another five and five more ones. Jamal's strategies are indicative of Level 4: Repeated Abstract Composite Grouping.

LEVEL 5: MULTIPLICATION AND DIVISION AS OPERATIONS

> **Level 5: Multiplication and Division as Operations.** Can regard both the number in each group and the number of groups as a composite unit. Can immediately recall or quickly derive many of the basic facts for multiplication and division.

The child at Level 5 can coordinate two composite units in the context of multiplication or division. In a task such as six threes or six groups of three, for example, the child is aware of both six and three as abstract composite units, whereas at Level 4 the child is aware of three as an abstract composite unit but is not aware of six as an abstract composite unit. The child at Level 5 can immediately recall or quickly derive many of the basic facts of multiplication and division and may use multiplication facts to derive division facts. At Level 5, the commutative principle of multiplication (for example $5 \times 3 = 3 \times 5$) and the inverse relationship between multiplication and division are within the child's zone of proximal development. Thus, for example, the child might be aware that six threes is the same as three sixes and might use $4 \times 8 = 32$ to work out $32 \div 4$.

Scenario 5: Richard and Aimee

R: There are twelve tables and four children are seated at each table. How many children are there?

A: Six times four is twenty-four so twelve times four is forty-eight.

R: Why did you use six times four?

A: I just doubled six times, so it's twelve times.

R: There are forty-two stickers to be shared fairly among seven children. How many stickers do they get each?

A: Three by seven is twenty-one, so forty-two divided by seven must be six.

R: Why did you use three by seven first?

A: Because three by seven is twenty-one so that's halfway. Twenty-one and twenty-one is forty-two. So it's double three.

Discussion of Scenario 5

In solving the first task when Aimee said 'six times four is twenty-four so twelve times four is forty-eight', 'six' and 'twelve' as well as 'four' were abstract composite units for her. Aimee simultaneously regarded 'six fours' as standing for one unit, that is, one lot of 'six fours' (which could be doubled), and as 'six lots of four'. Aimee's solutions were very sophisticated in relative terms because she used multiplication facts that she knew automatically (that is, $6 \times 4 = 24$ and $3 \times 7 = 21$ respectively) to work out 12×4 and $42 \div 7$. Using an automatized multiplication fact to solve a different multiplicative task or to solve a divisional task is indicative of Level 5: Multiplication and Division as Operations.

ASSESSMENT INTERVIEW SCHEDULE 3.1: EARLY MULTIPLICATION AND DIVISION

The Assessment Interview Schedule 3.1 for Early Multiplication and Division consists of five task groups. These are set out in Table 8.1

Table 8.1 Task Groups in Assessment 3.1

Task Group 1	Forming Equal Groups
Task Group 2	Tasks Involving FNWS of Multiples
Task Group 3	Tasks Involving Visible Items Arranged in Rows or Arrays
Task Group 4	Tasks Involving Equal Groups of Visible Items
Task Group 5	Tasks Involving Screened Items

TASK GROUP 1: Forming Equal Groups

Task Group 1 concerns the formation of equal groups and Task Groups 2, 3 and 4 involve multiplicative and divisional tasks with visible items. In Task Group 5 we move away from perceptual objects and use screened items. The tasks become progressively more difficult across the task groups.

Present a pile of 15 counters to the child. (Put them out randomly spaced and not in a line.)

Using these counters, make three groups with four in each group.

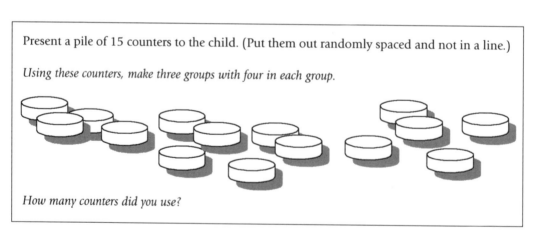

How many counters did you use?

A collection of counters, greater than the number of groups and units required, is presented to the child. The child is asked to make three groups with four in each group and to state the total of the counters used. It is important to attend carefully to the child's actions and words. For example, does the child solve the task? How does the child make the groups? Is it by moving one counter at a time or by moving multiples of counters? If by ones, how does the child cope with the surplus counters? Does the child know the total in each group without counting? Children may need to count from one when making, or checking, the number in a group and may have to repeat this behavior for all the groups (one, two, three, four, … one, two, three, four, … and so on). Some children might say the number in each group without counting by ones (four, four, four) or otherwise indicate that each group has the same number.

TASK GROUP 2: Tasks Involving FNWS of Multiples

To discover how facile the child is in the FNWS of multiples and where they stop or have problems.

(a) *Count by twos. I'll tell you when to stop.* (Stop at 20)

(b) *Count by tens. I'll tell you when to stop.* (Stop at 120)

(c) *Count by fives. I'll tell you when to stop.* (Stop at 55)

(d) *Count by threes. I'll tell you when to stop.* (Stop at 15)

No equipment is used for Task Group 2. It is posed verbally and is intended to see if the child has the FNWS in multiples and where the sequence of skip counting begins to break down with the child either halting or reverting to counting by ones. For example, three, … six, … nine, … ten, eleven, twelve, … thirteen, fourteen, fifteen, and so on. Some children may count from one and count on by ones emphasizing the multiples. This would appear as a rhythmic count such as one, *two*, three, *four*, five, *six*, seven, *eight*, and so on.

TASK GROUP 3: Tasks Involving Visible Items Arranged in Rows or Arrays

(a) Display a 10 × 2 array of dots, that is ten rows and two columns.

Can you tell me how many dots there are altogether?

(b) Display a 5 × 3 array of dots, that is five rows and three columns.

Can you tell me how many dots there are altogether?

(c) Display a 4 × 5 array, that is four rows and five columns. Indicate rows in turn.

How many rows are there?

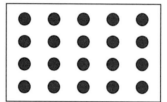

How many dots in each row?
How many dots altogether?

Turn the array through 90 degrees.
How many dots altogether now?

Task Group 3 uses visible items arranged in rows or arrays. These can be presented on card as shown above. For ease of administration we have found it helpful if the array can be made with magnetic counters on a baseboard. This mode of presentation allows for the child to make a slight movement of the counters consistent with touching counters in one-to-one correspondence activities. It is not advisable to place out twenty individual counters for 3(a) and then 15 for 3(b) because it is both time-consuming and detrimental to the climate of the interview as the child would need to look away from the display for far too long.

Tasks 3(a) and 3(b) are concerned with the counting of equal groups. The assessor should observe closely to see how the child counts the dots or counters. For example, do they count by ones or count by twos? If the latter, is the child able to complete the sequence and, if not, where do they revert to counting by ones? Listen carefully to ascertain whether the child uses rhythmic counting or skip counting. If they do count by ones it is advisable to ask if they have another way of counting the dots.

In task 3(c) the child needs to be introduced to the notion of 'row' and 'column'. These can be demonstrated on the array and checked by the first two questions. When these are answered correctly the third question, *'How many dots altogether?'* is posed. If answered correctly the 4 × 5 array is turned through 90 degrees and the child is asked *'How many dots altogether now?'* This task item is linked with conservation and the commutative principle in that reversing the order of two factors does not change the product. It is important to give the child sufficient time to reason and reflect on this task and to probe the response.

TASK GROUP 4: Tasks Involving Equal Groups of Visible Items

(a) Multiplication

Place out four plates with three counters on each plate.

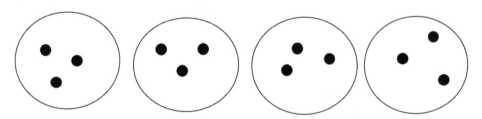

How many plates are there?
There are three counters on each plate, how many counters are there altogether?

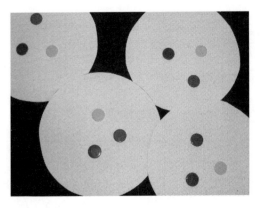

Task Group 4 continues the theme of counting in multiples but in a different context or **setting**, that of objects on plates. The counters can be placed on the plates or drawn on paper plates for ease of administration. The objective is to check the mode of counting. It is in Task Group 4(b), 4(c) and 4(d) that we first meet **partition division** and **quotition division**.

(b) Partition division.

Place out a pile of 15 counters.

Here are 15 counters. If we shared them equally among three children, how many would each child get?

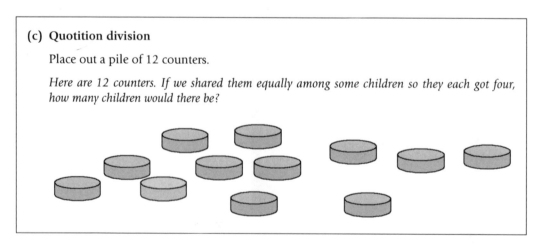

In Task 4(b), 15 counters are placed randomly on a surface. The child is told that there are fifteen counters and that they are to be shared equally among three children. They are asked to state how many each child will get. The assessor should observe how the child attempts to solve this problem. The tendency for some children is to share by ones. If so, observe if they can keep track of the total in each share or whether they have to count one or more groups to satisfy themselves of the total in a group and that each group has the same total. Some children will attempt to calculate the answer and then share by equal groups of a given number. This is quite difficult and may involve trial and error. For example the number word 'three' may trigger sharing by a group of three and then dealing with the remainder.

(c) Quotition division

Place out a pile of 12 counters.

Here are 12 counters. If we shared them equally among some children so they each got four, how many children would there be?

Task item 4(c) requires the child to share 12 counters so that each child gets four and to calculate how many children will be able to receive this share. This is quotition division, in that we know how many are in each share but we do not know how many people can receive shares. This task tends to be slightly easier than partition division. Note carefully how they make the share of four and how they solve the task.

The final item in this group involves partition division with larger numbers. The task is similar to 4(b) to administer. However, on completion of sharing the counters among three children the child is required to solve an additional problem. It is '*If I now shared them equally among 4 children how many would each get?*' This is challenging and the assessor should note if the child can answer without recourse to the counters. If they cannot the assessor should observe how they begin to rearrange the groups and whether a trial and error or methodological approach is used.

(c) **Partition division with redistribution**

Place out a pile of 24 counters.

Here are 24 counters. If we shared them equally among three children, how many would each child get?

If I now shared them equally among 4 children how many would each get?

GUIDELINES FOR LEVELS ARISING FROM TASK GROUPS 1–4

The task groups in Assessment 3.1 up to this point will indicate whether the child operates at Levels 1 or 2 on the model for multiplication and division. To help you decide the appropriate level we offer these guidelines which should be considered in conjunction with the descriptions and illustrations of each of the levels (as presented earlier in this chapter).

Level 1

Level 1 is characterized by perceptual counting by ones. A child is assessed at Level 1 if they are able to solve tasks such as those in Task Groups 1, 3 and 4 and in doing so, count by ones rather than count in multiples.

Level 2

Level 2 is characterized by the use of multiplicative counting strategies in cases where the items are visible. A child is assessed at Level 2 if they are able to solve tasks such as those in Task Groups 1, 3 and 4, and count in multiples when doing so.

TASK GROUP 5: Tasks Involving Screened Items

We now begin to work with assessment tasks where the items are screened. We will want to see if the child uses multiplicative counting strategies when they cannot see the objects. If the child can solve the following tasks they will be assessed at Level 3 at least. However, some may be only able to do this in multiplication but not in division. Therefore, it is important to note which aspects of this task group the child has difficulty with.

Task group 5 contains five subsections:

(a) Multiplication with equal groups.
(b) Partition division with equal groups.
(c) Quotition division with equal groups.
(d) Multiplication with an array.
(e) Quotition division with an array.

(a) Multiplication with Equal Groups

In this task the child is asked to look away while four sets of three objects are placed out and covered with four screens. The child is shown that three objects are under one screen and then told that *'Each screen has three counters under it. How many counters altogether?'* The assessor should note whether the child is able to use multiplicative counting now that the items are screened. The child might use their fingers to keep track of groups and the count.

(a) Multiplication with equal groups

Ask the child to look away while you place out four screens with three counters under each screen.

Each screen has three counters under it. How many counters altogether?

(b) Partition Division with Equal Groups

In this task we use equipment which we term 'covered opaque containers'. In essence these are containers with a slot in the top and no base so that the concealed objects can be easily retrieved and counted. They could be any container which will conceal the objects. A simple method is to use paper cups which can be covered with a lid or screen when the child has completed the partitioning. The key is that the child is not able to count the counters after having shared them.

(b) Partition Division with Equal Groups

Place out a pile of 12 counters and three covered opague containers.

Share these counters equally among the three containers and tell me how many counters there will be in each container?

Ensure that the child is not able to count the counters after having shared them.

(c) Quotition division with equal groups

For this task more counters and containers are placed out than are required to solve the task. The child has to use 20 of the counters to make containers with five counters in each and then tell the assessor how many containers will be used.

(c) Quotition Division with equal groups

Place out a pile of 30 counters and 7 containers.

Use 20 of these counters to make containers with five counters in each and tell me how many containers you will use?

(d) Multiplication with an array

This task focuses on determining how many dots there are in an array when two of five rows are unscreened. The child is shown the first two rows of three dots and told that there are a further three rows. The dots are then re-screened and the child is asked how many dots are there altogether. Observe whether the child counts in multiples and if, at some point, they revert to counting by ones. On completion allow the child to check their solution.

(d) Multiplication with an array
Using a 5 × 3 array, use one screen to screen the upper two rows and a second screen to screen the lower three rows. Unscreen the upper two rows for a few seconds. (Fig.1)

How many rows do you see? Rescreen the two rows. (Fig. 2)

There are three more rows under this screen. How many counters are there altogether?

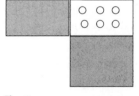

Fig. 1   **Fig. 2**

'How many rows do you see?'

Checking the solution

(e) Quotition Division with an Array

The child is shown a screened array in which one row of two dots is visible. They are told that there are 12 dots on the array and their task is to work out the total number of rows on the array. The task for the assessor is to see how they keep track of the number in each row and the number of rows.

(e) Quotition division with an array

Using a 6 × 2 array, screen five rows and leave the uppermost row unscreened. (Fig.1)

How many dots in this row? There are 12 dots altogether. How many rows altogether? Let the child check. (Fig. 2)

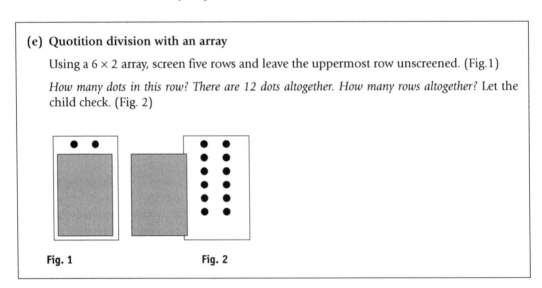

Fig. 1   **Fig. 2**

GUIDELINES FOR LEVELS ARISING FROM TASK GROUP 5

Level 3 is characterized by the use of multiplicative counting strategies in cases where items are screened. A child is assessed at Level 3 if they are able to solve tasks such as tasks (a), (b), (c) and (d) in Task Group 5, and count in multiples, or use addition or subtraction when so doing.

If the child is successful in answering 5(e) by counting in multiples, or the use of addition or subtraction they are judged to be at Level 4. Assessment 3.2 is used to confirm if the child is at Level 4 or 5.

ASSESSMENT INTERVIEW SCHEDULE 3.2: ADVANCED MULTIPLICATION AND DIVISION

Assessment Interview Schedule 3.2 has three task groups. These are:

1. Tasks presented without visible or screened items
2. Commutativity and Inverse relationship
3. Area Multiplication

The items include word and number problems on multiplication, the two aspects of division and division with a remainder. No equipment is required for task groups 1 and 2 other than the cards on which problems are written. The cards can be introduced by stating, '*Here is a problem for you to solve.*'

The assessor then reads the problem '*Six children have five marbles each. How many marbles altogether?*'

TASK GROUP 1: Tasks presented verbally without Visible or Screened Items

---

(a) **Multiplication**
   Six children have five marbles each. How many marbles altogether?

The objective is to see if the child can count in multiples by using knowledge of abstract composite units. That is they are simultaneously aware of both the composite and unitary aspects of 'five' for example. Some children may use repeated addition which is equivalent to using the composite unit a specified number of times. In the case of the above problem counting in multiples would usually involve counting by fives but some children might count by sixes. For example, 6, 12, 18, 24 and then 25, 26, 27, 28, 29, 30 before answering 'Thirty'. A child using repeated addition would say, 'Six and six is 12 and 6 is 18 and 6 is 24 and 6 is 30'. Children will need to keep track of the counts of six and the total number of counts. This is likely to involve the use of fingers.

(b) **Quotition division**
   There are 12 bananas and each child is given two bananas each.
   How many children are there?

Children will tend to use strategies similar to the above strategies when solving the following tasks. This might involve using repeated subtraction to solve division items.

(c) **Partition division**
   If we shared eighteen apples among three children, how many apples would each child get?

(d) Quotition division with remainder
There are 17 flowers and each person is given 5 flowers. How many people are there and how many flowers left over?

(e) Partition division with remainder
If we shared 14 cookies equally among four children, how many cookies would each child get and how many would be left over?

TASK GROUP 2: Commutativity and Inverse Relationship

The purpose of Task Group 2 is to determine whether the child is at Level 5 of the model for multiplication and division.

Initially, the tasks are posed using open-ended questions. The child is encouraged to demonstrate additional methods for solving the task. The task items in this group may allow the child to exhibit the following knowledge:

Task (a) Composite units
Task (b) Commutative principle of multiplication
Task (c) Inverse relationship between multiplication and division
Task (d) Multiplication facts to derive division facts.

(a) *What does this say? What does it make you think of?*

or

What do you see in your mind when you read 9×7?

$\boxed{9 \times 7}$

How would you work this out?

Can you tell me another way to work it out?

(b) *What does this say?*

$\boxed{3 \times 7}$

What does this say?

$\boxed{7 \times 3}$

What can you tell me about these two problems?

$\boxed{3 \times 7}$ $\boxed{7 \times 3}$

(c) *What is the answer to this problem?*

$$8 \times 4$$

Can you use that to help you do this problem?

$$32 \div 4$$

(d) *If I tell you that eight times seven is 56 (show the card)*

$$8 \times 7 = 56$$

Can you use these numbers and signs (symbols) to make a division (division sentence)?

8	7	56	=	÷

Can you make another division sentence?

TASK GROUP 3: Area Multiplication

Finally, in this group we look to see if the child can solve a multiplication problem related to area. The item uses a 7 × 3 rectangle which has unit lengths indicated on the perimeter. The child is shown the unit square and the rectangle and asked, 'How many squares like this one would you need to cover the rectangle completely?' Note that only one unit square is provided. The verbal instruction can be accompanied by a sweep of the hand to indicate the surface of the rectangle. The assessor observes whether the child reasons in terms of a unit of area. Alternatively the child's reasoning might focus on the perimeter of the rectangle. After the child has attempted to solve the task, a copy of the grid is presented and the child is asked to draw what the pattern of squares would look like. This may provoke a revision of the child's thinking.

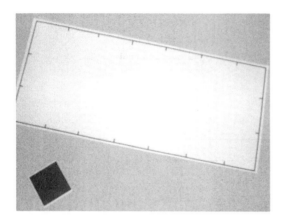

Area Multiplication

3. Area multiplication

Show the cardboard square unit and the 7×3 rectangle.

How many squares like this one would you need to cover the rectangle completely?

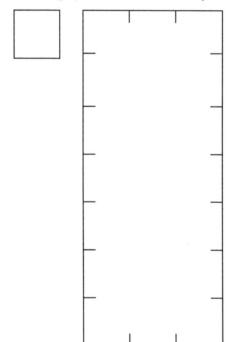

Provide the child with a copy of the grid and ask,

Can you draw what the squares would look like?

GUIDELINES FOR LEVELS ARISING FROM TASK GROUPS 1 AND 2

A child at Level 4, when solving, for example 5 × 3, is aware of 3 as an abstract composite unit but not aware of 5 as an abstract composite unit. Hence perhaps they would think of three and three and three and three and three (3 five times). They only have the grasp of one composite unit repeated so many times. The child at Level 5 can coordinate two composite units in the context of multiplication and division. They can also recall or quickly derive many of the basic facts of multiplication and division. They may use multiplication facts to derive division facts, may be aware of the commutative principle of multiplication, for example 4 × 3 = 3 × 4, and see the inverse relationship between multiplication and division.

CAN YOU IDENTIFY THE CHILD'S LEVEL OF EARLY MULTIPLICATION AND DIVISION KNOWLEDGE?

We have presented the five levels of the Model for Multiplication and Division. However, you may still need more exemplification and experience in coming to terms with the levels. This section is similar to Chapter 5 where the reader was challenged to apply the SEAL model to classify children on the basis of strategies used to solve numerical tasks. In this section, five scenarios describing children's solutions of multiplicative and divisional tasks are presented. Each of the five levels of early multiplication and division knowledge is exemplified by one scenario. The task for the reader is to identify the most appropriate level for each scenario. Solutions and explanations follow each scenario and identify the particular level for each. Included among the discussions are some important general points about children's early numerical strategies.

Practice Scenario 1: Charlotte and Anthony

In this scenario Anthony's first two tasks are to establish the numerosities of a screened 5 × 3 array and a partially screened 5 × 4 array. Following this Anthony is presented with a divisional task involving quotitive sharing.

C: (Places out a 5 × 3 array with one screen covering three rows and a second screen covering the other two rows. Briefly unscreens and then rescreens the three rows.) Under here there are three rows of three and under here there are two rows of three. How many rows are there altogether?

A: Five.

C: How many dots in each row?

A: Three.

C: How many dots are there altogether?

A: (After six seconds.) Fifteen!

C: How did you work that out?

A: I said, three, six, nine, and three more makes twelve and three more makes fifteen.

C: (Places out a 5 × 4 array on which twelve dots in a 4 × 3 array are screened.) I've covered part of this dot pattern. How many dots are there altogether?

A: (Looks at the array and moves his head from left to right and back five times in coordination with five subvocal counts.) There is – twenty!

C: How did you work that out?

A: I counted all the rows.

C: Tell me how you counted them.

A: (Points to each row of four in turn.) I went four, eight, twelve, umm –, sixteen, twenty!

C: There are twelve biscuits and the children are given two biscuits each. How many children would there be?

A: (Places his right hand on the desk and speaks softly.) Twelve biscuits –. (After 11 seconds.) There is –.

C: Pardon?

A: There is twelve biscuits (pauses) and we gotta share 'em.

C: Hmm, hmm. So that they get two biscuits each. How many children would there be?

A: (Looks ahead and then quickly moves his right hand twice along the desk.) One, two (subvocally. As before, quickly moves his hand twice), three, four (subvocally, and then moves his hand twice for a third time) five, six – (subvocally. Pauses for two seconds, and then makes four pairs of two movements on the desk in coordination with counting subvocally.) One, two –; three, four –; five, six; seven, eight –. (Pauses for one second, and then makes three pairs of two movements on the desk in coordination with counting subvocally.) One, two –; three, four –; five, six –. (Pauses briefly, and then taps the desk five times in a 2-2-1 pattern in coordination with counting subvocally.) One, two –; three, four –; five –. (Touches the desk three times.) Three children.

Answer to Practice Scenario 1: Charlotte and Anthony – Level 3

Anthony used skip counting and repeated addition to establish the numerosity of a screened 5×3 array and a partially screened 5×4 array. In explaining his solution of the task involving the 5×3 array he said 'three, six, nine, and three more makes twelve, and three more makes fifteen'. He similarly explained his solution of the task involving a 5×4 array. These solutions indicate that Anthony is at least at Level 3 because he solved tasks in which the items where not visible and in doing so counted equal groups by multiples. That the task involving quotitive sharing did not involve visible or screened items is significant in determining Anthony's level. Anthony did not use repeated subtraction or repeated addition when attempting to solve this task. Having done so would indicate that he could conceptualize 'two' as an abstract composite unit. He could regard 'two' simultaneously as two ones and one two. By way of contrast Anthony attempted to enact making groups of two using twelve imaginary biscuits. But he was unable to keep track of the number of groups and the number of biscuits remaining after he had enacted making three groups of two. In the absence of visible or screened items it was necessary for Anthony to attempt to enact making equal groups of two from twelve. Because 'two' was not an abstract composite unit for Anthony and because he could count in multiples to solve tasks involving equal groups, he is judged to be at Level 3: Figurative Composite Grouping.

Practice Scenario 2: Amanda and Joshua

In this scenario Joshua's first task is to produce the number word sequence of multiples of three, his second task is to establish the numerosity of a 5×3 array, and his third is to establish the numerosity of a 5×4 array. On the fourth task he is asked to count the 5×4 array by counting the rows of five rather than the rows of four.

A: Count by threes.

J: Three, six, (after four seconds) nine, (after three seconds) twelve, (after two seconds) fifteen, (after four seconds) fifteen.

A: Okay stop. Thank you. (Places out five rows of three counters arranged in a 5 × 3 array.) Can you count those now?

J: (Places a finger on each counter in the first row and moves the counters.) Three, (similarly moves the second row) six, (moves the next three rows in coordination with saying the number words) nine, twelve, fifteen.

A: (Places out a 5 × 4 array of dots.) How many dots are there altogether?

J: Four, and four makes eight, nine, ten, eleven, twelve, thirteen.

A: Can you count the rows in fives the other way (indicates appropriately)?

J: (Places hand on row of five.) That's five, ten, fifteen, (pauses briefly) sixteen, seventeen, eighteen, nineteen, twenty.

Answer to Practice Scenario 2: Amanda and Joshua – Level 2

Joshua counted a 5 × 3 array of counters by moving each row of three in coordination with saying the multiples of three. After unsuccessfully attempting to count a 5 × 4 array by fours he counted the array by fives to fifteen and continued by ones to count the fourth row of five. Because he could use multiples of three or five to count visible collections, Joshua is judged to be at Level 2: Perceptual Counting in Multiples. Joshua's strategies differ from Anthony's (Scenario 1) because they involved counting visible collections by multiples, whereas Anthony's strategies involved counting screened collections by multiples.

Practice Scenario 3: Steven and Aaron

In this scenario Aaron is presented with two tasks, each of which involves establishing the numerosity of an array (5 × 3 and 5 × 4). Following this he is presented with a divisional task involving quotitive sharing and a multiplicative task.

S: (Places out a 5 × 3 array with one screen covering three rows and a second screen covering the other two rows. Briefly unscreens and then rescreens the three rows.) Under here there are three rows of three and under here there are two rows of three. How many dots are there altogether?

A: (After five seconds.) Fifteen!

S: How did you work that out?

A: Because you said there were three rows down the bottom and there's two rows at the top. And that makes five. And you do five times three.

S: (Places out a 5 × 4 array on which twelve dots in a 4 × 3 array are screened.) Now this time, we've covered part of that pattern of dots. Can you tell me how many dots on that whole page?

A: (Looks at the array and counts subvocally.) One, two, three, four; one, two, three, four, five. (Looks up and answers after one second.) Twenty!

S: How did you know that?

A: Because I counted four up top and five along the side.

S: And how did that help?

A: Umm –, well you're –, five times four equals twenty.

S: Twelve cakes were shared among some children so that they got four each. How many children were there.

A: (After two seconds.) Three!

S: How did you get that answer?

A: Because four times three equals twelve.
S: Six children have five marbles each. How many marbles altogether?
A: (Immediately.) Six fives are thirty. Thirty.
S: Can you tell me how you got thirty?
A: I just timesed six by five. Six fives are thirty.

Answer to Practice Scenario 3: Steven and Aaron – Level 5

Aaron used automatized multiplication facts to solve two multiplicative tasks. The first of these involved a screened 5 × 3 array and the second involved a partially screened 5 × 4 array. Aaron also used automatized multiplication facts to solve a divisional and a multiplicative task. These tasks did not involve visible or screened items. In the case of the two tasks involving arrays, Aaron's strategies can be contrasted with Anthony's because Anthony counted in multiples whereas Aaron used automatized facts. Because of his prevalent use of automatized facts to solve tasks, Aaron is judged to be at Level 5: Known Multiplication and Division Facts.

Practice Scenario 4: Jeremy and Chantelle

In the this scenario Chantelle's first task is to produce the number word sequence of multiples of three and her second task is to establish the numerosity of a 5 × 3 array of counters.

J: Can you count by threes for me? I'll tell you when to stop.
C: (Immediately.) Three –. (Looks ahead. After four seconds.) Seven. (Looks at Jeremy, smiles and shakes her head.)
J: Would you like to start again?
C: (Immediately.) Three, six, (after three seconds) twelve.
J: (After six seconds.) You can stop there.
J: I'm going to put out some counters now. (Places out five rows of three counters arranged in a 5 × 3 array.) They're arranged in threes aren't they? Could you show me how you'd count those counters by threes? You can move them if you would like to.
C: (Counts subvocally from one to three in coordination with pointing to each counter in the first row in turn. Places a finger on each counter in the first row and moves them a small distance.) Three. (Counts subvocally from four to six in coordination with pointing to each counter in the second row in turn. Then moves the second row a small distance.) Six. (Similarly counts the counters in the third row subvocally and then moves them). Nine. (Similarly with the fourth and fifth rows.) Twelve, fifteen.

Answer to Practice Scenario 4: Jeremy and Chantelle – Level 1

Chantelle was not able to produce the number word sequence of multiples of three. In the task which involved establishing the numerosity of a 5 × 3 array of counters she appeared to produce the number word sequence of multiples of three up to fifteen in coordination with moving successive rows of three counters. Nevertheless, in doing this she subvocally counted each row by ones prior to uttering the appropriate multiple of three, for example she said 'seven, eight, nine' subvocally and then said aloud, 'nine'. This counting did not constitute counting by threes. Her inability to produce the number word sequence of multiples of threes on the first task provides a further indication that she could not count in multiples. Thus Chantelle is judged to be at Level

1: Initial Grouping. Chantelle's strategies differ from Joshua's (Practice Scenario 2) because they involve counting visible collections of equal groups by ones rather than counting by multiples as was the case with Joshua's strategies.

Practice Scenario 5: Meghan and Orana

In this scenario Orana's first task is to establish the numerosity of a screened 5 × 3 array. Her second task is to establish the numerosity of the screened 5 × 3 array after Meghan has turned it through 90 degrees (approximately). Her third task is a multiplicative task (4 × 3), her fourth is a divisional task involving quotitive sharing, and her fifth is a divisional task involving partitive sharing.

M: (Briefly displays and then screens a 5 × 3 array of dots.) How many dots are there in each row?

O: Five.

M: (Displays the array and points to a row of three dots.) This is a row here.

O: Oh. Three!

M: Three in each row. How many rows are there?

O: (After three seconds.) Five!

M: (Screens the array.) How many dots are there altogether?

O: (Looks at the screen and counts subvocally. After six seconds.) Fifteen!

M: How did you know that?

O: Because three and three makes six (waves her hand over the first two rows of the array), and another three makes (pauses for two seconds) nine, and another three makes umm twelve, and then another three makes fifteen!

M: Thank you! (Unscreens the array and rotates it through 90 degrees.) If I was to turn them around that way how many dots now?

O: (Immediately.) Umm, fifteen!

M: How did you know that?

O: Because when you turn it around there was fifteen and then when you turn it this way there's fifteen.

M: Four children have three pencils each. How many pencils altogether?

O: (After 3 seconds.) Twelve!

M: How did you work that out?

O: I was counting by – (pauses briefly) threes?

M: Hmm, hmm.

O: And it made twelve.

M: Orana there are twelve biscuits and children were given two biscuits each. How many children would there be?

O: Umm, two –, two, four, six, eight, ten, twelve. Six.

M: How did you know that?

O: Because two plus two plus two plus two plus two plus two equals twelve.

M: Good thinking. If we shared eighteen lollies among three children, how many would each child get?

O: (Looks to her left. After five seconds.) Six!

M: And what did you do to work that one out?

O: I was counting by sixes first.

Answer to Practice Scenario 5: Meghan and Orana – Level 4

Orana used repeated addition of three in explaining how she counted a 5 × 3 array. In similar vein, she said 'I was counting by – threes' to explain how she solved a multiplicative task involving three groups of four pencils and she counted by twos to twelve to solve a division task involving quotitive sharing. Her solution to the partitive sharing task (18 shared among 3) was relatively sophisticated because it seemed to involve using six as an estimation. Knowing that the 5 × 3 array contained the same number of dots after it was rotated as before (that is, 15) indicates she could conserve quantity rather than that she had a generalized knowledge of the commutative principle of multiplication. For these reasons Orana is judged to be at Level 4: Repeated Abstract Composite Grouping. Her solution of the task involving a 5 × 3 array can be contrasted with Aaron's (Practice Scenario 3) because Aaron used an automatized fact (5 × 3 = 15), whereas Orana used repeated addition of three. Anthony (Scenario 1) solved this task using a strategy similar to that used by Orana, that is, by counting in multiples of three to nine and then adding three twice to obtain fifteen. One can conclude that a task involving counting how many counters in all, in an array, that is, a multiplicative array task, is unlikely to discriminate between children at Level 3 and those at Level 4, whereas a divisional array task, that is, where the number of items in all and the number of items in each row is specified, might serve this purpose. Finally, Orana's solution of the divisional task involving quotitive sharing – 'there are twelve biscuits and the children are given two each, and so on' – can be contrasted with Anthony's (Practice Scenario 1). In this task Orana counted by twos whereas Anthony attempted to enact arranging twelve into groups of two. Orana could regard 'two' as a unit (that is, one 'two'), in other words, as an abstract composite unit that could be counted. For Anthony 'two' was a numerical composite (that is, two 'ones') that resulted when he enacted making successive groups of two.

9

Recording, Coding and Analyzing the Assessment Interview Schedules

Summary

This chapter is concerned with maximizing the use of video recording in the assessment interviews. Technical advice is presented to achieve high-quality recording and a coding system is set out to aid analysis and reporting. The chapter also refers to research on teachers' experience of video recording and the impact it has on their understanding of children's difficulties, their classroom organization and practice, and their role in developing numeracy in their school community.

Video recording of children solving number tasks was important in the development of the model of the Stages of Early Arithmetical Learning (Steffe, 1992a; Steffe and Cobb, 1988; Steffe et al., 1983) and in the development of other models of the Learning Framework in Number (Wright, 1989; 1991b). The use of video recording is an established aspect of assessment and teaching in the Mathematics Recovery Programme. In this chapter we set out why video recording is important. The completed assessment is used to develop a detailed report leading to the formation of a teaching plan for the child.

WHY USE VIDEO RECORDING?

The use of video recording has considerable advantages for the interviewer or teacher. These can be summed under five headings:

1. Data gathering
2. Analysis
3. Reflection
4. Communication
5. Accreditation.

Data Gathering

Video recording enables detailed observation of the child's responses to assessment tasks. There is no need for the interviewer to write notes during the interview. Total attention can be given to the child's responses to tasks. The interviewer can then decide to re-pose tasks, revisit items, and seek confirmation for a conjecture relating to the child's strategy or probe to ascertain the child's thinking.

Analysis

The recording can be viewed and rewound several times to allow a decision to be made regarding a child's response. Colleagues can view the tape to reach agreement on the behaviors, actions and utterances of the child and agree a stage or level of performance.

Reflection

Viewing tapes in a group is a most valuable activity in the training period and follow-up sessions. Colleagues can reflect on what has passed during the interview and offer interpretations of the child's reasoning and explanations.

Communication

Video recording can provide a powerful tool for communication with colleagues, parents and other professionals. Tapes have been used to form libraries of clips, which can be used for further dissemination or training. Developments in equipment mean that digital recordings can be reproduced and annotated in a variety of formats.

Accreditation

A trainee has the opportunity to become an accredited teacher or leader in the Mathematics Recovery Programme. The assignments require that tapes are submitted to demonstrate competence and expertise in the administration, analysis and reporting across a range of children's abilities.

GUIDELINES FOR VIDEOTAPING ASSESSMENT INTERVIEWS

It is common for teachers initially to be somewhat daunted by the prospect of videotaping their assessment interviews. At the same time the vast majority of teachers quickly gain a level of expertise and the process of videotaping assessment interviews becomes very routine. No doubt this process is helped by the fact that, after conducting and reviewing a series of interviews, teachers begin to appreciate the power of the videotaping process for learning about children's early numerical knowledge and strategies. Videotaping of the assessment interview does not require the presence of an additional person but during the training period it is helpful for trainees to work in groups. In this way one trainee can administer the tasks, one can observe the child and the interviewer, while the third monitors the camera operation. If only the interviewer and the child are present the use of digital video cameras with LCD screens that rotate through 180 degrees will allow for monitoring the image and camera operation.

Specific guidelines for videotaping assessment interviews are now presented under the following four subheadings: interview room and camera setup; camera operation; using and labeling videotapes; and conducting the interview.

Interview Room and Camera Setup

Schools are busy places and often space is at a premium. Therefore, it is not possible to legislate for specific rooms to be used. However, certain conditions are necessary. These relate to power, lighting, acoustics and space.

▶ Check beforehand that a power supply is available and conveniently located. Most cameras have a battery-operation feature that can be used if necessary.

▶ The camera should be pointed away from any outside light source such as windows and glass doors.

▶ Position the furniture and camera away from devices such as air-conditioners or lights to minimize interference.

▶ Turn off heating and air-conditioning fans or vents during the recording process, if possible.

▶ Obtaining high-quality sound recording is very important. The interviewer should attempt to ensure that the child's voice is audible and is recorded as clearly as possible.

▶ If possible, use an external microphone with the video camera, and a unidirectional or clip-on microphone for the child.

▶ Place a notice on the door to indicate recording is in progress.

▶ The teacher and child should be seated on the same side of the table and the camera should be placed to face the teacher and child.

▶ Angle the seating so the child and interviewer can see one another.

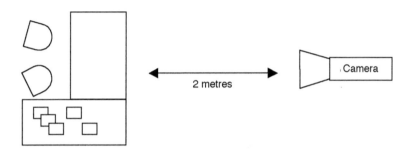

Figure 9.1 Optimum conditions for video recording

▶ Mount the camera on a tripod and be sure to remove the lens cap.

▶ A quick-release tripod is preferable.

▶ Position the camera approximately 2 metres from the table.

▶ Raise the camera to look down on the subjects and the tabletop.

▶ Space should be sufficient to allow both the teacher and the child to be included in the video frame.

▶ Use a wide-angle setting (that is, the W button) to locate the camera as closely as possible to the interview table.

▶ Adjust the zoom lens facility (that is, W and T buttons) so that the video picture includes the child, the teacher and the tabletop on which the tasks are presented.

▶ Ensure that a sufficient quantity of videotapes is available.

Camera Operation

▶ Set the date and time settings so that these appear on the video recording. In the case of cameras that do not show date and time displays together, put the time display on and place a sign on the interview table indicating the date.

▶ Ensure that you are familiar with the ON/OFF and STANDBY features of the camera. Some cameras automatically switch to a STANDBY setting during periods when they are not being used.

▶ Press the RECORD button prior to commencing the interview. The RECORD button is usually a red button and is often located between the W and T buttons on the right-hand side of the camera. When the RECORD button is activated a symbol, for example, 'rec', should appear on the recording screen.

▶ Some cameras may be supplied with a remote control device that enables you to switch the recording function on and off. Use of such devices is not particularly important in recording the interview.

Digital and Emerging Technology

▶ New technology continues to emerge, making the use of digital camcorders most appropriate. The digital formats are easily loaded onto most players and computers and make the highlighting of notable episodes easy for the novice. Cables and directions for this transfer and viewing are usually included with the camcorder.

▶ When utilizing the digital camcorder normal recording speed is SP and should be used to make the footage more easily transferred to DVDs or VHS tapes.

▶ Use the backlight feature when recording a subject that is darker than the surrounding scene.

▶ When using a digital camcorder it is easy to review the footage through the LCD panel. Also, digital camcorders have built-in adapters to block out surrounding interfering noises.

Using and Labeling Videotapes

▶ It is helpful to write the school name and date on the outside label and, on the inside label, the date of the interview(s), each child's name and the commencement time of the interview.

▶ Immediate labeling of videotapes on completion of filming is recommended.

▶ The assessment interviews for several children may be recorded on one videotape. Each child should be clearly identifiable via the list of names and times on the inside label.

▶ Typically, teachers commence the interview session by stating or asking the child's name and other particulars such as class teacher's name, school name and the child's birth date. This is a useful technique because it helps to ensure the accuracy of this kind of information.

Conducting the Interview

▶ Ensure you have parental or guardian permission to record the child.

▶ Prior to commencing the assessment interview, complete the required information at the top of the Assessment Interview Schedule. Do not write on the Assessment Interview Schedule when conducting the interview.

The Assessment Interview Script and Materials

▶ Scripts for the six assessment interview schedules and lists of materials can be found in the Appendices.

CODING THE ASSESSMENT INTERVIEW SCHEDULE

Analysis of the six Mathematics Recovery assessment interview schedules involves viewing the videotape of the assessment in conjunction with annotating the Assessment Interview Schedule. The analyzer works from the Assessment Interview Schedule, and each Task Group is analyzed in turn, using the coding system. In this way the completed Assessment Interview Schedule constitutes a written summary of the assessment interview. The final phase of analysis involves determining the child's stage and levels in terms of the models in the four strands of the Learning Framework in Number.

A coding system is used to derive the maximum information from a child's performance in the assessment interview. The codes indicate how the child responded as well as the answers given. The codes can also indicate how the interview was conducted. The codes are illustrated in Table 9.1.

Table 9.1 The Mathematics Recovery coding schedule

✓	correct
✓✓	correct and with certitude
??	needs time to think
?✓	needs some time, then correct
✗✓	initially incorrect, then correct
SC	child self-corrects
TTA	'Try that again'
∧	omission of a number in FNWS or BNWS
IDK	child says 'I don't know'
'..'	indicates the words used
Rev	assessor revisits an item
Red	Teacher redirects or teacher prompt
C.from 1	child counts from one
CO	child counts on
CDF	child counts down from
CDT	child counts down to

The code sheet is self-explanatory but it may be useful to exemplify certain aspects. For example, the interviewer wants to know not only the answer the child gives, but also the child's level of certitude. Correct answers are ticked but two ticks can be given indicating a swift, confident response. If an error is made it is advisable to write down the child's response. In this way the interviewer can see the incorrect response but we may also be able to detect patterns among the incorrect responses. For example, it is common in the Numeral Identification tasks for children to reverse responses, saying 'fifty-one' for 15 and 'thirty-one' for 13. It is also desirable to record omissions, or repetitions, in the utterance of number sequences.

It is interesting to note how much thinking time the child required before producing an answer. A question mark can be used for thinking time or multiple question marks for longer periods. Sometimes children answer incorrectly and then check themselves before giving a correct response. Where the child has corrected an answer without any prompting from the interviewer we use the code 'SC'. Often children say 'I don't know' and 'IDK' is recorded.

We want to give the children every opportunity to respond and questions can be restated and rephrased. A useful strategy is to note errors and where there is evidence that this may be an oversight or slip the question can be revisited at the end of a task group. The code used is 'Rev'. When a child's answer is incorrect it is advisable to let them have another attempt. This is particularly useful when they may be just one away from a correct answer. Since this may be due to inaccurate counting it is helpful to re-pose the task. Where the child has understood the question but given an incorrect response 'TTA' can be used, meaning would you like to try that one again?

It is advisable, particularly in the additive and subtractive tasks in Assessment 1.1, and later in the non-count-by-one task items in Assessment 1.2, to record the explanations the child offers. Indications of finger movements and specific non-verbal gestures often reveal the strategies a child is using and these should be noted. If a strategy is detected, then it is helpful to record this to serve as a reminder when analyzing and determining the final Stage of Early Arithmetical Learning and levels. For example, you may code the child's 'count-on' (CO) or 'count-down-from' (CDF) strategy.

Comprehensive application of coding will allow:

▶   the strengths and weaknesses of a child to be detected;
▶   the identification of patterns of response;
▶   the correct identification and allocation of levels and stages; and
▶   an accurate, concise description of the child's ability.

The application of coding will also allow the interviewer to reflect on his or her own performance in administering the task items. For example, one might check whether certain items could have been reposed or revisited. The ability to rewind the tape and watch the same episode again, especially with colleagues, enables accurate judgments to be made.

Determining the Child's Stage and Levels

Determining the child's stage or level on each of the six models is an important outcome of the assessment. The stage and levels constitute a succinct summary of the extent of the child's early number knowledge. Whereas the video recording gave very rich data and the coding produced a very comprehensive overview of the performance, the child's overall result can be summarized by a brief numerical statement indicating first a stage on SEAL and then levels in the other models. For example, the result for a typical Stage 2, Figurative child would be condensed to 2, 4, 3, 2, 0, 1. This would be indicated as in Table 9.2.

Table 9.2 The profile of a typical Figurative Child (Stage 2)

Model	Stage/level
Stage of Early Arithmetical Learning	2
Forward Number Word Sequences	4
Backward Number Word Sequences	3
Numeral Identification	2
Tens and Ones	0
Multiplication and Division	1

Learning to identify stages and levels, and skills in video recording and transfer, have allowed many trainees to compile video libraries. The models of the LFIN can be used to generate video-excerpt headings of strong, average and weak performances. Video excerpts can also highlight non-standard responses to task items and, therefore, research data can be compiled which show the range of children's responses and patterns within the responses.

DEVELOPING UNDERSTANDING THROUGH THE USE OF VIDEO RECORDING

Recent research in Scotland has shown how the use of the video recording when applying Mathematics Recovery Assessment schedules has been very important in helping teachers understand children's conceptual difficulties (Munn, 2005). Teacher thinking changes when they understand the reasons for children's mistakes. It is important that teachers can map this 'reason why' onto their understanding of number development. Munn found that the best and quickest way for teachers to develop a clear understanding of children's conceptual development is for them to analyze and discuss children's responses to verbally presented tasks. Initially, some teachers can feel very awkward and embarrassed about videotaping themselves. This decreases after a time, and mentors working with teachers have found that teachers' reactions to videotape and to implementation based on videotaped assessment go through three distinct stages.

In the first stage, the primary concern is with the self. Teachers worry about how to manage the assessments, and about the resources needed to produce the tapes. In the second stage, teachers focus on the tasks that they are designing for the children. In this stage, they are preoccupied with resourcing and arranging the tasks for their class. In the third stage, the teachers are wholly engaged with the impact on the children, and their focus has shifted from self to other (the other being, in this case, the child). In this final stage, teachers are focussed on the children's thinking, and are close observers of the task from the child's viewpoint. They find it relatively easy to note the children's level of understanding, and changes in these levels. During the time that teachers build up specific information of the development of children's knowledge of number, they develop the habit of reflecting critically on the children's interview responses and they become preoccupied with the way children understand and benefit from specific tasks.

Hird (2004) reports how teachers change their teaching style as a result of learning how to assess children. They describe how they present the children with more intensive and challenging tasks. They use open-ended questions initially to encourage responses. The teachers target their questions more purposefully and allow time for the children to think and respond. They also create a supportive climate in which it is acceptable to offer an answer. They describe how they use knowledge of the Stages of Early Arithmetical Learning to group the children and differentiate instruction. Through informed differentiation they are able to match the activities specifically to the children's needs.

Teachers have disseminated their training within their schools and use teacher assistants more specifically to assist with instruction involving practical and oral activities. Greater emphasis is put on discussion of tasks with a matching emphasis on vocabulary and developing children's confidence to express themselves and to listen to others. Most importantly, the teachers develop confidence to speak about early numeracy and to advise colleagues and parents.

In the final chapter we will show how the teaching programme in Mathematics Recovery is derived from the six assessment schedules and the Learning Framework in Number.

10
Linking the Assessment to Teaching

Summary

In this chapter we return to the three children who were having difficulty and show how a teaching approach can be made by linking the Learning Framework in Number to an Instructional Framework. The interrelationship of the frameworks is demonstrated and instructional phases, strands, key topics, procedures and settings outlined. The procedures and topics should not be seen in isolation. Rather we want the reader to note how the Key Topics in the Number Words and Numerals, Counting and Grouping Strands are interrelated. The distinctive approach to teaching in the Mathematics Recovery Programme is outlined and the chapter concludes with a summary of the nine guiding principles.

INTRODUCTION

In the previous chapter we showed how the child's strategies and number knowledge could be profiled using models of aspects of number knowledge. In Chapter 1 we introduced three children who were experiencing difficulties in early numeracy and at risk of falling behind their peers. Let us now return to Judy, Denise and Michael and consider how their teachers used the results of the assessment to plan the teaching. First, let us remind ourselves of their difficulties. If we generalize across the three cases we can see that they were operating at the Perceptual Stage. Their profile probably could be expressed as in Table 10.1.

Table 10.1 The profile of a typical Perceptual Child (Stage 1)

Model	Stage/level
Stage of Early Arithmetical Learning	1
Forward Number Word Sequences	3
Backward Number Word Sequences	1
Numeral Identification	1
Tens and Ones	0
Multiplication and Division	0

WHAT DOES THE CHILD PROFILE TELL US?

What does this mean and how can we use the information? First it tells us that the children are at the Perceptual Stage (Stage 1). When they completed Assessment Interview Schedule 1.1 they showed that they were able to count collections of counters in the range 13 to 18. However, they could not solve additive tasks involving two collections when either one or both collections were screened. In other words, they could count quite a large single collection, when it was visible, but had difficulty establishing the numerosity of two collections when one or both collections were covered, even when the numbers involved were less than 18.

Level 3 in forward number word sequences (FNWS) indicates that they had good facility with saying the sequence from 1 to 10 and beyond. Possibly they could say the sequence up to 29 though problems may be experienced with teens and crossing decade numbers. All had difficulty in saying the number word after (NWA) a given number word beyond 10, for example, after thirteen. The children were able to say the backward sequence from 10 to 1. However, they could not say the number word before a given number in the range 10 to 1. Some children need to say the sequence forward to find the number word before.

Level 1 in numeral identification shows that the children could recognize and identify numerals in the range 1 to 10 but had difficulty with numerals in the teens. For example, calling '12' twenty-one or reversing digits so '14' becomes 'forty-one'. No information is available for tens and ones and multiplication because these assessments would not be given to children at this level.

However, Assessment 2.1 would provide additional information about their number knowledge. This information would be summarized on the report sheet for 2.1. Typically, children with the above profile would be able to subitize in the range 1 to 4. By this we mean they could correctly ascribe number to irregular arrays when flashed for half a second. They may also have facile finger patterns for numbers in the range 1 to 5 and they could use finger patterns to solve additive tasks in cases were both the addends are in the range 1 to 5, for example, 4 + 3. This involves making a finger pattern for four on one hand, a finger pattern for three on the other hand, and then counting their fingers from one. We refer to this as 'counting from one three times'.

The children's number knowledge forms the basis for deciding the teaching objectives. The Learning Framework provides the overall focus and direction. We want the children to attain the next stage and this will be achieved by raising the levels of performance in FNWS, BNWS and numeral identification, and increased facility with spatial and finger patterns. So from a profile of 1 3 1 1 the target becomes 2 4 2 2. This in turn can be extended to 3 5 3 3 (Table 10.2). (Judy and Denise attained this profile and Michael exceeded it by reaching Stage 4.)

Table 10.2 Directionality and Focus provided by the Learning Framework

Model	Stage/level	Aim	Achievement
Stage of Early Arithmetical Learning	1	2	3*
Forward Number Word Sequences	3	4	5
Backward Number Word Sequences	1	2	3
Numeral Identification	1	2	3

Note: * at least Stage 3

In the case of FNWS, our goal is to consolidate the children's facility up to 10 and extend the range to 30 and beyond. In BNWS we want to advance facility in the range 1 to 10 and extend knowledge beyond 10. Knowledge of numerals can be consolidated up to 20 and the problems with the teens addressed. Finger patterns and spatial patterns will be strengthened for numbers beyond 5. The result will be that increased facility with the above will provide a basis for moving to Stage 2 where they will be able to use counting to solve additive tasks involving screened, or partially screened, collections and rows of counters where some are covered. However, in solving the problems they might still count from one.

Thus the Learning Framework has given us clear directions in which to take the children. We have been guided by the initial assessment and we know their strengths and weaknesses. We can plan instructional activities within their zones of potential development. The work will be challenging as we advance them to the next level of sophistication, but the tasks will be within their grasp with the help of the teacher. They will not get there by themselves nor should the teacher wait for developments. With good teaching they are likely to make appropriate progress. But how will we get there? This involves using another framework called the Instructional Framework for Early Number (**IFEN**), see Table 10.3.

Table 10.3 Instructional Framework for Early Number (IFEN)

Instructional Phase	Number Words and Numerals	Counting	Grouping
Phase 1 Emergent	▶ FNWS 1 to 20 ▶ BNWS 1 to 10 ▶ Numerals 1 to 10	▶ Count involving visible items in collections and in rows ▶ Temporal sequences and temporal patterns	▶ Early spatial patterns ▶ Early finger patterns
Phase 2 Perceptual	▶ FNWS 1 to 30 ▶ BNWS 1 to 30 ▶ Numerals 1 to 20	▶ Counting involving screened items in collections and rows	▶ Developing spatial patterns ▶ Developing finger patterns ▶ Equal groups and sharing
Phase 3 Figurative	▶ FNWS 1 to 100 ▶ BNWS 1 to 100 ▶ Numerals 1 to 100	▶ Counting-on and counting-back to solve additive and subtractive tasks	▶ Combining and partitioning using 5 and 10 ▶ Combining and partitioning in range 1–10 ▶ Early multiplication and division
Phase 4 Counting-on and Counting-back	▶ NWSs by 2, 10s, 5s, 3s, and 4s in the range 1–100 ▶ Numerals 1 to 1000	▶ Incrementing by 10s and 1s	▶ Adding and subtracting to and from decade numbers ▶ Adding and subtracting to 20 using 5 and 10 ▶ Developing multiplication and division
Phase 5 Facile	▶ NWSs by 10s on and off the decade ▶ NWSs by 100s on and off the 100 and on and off the decade	▶ Two-digit addition and subtraction through counting	▶ Two-digit addition and subtraction involving collections ▶ Non-canonical forms of two- and three-digit numbers ▶ Higher decade addition and subtraction ▶ Advanced multiplication and division

AN INSTRUCTIONAL FRAMEWORK FOR EARLY NUMBER (IFEN)

The Instructional Framework can be visualized as a series of files which can be seen as a typical early number curriculum. It is structured into Phases, Strands, Key Teaching Topics and Procedures, and these are explained below (see Figure 10.1).

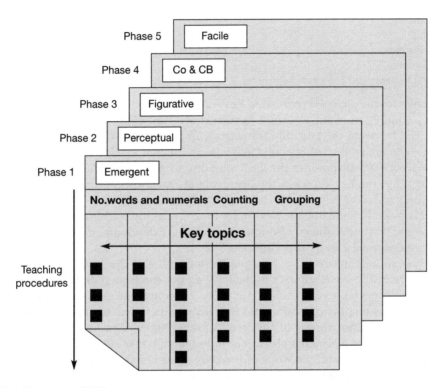

Figure 10.1 The phases of IFEN

Phases

The Instructional Framework is organized into five phases of early number instruction which refer to the Stages of Early Arithmetical Learning. For example, the first or Emergent Phase concerns moving a child from Emergent (Stage 0) to Perceptual (Stage 1). The IFEN is also organized into three strands: (a) number words and numerals, (b) counting and (c) grouping.

Strands

The three strands of the Instructional Framework are intended to be broad and inclusive of specific early number topics. Thus the IFEN is intended to be inclusive of topics such as addition, subtraction, multiplication, division and tens and ones knowledge. The IFEN also includes topics such as combinations to 10, knowing the basic facts (that is, number bonds), learning to derive facts from known facts, and mental strategies for two-digit addition and subtraction. Our intention is that these three strands should come close to encompassing a typical early number curriculum.

Key Topics

The three strands of the Instructional Framework are further subdivided into a progression of key teaching topics. For the sake of brevity these are referred to as Key Topics. The six Key Topics for the Emergent Phase are:

1. Number Word Sequences
2. Numerals
3. Counting
4. Spatial Patterns
5. Finger Patterns
6. Temporal Patterns and Temporal Sequences.

The key topics for the phases Perceptual to Facile are the same with the exception that Key Topic Six is 'Early Multiplication and Division'. As you can see, the Key Topics can be linked to particular stages and levels on the Learning Framework, in the sense that key topics are considered appropriate exemplars or starting points for teaching children at relevant stages or levels. Many of the Key Topics which appear in the IFEN arise directly from a specific strand of the Learning Framework. Thus the Key Topics in the Instructional Framework focusing on the teaching of number words and numerals arise directly from the Number Words and Numerals Strand of the Learning Framework. Similarly, the Key Topics focusing on the teaching of multiplication and division in the IFEN arise directly from the model of the development of multiplication and division knowledge presented in the Grouping Strand.

Much corresponds between the Learning Framework and the Instructional Framework. Nevertheless several of the Key Topics in the IFEN do not correspond directly with an aspect of the LFIN. This occurs for several reasons. First, Key Topics in some cases are more integrative of content in the early number curriculum precisely because they focus on teaching whereas the the LFIN focuses on distinct aspects of children's number knowledge. Second, some of the Key Topics (in Phases 4 and 5, for example) can be linked to aspects of children's number knowledge which are, in a sense beyond the scope of the LFIN. Thus Key Topics in Phases 4 and 5 which involve adding or subtracting two- and three-digit numbers and related Key Topics which link to notions of place value (for example, non-canonical forms of two- and three-digit numbers) are not strongly linked to aspects of the LFIN.

Procedures

The teaching activities within the key topics are referred to as instructional procedures. They provide exemplars of teaching which are closely attuned to a stage or level. A teaching procedure includes an objective, an activity, materials and teacher dialogue. A particular feature of teaching procedures in the Instructional Framework is that notes are provided to help the teacher to determine an appropriate focus and points of emphasis, together with descriptions of likely child responses. In this way the teacher is prepared for possible adaptations and extension work.

There can be several procedures within a Key Topic. For instance, Key Topic – Spatial Patterns at the Perceptual Phase contains the following procedures:

- ▶ Partitioning Visible patterns to 6
- ▶ Partitioning Flashed patterns to 6
- ▶ Partitioning Visible patterns to 10
- ▶ Partitioning Flashed patterns to 10

▶ Combining Patterns using 4-grids
▶ Combining Patterns using 6, 8, 10-grids.

SETTINGS

Each of the above can be presented to the child using a range of settings. Settings are devices and materials which are used to pose tasks to the child. Figure 10.2 gives an example of the relationships between Phases, Strands, Key Topics, Procedures and Settings. It shows how one procedure, Partitioning Flashed Patterns to 10, is presented through using a 6-grid with heart symbols. The teacher would ask the child what they had seen. More specific questions could be used, such as 'How many hearts on the top row? How many on the bottom row? How many altogether? How many squares with no hearts?' Changing the orientation of the flashed card produces a different setting for the same task. Flashing patterns is part of the Key Topic – Spatial Patterns, which is in the Grouping Strand of IFEN for the Perceptual child.

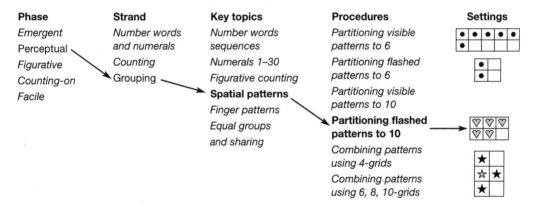

Figure 10.2 Linking a teaching activity for the Perceptual Child to the phases of IFEN

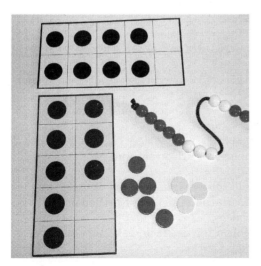

Thirty-two procedures are given for the six key topics at the Perceptual Stage. For a full discussion of the Instructional Framework see Wright et al. (2002) *Teaching Number: Advancing Children's Skills and Strategies.*

INTEGRATION OF KEY TOPICS

Before leaving the discussion on Key Topics it is important to set out a distinctive aspect of teaching in the Mathematics Recovery Programme. We refer to the integration of the Key Topics within single lessons. By this we mean that teaching activities are provided from four, five or even six Key Topics within close association. For example, in a 30-minute lesson the teacher may be working towards addition tasks with two collections, the first of which is covered with numbers in the range beyond 10, for example, 7 + 4. The lesson could commence with saying short, FNWSs commencing at 5, then 6, 7, 8, and so on. This could be followed by the teacher saying one number and the child saying the next two, three or four number words. For example, Five … 6, 7, 8; … Nine 10, 11, 12; Thirteen … 14, 15, 16; and so on. The activity could shade to saying the number word after a number or even saying two or three numbers after. Similarly activities could involve saying the number word before, two before, or even three before. A **numeral track**, or covered number line, would enable the same activities to be done in a different setting. Activities involving flashing spatial patterns using a filled Ten Frame and a partially filled Ten Frame with 2, 3, 4, or 5 dots could be used with the child being asked, 'How many altogether?' The Figurative Counting Key Topic involves a variety of settings such as seven animals in one barn and four animals in the field; seven bees in the hive and four flying around; seven letters in the post box and four more being posted, and so on. The key element of the activity is that the first collection is briefly displayed and then screened.

GUIDING PRINCIPLES IN MATHEMATICS RECOVERY TEACHING

The teaching sessions, whether for an individual, group or class, afford an opportunity to provide intensive, high-quality teaching. In order to do this the teacher must have a clear model of the children's current knowledge and strategies in early number, and a clear idea of the progress in learning that is a reasonable goal for them. The origins of Mathematics Recovery teaching lie in large part in research projects which involved longitudinal observation and study of children's developing strategies and learning as they occurred in interactive teaching sessions.

We conclude this chapter on how Judy, Denise and Michael were able to make such good progress by summarizing the teaching approach in the following set of nine guiding principles of Mathematics Recovery teaching.

1. The teaching approach is enquiry-based, that is, problem-based. Children are routinely engaged in thinking hard to solve numerical problems which for them, are quite challenging.
2. Teaching is informed by an initial, comprehensive assessment and ongoing assessment through teaching. The latter refers to the teacher's informed understanding of the child's current knowledge and problem-solving strategies, and continual revision of this understanding.
3. Teaching is focused just beyond the 'cutting-edge' of the child's current knowledge.
4. Teachers exercise their professional judgment in selecting from a bank of teaching procedures, each of which involves particular instructional settings and tasks, and varying this selection on the basis of ongoing observations.
5. The teacher understands children's numerical strategies and deliberately engenders the development of more sophisticated strategies.
6. Teaching involves intensive, ongoing observation by the teacher and continual micro-adjusting or fine-tuning of teaching on the basis of her or his observation.
7. Teaching supports and builds on the child's intuitive, verbally based strategies and these are used as a basis for the development of written forms of arithmetic which accord with the child's verbally based strategies.
8. The teacher provides the child with sufficient time to solve a given problem. Consequently, the child is frequently engaged in episodes which involve sustained thinking, reflection on her or his thinking and reflecting on the results of her or his thinking.
9. Children gain intrinsic satisfaction from their problem-solving, their realization that they are making progress, and from the verification methods they develop.

Appendix 1

The Mathematics Recovery Programme

Assessment Interview Schedule 1.1
Early Arithmetical Strategies
and Numerical Knowledge

Child's name: ....

DoB: ....   Age: .... years ....months

Interviewer's name: ....

Date of interview: ....

Teacher/class: ....

	SEAL	FNWS	No. Id.	BNWS
Stage/level				

1 Forward Number Word Sequence

*Start counting from ** and I'll tell you when to stop.*

(a) 1 (to 32)	(b) 48 (to 61)
(c) 76 (to 84)	(d) 93 (to 112)

2 Number Word After

*Say the word that comes straight after ***. Example: Say the word that comes straight after one.*

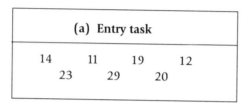

(a) Entry task

14   11   19   12

23   29   20

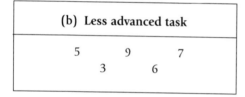

(b) Less advanced task

5   9   7

3   6

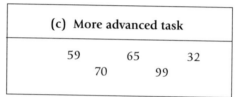

(c) More advanced task

59   65   32

70   99

3 Numeral Identification

Show each card in turn, saying, *What number is this?*

(a) Entry task

10   15   47   13   21

80   12   17   99   20   66

(b) Less advanced task

8   3   5   7   9

6   2   4   1

(c) More advanced task

100   123   206

341   820

4 Numeral Recognition

Arrange the cards from 1 to 10 randomly. Which number is ... ?

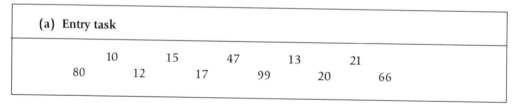

6   4   7   9   8

5 Backward Number Word Sequence

Example: *Count backwards from 3. Three, two, one.*

*Now count backwards from ** and keep going until I say stop.*

(a) 10 (down to 1)	(b) 15 (down to 10)
(c) 23 (down to 16)	(d) 34 (down to 27)
	(e) 72 (down to 67)

6 Number Word Before

*Say the number word that comes just before ***. Example: Say the number just before 2.*

(a) Entry task

24	17	20	11
13	21	14	30

(b) Less advanced task

7	10	4
8	3	

(c) More advanced task

67	50	38	100
83	41	99	

7 Sequencing Numerals

Show the ten numbered cards face up in random order, asking the child to identify each number as you put it out. Then say, *Can you place the cards in order? Start by putting the smallest down here.*

(a) Entry task

Cards from 46 to 55

(b) More advanced task

Cards from 1 to 10

8 Additive Tasks (screened, use counters of two colours)

Introductory task:

There are three red counter under here, and one yellow counter under here. How many counters are there altogether?

3	+	1

(a) Entry tasks (both collections screened)

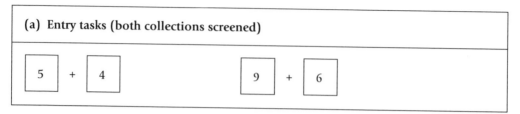

If one or more incorrect continue below to **8(b)**. If both correct go to **8(e)**.

(b) Less advanced task (first collection screened)

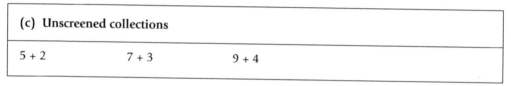

If **(b)** is too difficult go to **(c)**

(c) Unscreened collections

5 + 2   7 + 3   9 + 4

(d) Perceptual counting
   Would you count to see how many counters there are altogether in this group?

   Place out 13 counters.   Place out 18 counters

(e) Supplementary additive tasks (screened, use counters of two colours)
   Supplementary tasks to **(a)** if further clarification is needed. The tasks are presented
   totally screened.

(f) Missing addend
   *Here are four red counters. Now look away. While you were looking away I put some more yellow
   counters under here. Now there are 6 counters altogether. How many yellow counters did I put
   under here?*

Introductory task 4 + [ ] = 6

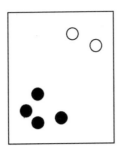

Tasks 7 + [ ] = 10   12 + [ ] = 15

9 Subtractive Tasks

(a) Subtraction sentences

Present the tasks as a written number sentence on card. Say to the child, *What does this say? Do you have a way to work out what the answer is?* [Note: using counters is not an option]

Entry task	Supplementary task
16 – 12	17 – 14

(b) Missing subtrahend

[Note: use counters of one colour only]

Here are five counters. (Ask the child to look away. Remove and screen two counters.) *There were five counters. While you were looking away I took some away. Now there are only three. How many did I take away?*

(i)	**Introductory task**	5 to 3	{ 5 – [ ] = 3}
(ii)	**Entry tasks**	10 to 6	{10 – [ ] = 6}
		12 to 9	{12 – [ ] = 9}
(iii)	**More advanced task**	15 to 11	{15 – [ ] = 11}

(c) Removed items

Here are three counters. (briefly display, then screen). *If I take away one,* (remove one counter, display briefly, then re-screen) *how many are left under here?* (Indicate the first screen.)

(i)	**Introductory task**	3 – 1		

(ii)	**Entry tasks**	6 – 2	9 – 4	15 – 3

(iii)	**More advanced task**	27 – 4		

Mathematics Recovery Programme: 1.1 – pupil profile sheet

Pupil:	DoB:	Teacher:	Class:
Age: yrs months	Assessment date:	Assessor:	

Aspect/Task Item	Level	Comments
FNWS and NWA	1 2 3 4 5	
Numeral Id.	1 2 3 4	
BNWS and NWB	1 2 3 4 5	
Sequencing Nos		

Additive Tasks and Subtractive tasks. Use the information on each section to arrive at the Stage.

Additive Tasks	
Missing Addends	
Subtractive Tasks	
Missing Subtrahends	
Removed Items	
STAGE on SEAL	1 2 3 4 5

Appendix 2

The Mathematics Recovery Programme

Assessment Interview Schedule 1.2
Base-Ten and Advanced Arithmetical Strategies

Child's name: ....

DoB: ....   Age: .... years ....months

Interviewer's name: ....

Date of interview: ....

Teacher/class: ....

Tasks	Comments
Tens and Ones Level 0 1 2 3	
Non-Count-By-Ones strategies	

1   **Tens and Ones Tasks**

(a)   Counting by tens with 'strips' – informal familiarization with material

---

(i)   Put down a ten strip. *How many do we have?* If the child says 'one', ask, *How many dots are there?*

(ii)   *'How many altogether?'* Put down one ten strip at a time to 8 strips.

   10   20   30   40   50   60   70   80

(iii)   Pick up all the strips.
   How many dots do we have?
   How many strips are there?

(b) Incrementing by ten

(i)   Place out the 'four dot' strip. *How many dots are there?*

(ii)   Place out a ten strip to the right of the four strip. *How many dots are there altogether?*

(iii)   Continue placing ten strips to the right of the four strip. *How many dots are there altogether?*   24   34   44   54   64   74

(iv)   If necessary, repeat the whole task with either the 3 strip or the 7 strip.

(c) Uncovering tasks: Board One
   Upon each uncovering ask, *How many dots are there now?*

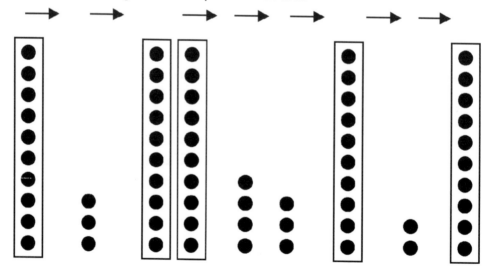

(d) **Uncovering tasks: Board Two**

Upon each uncovering ask, *How many are there now?*

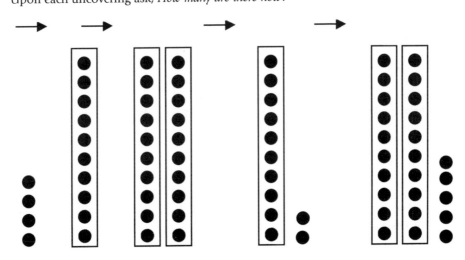

Example of Uncovering tasks: Board One, fourth move

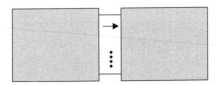

2	Horizontal Sentences
(a) *Do you have a way to figure out what is?* *So what is 16 + 9?*	16 + 10 =
(b) *Do you have a way to figure out what is?* *If correct ask, Do you have another way to work it out or check?*	42 + 23
(c) *Do you have a way to figure out what is?* *If correct ask, Do you have another way to work it out or check?*	38 + 24
(d) Repeat the above questions for:	39 + 53
(e)	56 – 23
(f)	43 – 15
(g)	73 – 48

3 Tasks to Elicit Non-Count-By-Ones Strategies and Relational Thinking

(a)

9 + 3

*Can you use ...
to help you do?*

9 + 4

9 + 5

9 + 6
and so on
if necessary

(b)

6 + 6

*Can you use ...
you help you do?*

7 + 5

8 + 4

9 + 3
and so on
if necessary

(c)

7 – 5

*Can you use ...
to help you do?*

27 – 5

47 – 5

*What do you think
the next take-away
will be?*

(d)

15 + 3

*Can you use ...
to help you do ...?*

18 – 3?

*How do you use
... to help you?*

(e)

If I tell you

21 – 16 = 5
*Can you use ...
to help you do ...?*

21 – 5?

(f)

14 + 4 = 18

*There are three numbers here.
Can you use these to make
a take-away sum?*

*Can you make
another one?*

Appendix 3

The Mathematics Recovery Programme

Assessment Interview Schedule 2.1
Early Grouping: Structuring Numbers 1 to 10

Child's name: ....

DoB: ....   Age: ....   years ....months

Interviewer's name: ....

Date of interview: ....

Teacher/class: ....

Subitizing and Spatial Patterns	Regular	Irregular	Domino
Finger Patterns	1 to 5		6 to 10
Five Frame Patterns	1 to 5		
Pair-wise Patterns on a Ten Frame	1 to 5		6 to 10
Five-wise Patterns on a Ten Frame	1 to 5		6 to 10
Combining to make Five			
Combining to make Ten			

1 Subsitizing and Spatial Patterns

Show each card briefly, for about half a second, saying, *I'm going to show you some cards very quickly. Tell me how many spots are on each one.*

(a)	Flashed Regular	4	3	2	5	6
(b)	Flashed Irregular	6	7	4	5	8
(c)	Domino Cards					

Show each card briefly, for about half a second, saying, *I'm going to show you some cards very quickly.*

(i)   *What did you see?*
(ii)   *Tell me how many spots are on one side.*
(iii)   *Tell me how many spots are on the other side.*
(iv)   *How many are there altogether?*

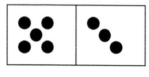
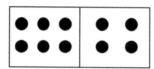
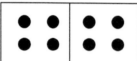
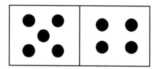

2 Finger Patterns 1 to 5

(a)   *Show me three on your fingers.*
      3   2   5   1   4
(b)   *Using two hands show me.*
      3   2   5   4

3 Finger Patterns 6 to 10

(a)   *Show me 6 on your fingers.*
(b)   *Show me 6 a different way.*
(c)   *Show me 9 on your fingers.*
(d)   *Show me 10 on your fingers.*
(e)   *Show me 8 on your fingers.*
(f)   *Show me 8 a different way.*

4 Five Frame Patterns

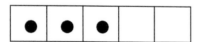

Flash the Five Frame.
(a)   *What did you see?*
(b)   *How many spots did you see?*
      3   2   5   1   4

5 Five-wise Patterns on a Ten Frame

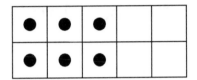

Flash five-wise cards 1–10

(a)   *What did you see?*
(b)   *How many spots did you see?*

     7   10   8   6   9

6 Pair-wise Patterns on a Ten Frame

Flash pair-wise cards 1–10

(a)   *What did you see?*
(b)   *How many spots did you see?*

     4   2   5   1   3
     7   10   8   6   9

7 Combining to make five

I will say a number and you say the number that goes with it to make five.

     4   2   1   3   5

8 Combining to make ten

(a)   *Tell me two numbers that add up to 10.*
(b)   *Tell me 2 other numbers that add up to 10.*
(c)   *Can you tell me another two?*
(d)   *I have 8 apples, how many more do I need to make 10?*
(e)   *I have 4, how many more to make 10?*
(f)   *I have 7, how many more to make 10?*

The Mathematics Recovery Programme

Assessment Interview Schedule 2.2
Advanced Grouping: Structuring Numbers 1 to 20

Child's name: ....

DoB: .... Age: .... years ....months

Interviewer's name: ....

Date of interview: ....

Teacher/class: ....

Tasks	Comments
Doubles	
Near Doubles	
Addition using five, ten or doubles, and so on	
Subtraction using five, ten or doubles, and so on	
Addition and subtraction with one addend/subtrahend > 10	
Relational Thinking	

Assessment Interview 2.2
Advanced Grouping: Structuring Numbers 1 to 20

1 Doubles

Show spot cards (two seconds)

(a) 5 + 5   (b) 4 + 4   (c) 2 + 2
(i)   *What do you see?*
(ii)   *How many on the top row?*
(iii) *How many on the bottom row?*
(iv)   *How many altogether?*

(d) 7 + 7   (e) 9 + 9   (f) 6 + 6   (g) 8 + 8
(v)   *What do you see?*
(vi)   *How many on the top row?*
(vii) *How many on the bottom row?*
(viii) *How many altogether?*

2 Near Doubles

Show the number problem.
Can you work this problem out?
How did you do that?
Do you have another way to work it out?

(a) 5 + 6   (b) 4 + 3   (c) 7 + 6
(d) 9 + 8   (e) 8 + 7   (f) 3 + 2

3 Addition Using Five, Ten or Doubles, and so on

Show the number problem. *Do you have a way to work out this problem?*
How did you do that?

(a) 9 + 3   (b) 8 + 5   (c) 9 + 6
(d) 8 + 6   (e) 5 + 7   (f) 4 + 9

4 Subtraction using five, ten or doubles, and so on

Show the number problem. *Do you have a way to work out this problem?*
How did you do that?
(a) 17 – 7   (b) 11 – 4   (c) 12 – 9
(d) 17 – 8   (e) 13 – 5   (f) 14 – 8

5 Addition and Subtraction with One Addend/Subtrahend Greater than Ten

Show the number sentence. *Do you have a way to work out this problem?*
How did you do that?
(a) 13 + 5   (b) 11 + 8
(c) 19 − 7   (d) 17 − 15

6 Relational Thinking

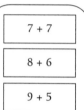

(a) Present the card
     What does this say?
     Can you work it out?

     Can you use this number problem to help you work out …?

(b) Present the card
     What does this say?

     Can you use this … to help you do …

     Can you use this … to help you do …

     And so on … if necessary.

(c) Present the card
     What does this say? Do you have a
     way to work this number problem out?
     Can you use this number problem to
     help you work out this?

     How did you do that?

(d) Present the card

     Can you use this number problem to help you work out this? $6 + 8 = 14$

     (i) $8 + 6$ (ii) $14 − 6$

     (iii) *What other number facts would you know from this?*

Appendix 5

The Mathematics Recovery Programme

Assessment Interview Schedule 3.1
Early Multiplication and Division

Child's name: ....

DoB: ....   Age: .... years ....months

Interviewer's name: ....

Date of interview: ....

Teacher/class: ....

Forming Equal Groups	
FNWS in multiples	
Rows and Arrays	
Equal groups of visible Items (a) Multiplication (b) Partition Division (c) Quotition Division	
Screened Items (a) Multiplication (equal groups) (b) Partition Division (equal groups) (c) Quotition Division (equal groups) (d) Multiplication (array) (e) Quotition Division (array)	

Level   0   1   2   3

Assessment Interview 3.1
Early Multiplication and Division

TASK GROUP 1. FORMING EQUAL GROUPS

Present a pile of 15 counters to the child. (Put them out randomly spaced and not in a line.)
Using these counters, make three groups with four in each group.

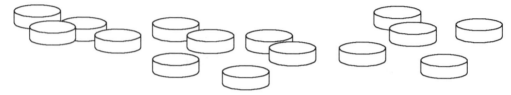

How many counters did you use?

TASK GROUP 2. TASKS INVOLVING FNWS OF MULTIPLES

To discover how facile the child is in the FNWS of multiples and where they stop or have problems.

(a) *Count by twos. I'll tell you when to stop.* (Stop at 20)
(b) *Count by tens. I'll tell you when to stop.* (Stop at 120)
(c) *Count by fives. I'll tell you when to stop.* (Stop at 55)
(d) *Count by threes. I'll tell you when to stop.* (Stop at 15)

TASK GROUP 3. TASKS INVOLVING VISIBLE ITEMS ARRANGED IN ROWS OR ARRAYS

(a) Display a 10×2 array of dots, that is ten rows and two columns.
   Can you tell me how many dots there are altogether?

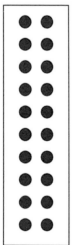

(b) Display a 5 × 3 array of dots, that is five rows and three columns.
Can you tell me how many dots there are altogether?

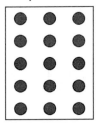

(c) Display a 4 × 5 array, that is four rows and five columns. Indicate rows in turn.
How many rows are there?

How many dots in each row?
How many dots altogether?

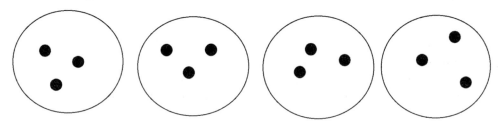

Turn the array through 90 degrees.
How many dots altogether now?

TASK GROUP 4. TASKS INVOLVING EQUAL GROUPS OF VISIBLE ITEMS

(a) Multiplication
Place out four plates with three counters on each plate.

How many plates are there?
There are three counters on each plate, how many counters are there altogether?

(b) Partition division
Place out a pile of 15 counters.
Here are 15 counters. If we shared them equally among three children, how many would each child get?

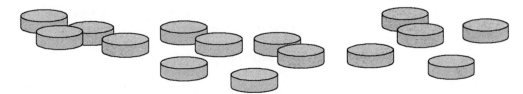

(c) Quotition division
Place out a pile of 12 counters.
Here are 12 counters. If we shared them equally among some children so they each got four, how many children would there be?

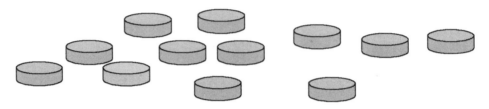

(d) Partition division with redistribution
Place out a pile of 24 counters.
Here are 24 counters. If we shared them equally among three children, how many would each child get?
If I now shared them equally among 4 children how many would each get?

TASK GROUP 5. TASKS INVOLVING SCREENED ITEMS

(a) Multiplication with equal groups
Ask the child to look away while you place out four screens with three counters under each screen.

Each screen has three counters under it. How many counters altogether?

(b) Partition division with equal groups
Place out a pile of 12 counters and three covered opaque containers.
Share these counters equally among the three containers and tell me how many counters there will be in each container?
Ensure that the child is not able to count the counters after having shared them.

(c) Quotition division with equal groups
Place out a pile of 30 counters and 7 covered containers.
Use 20 of these counters to make containers with five counters in each and tell me how many containers you will use?

(d) Multiplication with an array.
Using a 5 × 3 array, use one screen to screen the two upper rows and a second screen to screen the lower three rows. Unscreen the upper two rows for a few seconds. (Fig. 1)

How many rows do you see? Re-screen the two rows. (Fig. 2)

There are three more rows under this screen. How many counters are there altogether?

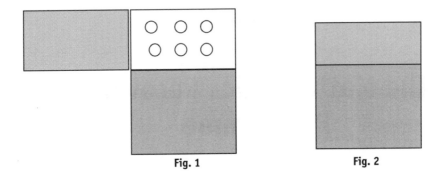

| Fig. 1 | Fig. 2 |

(e) Quotition division with an array

Using a 6 × 2 array, screen five rows and leave the uppermost row unscreened. (Fig. 3)
How many dots in this row? There are 12 dots altogether. How many rows altogether? Let the child
check. (Fig. 4)

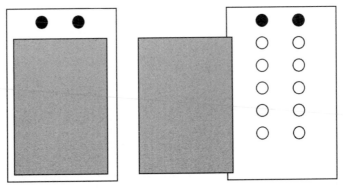

Fig. 3   Fig. 4

Appendix 6

Assessment Interview Schedule 3.2
Advanced Multiplication and Division

Child's name: ....

DoB: ....   Age: .... years ....months

Interviewer's name: ....

Date of interview: ....

Teacher/class: ....

Written sentences

(a) Multiplication

(b) Quotition division

(c) Partition division

(d) Quotition division with remainder

(e) Partition division with remainder

Communtativity and Inverse relationship

Applied Multiplication

Level   3 4 5

Assessment Interview 3.2
Advanced Multiplication and Division

TASK GROUP 1: TASKS PRESENTED VERBALLY WITHOUT MATERIALS

(a) Multiplication

> *Six children have five marbles each. How many marbles altogether?*

(b) Quotition division

> *There are 12 bananas and each child is given two bananas.*
> *How many children are there?*

(c) Partition division

> *If we shared eighteen apples among three children,*
> *how many apples would each child get?*

(d) Quotition division with remainder

> *There are 17 flowers and each person is given 5 flowers. How*
> *many people are there and how many flowers left over?*

(e) Partition division with remainder

> *If we shared 14 cookies equally among four children, how*
> *many cookies would each child get and how many would be left over?*

TASK GROUP 2: COMMUNTATIVITY AND INVERSE RELATIONSHIP

(a) *What does this say? What does it make you think of?*
    or

   What do you see in your mind when you read 9 × 7? 9×7

   How would you work this out?
   Can you tell me another way to work it out?

(b) *What does this say?* 3×7

   What does this say? 7×3

What can you tell me about these two problems?

| 3 × 7 | 7 × 3 |

(c) *What is the answer to this problem?* | 8 × 4 |

Can you use that to help you do this problem? | 32 ÷ 4 |

(d) *If I tell you that eight times seven is 56* (show the card) | 8 × 7 = 56 |

Can you use these numbers and signs (symbols) to make a division (division sentence)?

| 8 | | 7 | | 56 | | = | | ÷ |

Can you make another division?

TASK GROUP 3: AREA MULTIPLICATION

Show the cardboard square unit and the 7 × 3 rectangle.
How many squares like this one would you need to cover the rectangle completely?

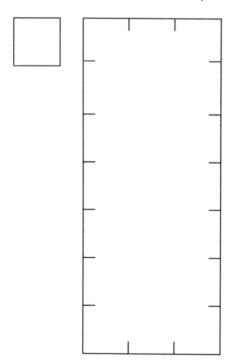

Provide the child with a copy of the grid and ask,
Can you draw what the squares would look like?

Levels in the Development of Multiplication and Division

Level 1: Forming Equal Groups or Initial Grouping

The child uses perceptual counting and sharing (that is, by ones) to form or make groups of specific sizes; to share items into groups of a given size (quotitive sharing); to share items into a given number of groups (partitive sharing). The child does not see the groups as composite units and thus counts each item by ones instead of in multiples. (Similar to Stage 1 in SEAL)

Level 2: Perceptual Counting in Multiples

The child uses a multiplicative counting strategy to count visible items arranged in equal groups. The child cannot count screened groups. Strategies used can be rhythmic, skip counting and double counting. All are called perceptual because the child is reliant on seeing the items.

Level 3: Figurative Composite Grouping

The child uses a multiplicative counting strategy to count items arranged in equal groups where the individual items are not visible. The child is not dependent upon direct sensory experience where he or she relies on counting by ones. (Equivalent to Stage 3 – Counting-on, in SEAL)

Level 4: Repeated Abstract Composite Grouping

The child counts composite units in repeated addition or subtraction tasks, that is, he or she uses the composite unit a specified number of times. Double counting is a common strategy at this stage.

Level 5: Multiplication and Divisions as Operations

Can regard both the number in each group and the number of groups as a composite unit. Can immediately recall or quickly derive many of the basic facts for multiplication and division, for example, three sixes. A child at this level may possess the commutative principle of multiplication ($5 \times 3 = 3 \times 5$) and/or see the inverse relationship of multiplication and division.

Appendix 7: The Learning Framework in Number

Part A	Part B	Part C	Part D
Early Arithmetical Strategies Base-Ten Arithmetical Strategies	Forward Number Word Sequences and Number Word After Backward Number Word Sequences and Number Word Before Numerals	Structuring Numbers 1–20	Early Multiplication and Division
Stages: **Early Arithmetical Strategies** 0 – Emergent Counting 1 – Perceptual Counting 2 – Figurative Counting 3 – Initial Number Sequence 4 – Intermediate Number Sequence 5 – Facile Number Sequence **Levels:** **Base-Ten Arithmetical Strategies** 1 – Initial Concept of Ten 2 – Intermediate Concept of Ten 3 – Facile Concept of Ten	**Levels:** **Forward Number Word Sequences (FNWSs) and Number Word After** 0 – Emergent FNWS. 1 – Initial FNWS up to 'ten' 2 – Intermediate FNWS up to 'ten' 3 – Facile with FNWSs up to 'ten' 4 – Facile with FNWSs up to 'thirty' 5 – Facile with FNWSs up to 'one hundred' **Levels:** **Backward Number Word Sequences (BNWSs) and Number Word Before** 0 – Emergent BNWS. 1 – Initial BNWS up to 'ten' 2 – Intermediate BNWS up to 'ten' 3 – Facile with BNWSs up to 'ten'. 4 – Facile with BNWSs up to 'thirty'. 5 – Facile with BNWSs up to 'one hundred'. **Levels:** **Numeral Identification** 0 – Emergent Numeral Identification. 1 – Numeral to '10' 2 – Numerals to '20' 3 – Numerals to '100' 4 – Numerals to '1000'	Combining and Partitioning Spatial Patterns and Subitizing Temporal Sequences Finger Patterns Five-based (Quinary-based) Strategies	**Levels:** 1 Initial Grouping 2 Perceptual Counting in Multiples 3 Figurative Composite 4 Repeated Composite Grouping 5 Multiplication and Division as Operations

Source: adapted from Wright et al., 2002, p. 10.

Appendix 8: Instructional Framework for Early Number

Instructional Phase	Number Words and Numerals	Counting	Grouping
Phase 1 Emergent	▶ FNWS 1 to 20 ▶ BNWS 1 to 10 ▶ Numerals 1 to 10	▶ Count involving visible items in collections and in rows ▶ Temporal sequences and temporal patterns	▶ Early spatial patterns ▶ Early finger patterns
Phase 2 Perceptual	▶ FNWS 1 to 30 ▶ BNWS 1 to 30 ▶ Numerals 1 to 20	▶ Counting involving screened items in collections and rows	▶ Developing spatial patterns ▶ Developing finger patterns ▶ Equal groups and sharing
Phase 3 Figurative	▶ FNWS 1 to 100 ▶ BNWS 1 to 100 ▶ Numerals 1 to 100	▶ Counting-on and counting-back to solve additive and subtractive tasks	▶ Combining and partitioning using 5 and 10 ▶ Combining and partitioning in range 1–10 ▶ Early multiplication and division
Phase 4 Counting-on and Counting-back	▶ NWSs by 2, 10s, 5s, 3s, and 4s in the range 1–100 ▶ Numerals 1 to 1000	▶ Incrementing by 10s and 1s	▶ Adding and subtracting to and from decade numbers ▶ Adding and subtracting to 20 using 5 and 10 ▶ Developing multiplication and division
Phase 5 Facile	▶ NWSs by 10s on and off the decade ▶ NWSs by 100s on and off the 100 and on and off the decade	▶ Two-digit addition and subtraction through counting	▶ Two-digit addition and subtraction involving collections ▶ Non-canonical forms of two- and three-digit numbers ▶ Higher decade addition and subtraction ▶ Advanced multiplication and division

Appendix 9: Linking the Diagnostic Assessment Interviews to the Learning Framework in Number

Assessment 1.1

Outcomes of the assessment
1 To determine the child's Stage of Early Arithmetical Learning in addition and subtraction within the range Stage 0 to Stage 4.
2 To gain extensive information on the child's facility with number word sequences and numerals.

Assessment 1.2

Outcomes of the assessment.
1 To determine the child's Stage of Early Arithmetical Learning in addition and subtraction within the range Stage 3 to Stage 5.
2 To determine the child's level of development of Base-Ten Arithmetical Stategies.

Assessment 2.1

Outcomes of the assessment
1 To gain extensive information on the child's ability to structure numbers in the range one to ten.

Assessment 2.2

Outcomes of the assessment
1 To gain extensive information on the child's ability to structure numbers in the range one to twenty.

Assessment 3.1

Outcomes of the assessment
1 To determine the child's level of knowledge in the early stages of Multiplication and Division.

Assessment 3.2

Outcomes of the assessment
1 To determine the child's level of knowledge in the advanced stages of Multiplication and Division.

Appendix 10: Materials Required

1.1 Number Words and Numerals and Addition and Subtraction
Numeral Identification Cards 1, 2 and 3 digits [25 cards]
Numeral Recognition Cards 1–10 [10 cards]
Sequencing Number Cards 1–10; 46–55 [20 cards]
18 red counters; 10 yellow counters
2 screens of card
Subtraction Sentence Cards

1.2 Tens and Ones and Non-Count-by-Ones
$8 \times$ ten strips
Dot strips: 1×4; 1×3; 1×7
Uncovering Tasks: Board 1; Board 2
Horizontal Number cards: 16 + 10; 16 + 9; 42 + 23; 38 + 24; 39 + 53;
56 – 23; 43 – 15; 73 – 48
Non-Count-by-Ones cards: 9 + 3, 9 + 4, 9 + 5, 9 + 6; 6 + 6, 7 + 5, 8 + 4, 9 + 3;
7 – 5, 27 – 5, 47–5; 15 + 3, 18 – 3; 21 –16 = 5, 21 – 5; 14 + 4 = 18
Numbers and signs on cards: 18, 4, 14, =, –

2.1 Early Grouping Structuring Numbers 1–10
Subitizing and Spatial Pattern cards [14 cards]
Regular: 4; 3; 2; 5; 6
Irregular: 6; 7; 4; 5; 8
Domino Cards: 5 and 3; 6 and 4; 4 and 4; 5 and 4
Five Frames [5 cards]
Five-wise patterns on a Ten Frame [10 cards]
Pair-wise patterns on a Ten Frame [10 cards]

2.2 Advanced Grouping Structuring Numbers 1–20
Spot Cards: Doubles [7 cards]
Number Sentence cards: Near Doubles; Addition in Five, Ten or Doubles; [12 cards]
Subtraction using Five, Ten or Doubles; Addition and Subtraction with one addend/subtrahend
greater than 10 [10 cards]
Relational Thinking cards [10 cards]

3.1 Early Multiplication and Division
Counters: thirty of one colour.
Arrays: 10×2; 4×5; 5×3; [3 cards]
Screens: four smaller size pieces of cardboard (for example, 10 cm $\times$ 12 cm).
Paper plates: four.
Covered containers: seven
Screened arrays: 5×3; 6×2

3.2 Advanced Multiplication and Division
Screens: two larger size pieces of cardboard (for example, 20 cm $\times$ 30 cm).
Written Problems on cards
Number Problems on cards: 9×7; 3×7; 7×3; 8×4; $32 \div 4$; $8 \times 7 = 56$.
Numbers and signs on cards: 8, 7, 56, =, $\div$
7×3 rectangle and one unit square

Appendix 11: The Mathematics Recovery Coding Schedule

✓	correct
✓✓	correct and with confidence
??	needs time to think
? ✓	needs some time, then correct
✗✓	initially incorrect, then correct
SC	child self-corrects
TTA	'Try that again'
∧	omission of a number in FNWS or BNWS
IDK	child says 'I don't know'
'...'	indicates the words used
Rev	assessor revisits an item
Red	teacher redirects or teacher prompt
C.from 1	child counts from one
CO	child counts-on
CDF	child counts-down-from
CDT	child counts-down-to

Glossary

Additive task. A generic label for tasks involving what adults would regard as addition. The label 'additive task' is used to emphasize that children will construe such tasks idiosyncratically, that is, differently from each other and from the way adults will construe them.

Advanced counting-by-ones strategies. These strategies are used by a child who has attained at least Stage 3, for example counting-on, counting-down-from and counting-down-to.

Arithmetic rack. An abacus-like instructional device consisting of two rows of ten beads. In each row the beads appear in two groups of five, that is using two different colours for the beads.

Aspect. A key element of a part of the Learning Framework in Number.

Backward number word sequence (BNWS). A regular sequence of number words backward, typically but not necessarily by ones, for example, the BNWS from ten to one, the BNWS from eighty-two to seventy-five, the BNWS by tens from eighty-three.

Combining. An arithmetical strategy involving combining (that is, adding in a sense) two numbers in the range one to five, without counting, for example, 3 and 2, 4 and 4.

Count Me In Too. An innovative project in early mathematics undertaken in the government (public) schools of New South Wales, Australia.

Counting-by-ones. Initial or advanced arithmetical strategies which involve counting-by-ones only. Examples of initial counting-by-ones strategies are perceptual and figurative counting, which involve counting-from-one. Examples of advanced counting-by-ones strategies are counting-on, counting-down-from and counting-down-to.

Counting-down-from. A strategy used by children who have attained at least Stage 3 and typically used to solve Removed Items tasks, for example, 11 remove 3 – 'eleven, ten, nine – eight!' Also referred to as counting-off-from or counting-back-from.

Counting-down-to. Regarded as the most advanced of the counting-by-ones strategies and used by children who have attained at least Stage 4. Typically used to solve Missing Subtrahend tasks, for example, have 11, remove some, and there are eight left – 'eleven, ten, nine – three'. Also referred to as counting-back-to.

Counting-on. An advanced counting-by-ones strategy, indicative of having attained Stage 3, and used to solve additive tasks or Missing Addend tasks involving two hidden collections. Counting-on can be differentiated into counting-up-from for additive tasks and counting-up-to for subtractive tasks. Counting-on is also referred to as counting-up.

Counting-up-from. An advanced counting-by-ones strategy, indicative of having attained Stage 3, and used to solve additive tasks involving two hidden collections, for example, seven and five is solved by counting up five from seven.

Counting-up-to. An advanced counting-by-ones strategy, indicative of having attained Stage 3, and used to solve Missing Addend tasks, for example, seven and how many make twelve is solved by counting from seven up to twelve, and keeping track of five counts.

Difference. See Minuend.

Digit. The digits are the ten basic symbols in the modern numeration system, that is '0', '1', . . . '9'.

Early number. A generic label for the number work in the first three years of school and learned by children around four to eight years of age. Also known as 'Early Arithmetic'.

Facile. Used in the sense of having good facility, that is, fluent or dexterous, for example, a facile counting-on strategy, or facile with the backward number word sequence.

Figurative. The label for Stage 2. Figurative thought involves re-presentation of a sensory-motor experience, that is, a mental replay of a prior experience involving seeing, hearing, touching, and so on. Figurative counting may be figural, in which visualized items constitute the material which is counted; motor, in which movements constitute the material which is counted; or verbal, in which number words constitute the material which is counted.

Forward number word sequence (FNWS). A regular sequence of number words forward, typically but not necessarily by ones, for example, the FNWS from one to twenty, the FNWS from eighty-one to ninety-three, the FNWS by tens from twenty-four.

IFEN. An instructional framework for early number

Learning Framework in Number. A foundational structure for assessment and teaching in early number developed by the Mathematics Recovery Programme and adapted for the Count Me In Too project.

Level. The terms 'Level' and 'Stage' are used in a technical sense. A 'Level' is a point on a continuum, for example Level 3 in knowledge of FNWSs. A 'Stage' is like a plateau. Each new stage is characterized by a qualitative advancement in knowledge, that is, a conceptual reorganization of strategies, and in the way tasks are construed.

Minuend. In subtraction of standard form, for example $12 - 3 = 9$, 12 is the minuend, 3 is the subtrahend and 9 is the difference. Thus the difference is the answer obtained in subtraction, the subtrahend is the number subtracted and the minuend is the number from which the subtrahend is subtracted.

Missing addend. A subtractive task posed in the form of addition with one addend missing, for example, 12 and how many make 15.

Non-count-by-ones. A class of strategies which involve aspects other than counting-by-ones and which are used to solve additive and subtractive tasks. Part of the strategy may involve counting-by-ones but the solution also involves a more advanced procedure. For example, $6 + 8$ is solved by saying 'six and six is twelve – thirteen, fourteen'. These strategies are characteristic of Stage 5.

Number. A number is the idea or concept associated with, for example, how many items in a collection. We distinguish among the number 24 – that is, the concept, the spoken or heard number word 'twenty-four', the numeral '24' and also the read or written number word 'twenty-four'. These distinctions are important in understanding children's early numerical strategies.

Number word. Number words are names or words for numbers. In most cases in early number the term 'number word' refers to the spoken and heard names for numbers rather than the read or written names.

Numeral. Numerals are symbols for numbers, for example '5', '27'.

Numeral identification. Stating the name of a displayed numeral. The term is used similarly to the term 'letter identification' in early literacy. When assessing Numeral Identification, numerals are not displayed in numerical sequence.

Numeral recognition. Selecting a nominated numeral from a randomly arranged group of numerals.

Numeral track. An instructional device consisting of a sequence of numerals and, for each numeral, a hinged lid which may be used to screen or display the numeral.

Numerosity. The numerosity of a collection is the number of items in the collection.

Partitioning. An arithmetical strategy involving partitioning a small number into two parts without counting, typically with both parts in the range 1 to 5, for example partitioning 6 into 5 + 1, 4 + 2, and so on.

Partition division. In partition division tasks the dividend and the number of divisors are given and the problem is to work out the quotient; for example, 'How many sweets will each person get if I share 16 sweets among 4 people?'

Perceptual. Involving direct sensory input – usually seeing but may also refer to hearing or feeling. Thus perceptual counting involves counting items seen, heard or felt.

Procedure. See Strategy.

Quinary. This term refers to the use of five as a base in some sense, and typically in conjunction with, rather than instead of, ten as a base. The Arithmetic Rack may be regarded as a quinary-based instructional device.

Quotition division. In quotition division tasks the dividend and the quotient are given and the problem is to work out the number of divisors; for example, 'I have 20 chocolates and I want to give 5 to each person. How many children can I give 5 chocolates to?'

Re-presentation. A re-presentation can be thought of as a mental replay of a prior experience – that is, in reflection, distinct from and separated in time from the experience itself.

Setting. A physical situation used by a teacher in posing numerical tasks, for example, collections of counters, Numeral Track, Hundreds Chart, Ten Frame.

Stages. See Levels.

Standard number word sequence (SNWS). The forward sequence of number words from one onward.

Strand. One of four major threads of the Learning Framework In Number.

Strategy. A generic label for a method by which a child solves a task. A strategy consists of one or more constituent procedures. A procedure is the simplest form of a strategy, that is, a strategy that cannot be described in terms of two or more constituent procedures. For example, on an additive task involving two screened collections a child might use the procedure of counting the first collection from one and then use the procedure of continuing to count by ones, in order to count the second collection.

Subitizing. The immediate, correct assignation of a number word to a small collection of perceptual items.

Subtractive task. A generic label for tasks involving what adults would regard as subtraction. The label 'subtractive task' is used to emphasize that children will construe such tasks idiosyncratically, that is, differently from each other and from the way adults will construe them.

Subtrahend. See Minuend.

Task. A generic label for problems or questions presented to a child.

Temporal sequence. A sequence of events that occur sequentially in time, for example sequences of sounds or movements.

Bibliography

Anghileri, J. (1989) An investigation of young children's understanding of multiplication. *Educational Studies in Mathematics*, **20**, 367–85.

Aubrey, C. (1993) An investigation of the mathematical knowledge and competencies which young children bring into school. *British Educational Research Journal*, **19**(1), 27–41.

Bobis, J. (1996) Report of the Evaluation of the Count Me In Too Project. An unpublished report to the NSW Department of Education and Training.

Bobis, J., Clarke, B., Clarke, D., Thomas, G., Wright, R., Young-Loveridge, J. and Gould, P. (2005) Supporting teachers in the development of young children's mathematical thinking: three large-scale cases. *Mathematics Education Research Journal*, **16**(3), 27–57.

Carpenter, T.R, Ansell, E., Franke, K.L., Fennema, E. and Weisbeck, L. (1993) Models of problem solving: a study of kindergarten children's problem-solving processes. *Journal for Research in Mathematics Education*, **24**, 428–41.

Clark, E.B. and Kamii, C. (1996) Identification of multiplicative thinking in children in grades 1–5. *Journal for Research in Mathematical Education*, **27**, 41–51.

Cobb, P. and Steffe, L.P. (1983) The constructivist researcher as teacher and model builder. *Journal for Research in Mathematics Education*, **14**, 83–94.

Cobb, P. and Wheatley, G. (1988) Children's initial understandings of ten. *Focus on Learning Problems in Mathematics*, **10**(3), 1–26.

Cobb, P., Boufi, A., McClain, K. and Whitenack, J. (1997a) Reflective discourse and collective reflection. *Journal for Research in Mathematics Education*, **28**, 258–77.

Cobb, P., Gravemeijer, K., Yackel, E., McClain, K. and Whitenack, J. (1997b) Mathematizing and symbolizing: the emergence of chains of signification in one first-grade classroom, in D. Kirshner and J. A. Whitson (eds) *Situated Cognition Theory: Social, Semiotic and Neurological Perspectives* (pp. 151–233). Mahwah, NJ: Lawrence Erlbaum.

Cobb, P., McClain, K., Whitenack, J. and Estes, B. (1995) Supporting young children's development of mathematical power, in A. Richards (ed.) *Proceedings of the Fifteenth Biennial Conference of the Australian Association of Mathematics Teachers* (pp. 1–11) Adelaide: Australian Association of Mathematics Teachers.

Cobb, P., Wood, T. and Yackel, E. (1991) A constructivist approach to second grade mathematics, in E. von Glasersfeld (ed.) *Radical Constructivism in Mathematics Education* (pp. 157–76). Dordrecht: Kluwer.

Cobb, P., Wood, T. and Yackel, E. (1992) Interaction and learning in classroom situations. *Educational Studies in Mathematics*, **23**, 99–122.

Cockcroft, W.H. (1982) (Cockcroft Report) *Mathematics Counts: Report of the Committee of Inquiry into the Teaching of Mathematics in Schools*. London: HMSO.

Confrey, J. (1994) Splitting, similarity, and rate of change: a new approach to multiplication and exponential functions, in G. Harel and J. Confrey (eds) *The Development of Multiplicative Reasoning in the Learning of Mathematics* (pp. 291–330). Albany, NY: State University of New York Press.

Denvir, B. and Brown, M. (1986a) Understanding of number concepts in low attaining 7–9 year olds: Part I. Development of descriptive framework and diagnostic instrument. *Educational Studies in Mathematics*, **17**, 15–36.

Denvir, B. and Brown, M. (1986b) Understanding of number concepts in low attaining 7–9 year olds: Part II. The teaching studies. *Educational Studies in Mathematics*, **17**, 143–64.

DETYA (2000) *Mapping the Territory: Primary Students with Learning Difficulties.* (Vol 1, pp. 11–12) Canberra: DETYA.

Department for Education and Employment (DfEE) (1999a) *Framework for Teaching Mathematics from Reception to Year 6.* Cambridge: Cambridge University Press.

Department for Education and Employment (DfEE) (1999b) *National Numeracy Strategy: Mathematical Vocabulary.* London: DfEE.

Department for Education and Skills (DfES) (2004) *What Works for Children with Mathematical Difficulties, Research Brief RB554.* London: DfES.

Department for Education and Skills (DfES) (2005) *Targeting Support: Implementing Interventions for Children with Significant Difficulties in Mathematics,* Primary National Strategy, 1083–2005. London: DfES.

Dowker, A.D. (2003) Interventions in numeracy: individualized approaches, in I. Thompson (ed.) *Enhancing Primary Mathematics Teaching* (pp. 127–35). Maidenhead, UK: Open University Press.

Dowker, A.D. (2004) *Children with Difficulties in Mathematics: What Works?* London: DfES.

Dowker, A.D. (2005) *Individual Differences in Arithmetic: Implications for Psychology, Neuroscience and Education.* Hove: Psychology Press.

Glasersfeld, E. von (1982) Subitizing: the role of figural patterns in the development of numerical concepts. *Archives de Psychologie*, **50**, 191–218.

Glasersfeld, E. von and Kelley, M. (1982) On the concepts of period, phase, stage and level. *Human Development*, **25**, 152–60.

Gravemeijer, K.P.E. (1994) *Developing Realistic Mathematics Education.* Utrecht: CD-B Press.

Gravemeijer, K.P.E., Cobb, P., Bowers, J., & Whitenack, J. (2000). Symbolizing, modeling, and instructional design. In P. Cobb, E. Yackel, & K. McClain (Eds.), *Symbolizing and communicating and in mathematics classrooms: Perspectives on discourse, tools, and instructional design,* (pp. 335–73). Mahwah, NJ: Erlbaum.

Hird, D. (2004) An evaluation of the impact of the Mathematics Recovery Programme on the staff and pupils in Sefton LEA. Unpublished M.Ed. thesis, University of Liverpool.

Hunting, R.R, Davis, G. and Pearn, C. (1996) Engaging whole-number knowledge for rational-number learning using a computer-based tool. *Journal for Research in Mathematics Education*, **27**, 354–79.

Kouba, V.L. (1989) Children's solution strategies for equivalent set multiplication and division word problems. *Journal for Research in Mathematics Education*, **20**, 147–58.

Mitchelmore, M.C., and White, P. (2003). Count Me In Too and the Basic Skills Test in New South Wales, in L. Bragg, C. Campbell, G. Herbert, and J. Mousley (eds) *Mathematics Education Research: Innovation, Networking, Opportunity* (Proceedings of the 26th annual conference of the Mathematics Education Research Group of Australasia, Geelong) (pp. 515–22). Sydney: MERGA.

Mulligan, J.T. (1998) A research-based framework for assessing early multiplication and division, in C. Kanes, M. Goos and E. Warren (eds) *Proceedings of the 21st Annual Conference of the Mathematics Education Research Group of Australasia* (vol. 2, pp. 404–11). Brisbane: Griffith University.

Mulligan, J.T. and Mitchelmore, M.C. (1997) Young children's intuitive models of multiplication and division. *Journal for Research in Mathematics Education*, **28**, 309–30.

Munn, P. (2005) The teacher as a learner, in R.J. Wright, G. Stanger, A.K. Stafford and J.R. Martland, *Teaching Mathematics in the Classroom with 4–8 Year Olds*, (Ch.11) London: Paul Chapman Publishing.

National Council for Teachers of Mathematics (NCTM) (2000) *Principles and Standards for School Mathematics*. Reston, VA: NCTM.

National Numeracy Project (NNP) (1999) *Numeracy Lessons*. Reading: National Centre for Numeracy.

NSW Department of Education and Training (1998) *Count Me In Too: A Professional Development Package*. Sydney: NSWDET.

Numeracy = Everyone's Business (1997) Report of the Numeracy Education Strategy Development Conference. Adelaide: Australian Association of Mathematics Teachers.

Qualifications and Curriculum Authority (QCA) (1999a) *Standards in Mathematics: Exemplification of Key Learning Objectives from Reception to Year 6*. London: QCA.

Qualifications and Curriculum Authority (QCA) (1999b) *The National Numeracy Strategy: Teaching Mental Calculation Strategies; Guidance for Teachers at Key Stages 1 and 2*. London: QCA.

Smith, J.R. (1996) Efficacy and teaching mathematics by telling: a challenge for reform. *Journal for Research in Mathematics Education*, **27**, 387–402.

Steffe, L.P. (1992a) Learning stages in the construction of the number sequence, in J. Bideaud, C. Meljac and J. Fischer (eds) *Pathways to Number: Children's Developing Numerical Abilities* (pp. 83–8). Hillsdale, NJ: Lawrence Erlbaum.

Steffe, L.P. (1992b) *Schemes of action and operation involving composite units. Learning and Individual Differences*, **4**, 259–309.

Steffe, L.P. (1994) Children's multiplying schemes, in G. Harel and J. Confrey (eds) *The Development of Multiplicative Reasoning in the Learning of Mathematics* (pp. 3–41) Albany, NY: State University of New York Press.

Steffe, L.P. and Cobb, P. (with E. von Glasersfeld) (1988) *Construction of Arithmetic Meanings and Strategies*. New York: Springer-Verlag.

Steffe, L.P. von Glasersfeld, E., Richards, J. and Cobb, P. (1983) *Children's Counting Types: Philosophy, Theory and Application*. New York: Praeger.

Wright, R.J. (1989) Numerical development in the kindergarten year: a teaching experiment. Doctoral dissertation, University of Georgia.

Wright, R.J. (1991a) An application of the epistemology of radical constructivism to the study of learning. *Australian Educational Researcher*, **18**(1), 75–95.

Wright, R.J. (1991b) What number knowledge is possessed by children entering the kindergarten year of school? *Mathematics Education Research Journal*, **3**(1), 1–16.

Wright, R.J. (1994) A study of the numerical development of 5-year-olds and 6-year-olds. *Educational Studies in Mathematics*, **26**, 25–44.

Wright, R.J. (1996) Problem-centred mathematics in the first year of school, in J. Mulligan and M. Mitchelmore (eds) *Children's Number Learning: A Research Monograph of the Mathematics Education Research Group of Australasia* (pp. 35–54). Adelaide: AAMT.

Wright, R.J. (2000) Professional development in recovery education, in L.P. Steffe and R.W. Thompson (eds) *Radical Constructivism in Action: Building on the Pioneering Work of Ernst von Glasersfeld.* (pp. 134–151). London: Falmer.

Wright, R.J., Cowper, M., Stafford, A., Stanger, G. and Stewart, R. (1994) The Maths Recovery Project: a progress report, in G. Bell, R. Wright, N. Leeson and J. Geake (eds) *Proceedings of the Seventeenth Annual Conference of the Mathematics Education Research Group of Australasia* (vol. 2, pp. 709–16). Lismore, NSW: Southern Cross University.

Wright, R.J., Martland, J., Stafford, A.K. and Stanger, G. (2002) *Teaching Number: Advancing children's skills and strategies.* London: Paul Chapman Publishing.

Wright, R.J., Stanger, G., Cowper, M. and Dyson, R. (1996) First-graders' progress in an experimental mathematics recovery program, in J. Mulligan and M. Mitchelmore (eds) *Children's Number Learning: A Research Monograph of the Mathematics Education Research Group of Australasia* (pp. 55–72). Adelaide: AAMT.

Wright, R.J., Stewart, R., Stafford, A. and Cain, R. (1998) Assessing and documenting student knowledge and progress in early mathematics, in S.B. Berenson, K.R. Dawkins, M. Blanton, W.N. Coulombe, J. Kolb, K. Norwood and L. Stiff (eds) *Proceedings of the Twentieth Annual Meeting of the North American Chapter of the International Group for the Psychology of Mathematics Education* (vol. 1, pp. 211–16). Columbus, OH: ERIC Clearinghouse for Science, Mathematics and Environmental Education.

Yackel, E., Cobb, P. and Wood, T. (1991) Small group interactions as a source of learning opportunities in second grade mathematics. *Journal for Research in Mathematics Education,* **22**, 390–408.

Young-Loveridge, J. (1989) The development of children's number concepts: the first year of school. *New Zealand Journal of Educational Studies,* **24**(1), 47–64.

Young-Loveridge, J. (1991) *The Development of Children's Number Concepts from Ages Five to Nine, Volumes 1 and 2.* Hamilton: University of Waikato.

Index